Henry Scott Holland

Logic and Life

With other Sermons

Henry Scott Holland

Logic and Life
With other Sermons

ISBN/EAN: 9783744742221

Printed in Europe, USA, Canada, Australia, Japan

Cover: Foto ©Lupo / pixelio.de

More available books at **www.hansebooks.com**

With other Sermons

BY THE REV.

H. S. HOLLAND, M.A.

CANON AND PRECENTOR OF ST. PAUL'S

NEW EDITION

LONDON
LONGMANS, GREEN, AND CO.
AND NEW YORK: 15 EAST 16TH STREET
1894

PREFACE.

The publication of Sermons needs always an apology. Sermons are written, and given, for a momentary purpose, without any intention that they should assume, in print, a permanent existence, or be detached from the occasion and the congregation for which they were originally designed. Why, then, give them this unintended permanence, this unforeseen detachment? Why address the reading public as if it were a gathered congregation? Why throw loosely abroad what was delivered within the shelter of a Church? That which was appropriate under the one set of circumstances is hardly likely to be appropriate in the other.

This is true; and, yet, I would attempt a defence.

We, clergy, suffer under difficulties in this matter. We cannot lie quiet, while we slowly accumulate the materials for a book. We, of necessity, find ourselves preaching: and, naturally, we speak of what is uppermost in our minds; and so we tell our secrets; we announce ourselves as we move. If we happen to be following out certain directions of theological thought, then, just as the molehills tell the lines of the burrowing mole, so we throw out, in sermons, the manifest tokens of our path. Those, therefore, of us, to whom it is, in any small way, given of God to write a book, practically write it in bits. We cannot store our material: such thinking as is possible to us manifests itself, step by step, under the pressure of immediate demands.

What, then, are we to do, when we see that it might be right for us to believe that our work would not be quite useless or unhelpful to others than those who heard us speak? Are we to recast it all? A good deal might be said for this; and yet, it would be to us ourselves an irksome and unhealthy task. It is one thing to delay production: it is quite another to reproduce and refashion what has once already taken form and shape. Again, we have moved on: we are occupied with other conditions of the problem: we cannot easily revive the old ardour with which we expressed our first intuition of this or that aspect of things. The result, therefore, of re-writing our own productions would be an inevitable deadening of all the work: we should re-write them, wearied and bored; for though, perhaps, the public will not believe it, very few of us are fond enough, or proud enough, of our own handiwork, to be able to enjoy the process of remaking it. We should be heartily sick of it before we had done; and if it was written wearily, it would be read wearily. It might gain, in arrangement, in unity, in completeness: it would lose in everything else.

I therefore venture to put out these sermons, just as they were delivered: only, I would say, that they are printed for the purpose with which books are written, rather than for that with which sermons are preached. They are offered, not as hortative addresses, so much as for the sake of laying before the minds of many who now find themselves astray, or in peril, amid the tangle of life, some such interpretation of the natural and spiritual worlds in which we move, as may possibly assist them in detecting their coherence with the truth, as it is in Christ Jesus. It is presumptuous to use such high words about an interpretation so partial, and fragmentary, and slight, as is given in this book: it does but attempt to suggest how strongly and how masterfully the faith which was held by St. Athanasius, the faith in Christ of St. Paul and of St. John, would, if known as they knew it, lay hold of the wealth of modern science, and of the secrets of modern culture, and of the desires and the necessities of modern spirit. We have lost much of that rich splendour, that large-hearted fulness of power, which characterizes the great Greek masters of theology. We have suffered our faith for so long to accept the pinched and narrow limits of a most unapostolic divinity, that we can hardly persuade people to recall how wide was the sweep of Christian thought in the first centuries, how largely it dealt with these deep problems of spiritual existence and development, which now once more impress upon us the seriousness of the issues amid which our souls are travelling. We have let people forget all that our Creed has to say about the unity of all creation, or about the evolution of history, or about the universality of the Divine action through the Word. We have lost the power of wielding the mighty language with which Athanasius expands the significance of Creation and Regeneration, of Incarnation and Sacrifice, and Redemption, and Salvation, and Glory.

It is needless to say that this little book does not pretend to attempt the task here suggested. But it may, possibly, just serve to remind some, who could undertake it more worthily, that such a task ought to be done: or it may happen, by good grace, to relieve a little the difficulties that haunt many souls, by hinting to them the possibility that Christianity holds in its heart solutions that they have disregarded, and which it would be well worth while for them to consider and examine. It may just help to recall with what vivid reality the faith of Christ could speak, if we only would let it, to the actual needs of the day and of the hour; and with how close a touch, with how clear a mastery, it could show itself at home in a world that we fancied so strange to its spirit, and so remote from its words and its habits. If here and there it could make this credible to some who now suffer and are distressed through the traditions that have cramped the large significance of the Catholic creed, then all will be well with it; it will have done such work as was possible for it.

The Sermons, though detached, follow a certain sequence. The first three, which were preached before the University of Oxford, attempt to suggest some of the conditions under which the *intellectual* approaches to a creed must be made. The two following touch on the *moral* needs and efforts which are presupposed by the coming of Christ; and the next four attempt to interpret the nature of the response made to these moral necessities by the Sacrifice of the Cross. After this follow four sermons on the spiritual temper which is essential to any realization of the faith,—the seeing eye, the awakened spirit, the upward look, the instinctive kinship. I then make an effort to exhibit and justify, in some slight measure, one or two of the central dogmas of the Creed,—*e.g.*, the Trinity, the Incarnation: and after these sermons follow three attempts to show some aspects of the office and work of the Christian society at large, and of its responsibilities in face of the civil and social facts of the time. The last two sermons touch on the nature of the soul's advance in faith, and on its outlook to a better land.

The rough sequence here indicated does not pretend

to give to the book the integrity and fulness of a complete treatise. It does but thread loosely together a few fragmentary suggestions, which may possibly make the growth of faith easier to some who now find their free movements hampered by masses of facts, which they know not how to array into harmony with the life which the spirit desires. Such might feel themselves released from the bondage of fear, and might go forward with a gladder confidence, if they could once put their inward belief into an intelligible relation to the world of outer fact. Even a mere glimpse into the possibilities of such a consistency, within and without, is a relief to the hindering pressure, and carries with it good cheer. But it must not be supposed for one moment that any such glimpses or suggestions will be sufficient to make faith exist in those who, as yet, have it not. Faith is not made by argument. It seeks, indeed, for rational solutions of life's mysteries; it grows through gaining hold of them; but its origin, its creation, is not in these. "The depth said, It is not in me." Not from things without, but from the heart within, cometh wisdom: there, in the inner places of the soul, in the secret will with which a man fears the Lord, and departs from evil, is the true place of spiritual understanding. Intellectual solutions can only be of value to those whose whole being already hungers after righteousness, and loathes sin, and wills to do the will of God, and abides loyally in such truth as has been made open to it, and seeks, with earnest, prayerful zeal, deliverance from an unworthy slavery in which it knows the good and does the evil. It is Christ, not reason, that makes the believer free: and it is the Spirit of God alone Who knoweth the deep things of God. Faith, then, is not created by reason, but "cometh of God" only. But, since the Christ in Whom we are made free is the Word of God, therefore, all the working of reason is prophetic of Him Who should come: and, by His coming, it is made perfect in Him Who is the Power and Wisdom of God. Here, then, is at once the limitation, and also the justification, of all our efforts to exhibit the intelligibility of our creed.

Deus, vera et summa Vita, Qui inveniri Te facis, et pulsanti aperis; Quem nemo quærit, nisi admonitus: nemo invenit, nisi purgatus; Quem nosse, vivere est: Te labiis et corde laudo, benedico, adoro.

PREFACE TO SECOND EDITION.

I ATTEMPTED in my former Preface an apology for the publication of Sermons. I find myself driven, by much criticism, to apologize for my apology. It shall be in as few words of explanation as possible.

I had spoken of the irksome labour of re-writing that which had already been delivered from the pulpit, and in so speaking, I have appeared to be under-estimating the value of painstaking and rigorous workmanship. That was, if I may venture to say so, as far as possible from my intention. Work—good, careful, incessant, laborious work—this, surely, is precious beyond all price.

But it is one thing to hold back a piece of work until all possible labour and polish have been bestowed upon it; it is another thing to have to repeat a work already produced—to have to throw it out of one form into another. My plea is that we preachers cannot hold back our thoughts in peace until we have given them all the slow pains and watchful postponement that perfect work requires. We cannot keep silence until we are thoroughly prepared at all points. We must still be speaking as we work : and the question for us is, not how long we will spend labour upon our work, but whether we are to re-write that which already has gone from us. This is where the possibility of irksomeness enters.

And more than this. The spoken word seems to necessitate a certain rapidity of production. Unless it is prepared with some pressure of speed and effusion, it is too cold for speech, it is apt to lose spontaneity. It is against the grain of a preacher to write a sermon long before the occasion of delivering it. It needs to be written in immediate contact with the condition of its delivery—in direct view of the circumstances to be dealt with, of the surroundings, of the character of the probable congregation. Some speed is essential to its freshness, to its fire. Otherwise it becomes an essay, not a sermon ; it passes out of the conditions of oratory—or, at least, is only possible in a University pulpit, and then, is usually criticised as " Academic." All this will often deprive a sermon of the chance of that perfect workmanship which would be essential in a calmer writing. It cannot endure more labour than is consistent with a certain free rapidity of production.

No doubt, to say this is to make Sermons incapable, except in the very rarest instances, of the highest literary excellence. I cannot deny it, it seems to me perfectly true; and I therefore should greatly doubt whether it would ever be wholly right to put any intellectual work that demanded very laborious and excellent finish into the form of Sermons, except under the authority of such rare and exceptional gifts as carried us beyond all critical canons and made all apology needless. In the absence of such authority, sermons that deal with intricate subjects will always need excusing; and it was because of this need that I ventured to apologize for work that took, as I cannot but think, a form inadequate to its complete task, and yet a form most 'difficult to avoid. That apology I now beg to repeat, with an increased sense of its needfulness and of its urgency.

CONTENTS.

SERMON I.
Logic, and Life.

PAGE

The Word was with God.—St. John i. 1 1

SERMON II.
The Venture of Reason.

Through faith, we understand that the worlds were framed by the Word of God.—Heb. xi. 3 21

SERMON III.
The Spirit, and its Interpretation.

What man knoweth the things of a man, save the spirit of man which is in him? Even so the things of God knoweth no man, but the Spirit of God.—1 Cor. ii. 11 41

SERMON IV.
The Cost of Moral Movement.

Unto whomsoever much is given, of him shall be much required: and to whom men have committed much, of him they will ask the more.—St. Luke xii. 48 62

SERMON V.

Christ, the Justification of a Suffering World.

PAGE

Having made known unto us the mystery of His will, according to His good pleasure which He hath purposed in Himself: that in the dispensation of the fulness of times He might gather together in one all things in Christ. In Whom also we have obtained an inheritance.—EPH. i. 9-11 81

SERMON VI.

The Sacrifice of Innocence.

That I may go unto the altar of God, even unto the God of my joy and gladness.—PS. xliii. 4 99

SERMON VII.

The Sacrifice of the Fallen.

Then said I, Lo, I come!—PS. xl. 7 110

SERMON VIII.

The Sacrifice of the Man.

A body hast Thou prepared me.—HEB. x. 5.
By the which will we are sanctified through the offering of the body of Jesus Christ.—HEB. x. 10 121

SERMON IX.

The Sacrifice of the Redeemed.

Unto you it is given in the behalf of Christ, not only to believe on Him, but also to suffer for His sake.—PHIL. i. 29 . . . 133

SERMON X.
The Spiritual Eye.
PAGE

They are not of the world, even as I am not of the world. . . .
*As Thou hast sent Me into the world, even so have I also sent them
into the world.*—ST. JOHN xvii. 16, 18 144

SERMON XI.
The Breaking of Dreams.

Walk as children of light.—EPH. v. 8 163

SERMON XII.
Sheep and Shepherd.

*For judgment I am come into this world, that they which see not
might see; and that they which see might be made blind.*—ST.
JOHN ix. 39 182

SERMON XIII.
Love, the Law of Life.

Thou shalt love the Lord thy God; and thy neighbour as thyself.—
ST. LUKE x. 27 199

SERMON XIV.
The Blessing of God Almighty, the Father, the Son, and the Holy Ghost.

I looked, and behold, a door was opened in heaven.—REV. iv. 1 . 212

SERMON XV.
The Meekness of God.

*The Son of Man came not to be ministered unto, but to minister,
and to give His life a ransom for many.*—ST. MATT. xx. 28 . 227

SERMON XVI.

The Powers that be.

PAGE

There is no power but of God: the powers that be are ordained of God.—ROM. xiii. 1 240

SERMON XVII.

The Sword of St. Michael.

There was war in heaven: Michael and his angels fought against the Dragon.—REV. xii. 7 254

SERMON XVIII.

The Kingdom of Righteousness.

Are your minds set upon righteousness, O ye congregation: and do ye judge the thing that is right, O ye sons of men.—PS. lviii. 1 . 271

SERMON XIX.

The Pruning of the Vine.

I am the true Vine, and My Father is the Husbandman: Every branch in Me that beareth not fruit He taketh away, and every branch that beareth fruit, He purgeth it that it may bring forth more fruit.—ST. JOHN xv. 1, 2 285

SERMON XX.

The Sleep, and the Waking.

Then shall the Kingdom of Heaven be likened unto ten virgins, which took their lamps, and went forth to meet the Bridegroom.—ST. MATT. xxv. 1 305

SERMON I.

LOGIC, AND LIFE.

"The Word was with God."—St. John i. 1.

ONE main lesson that all of us are steadily learning from many teachers, and with varying effect, is the reality, and universality, of movement. That fixed and solid framework of things which men called Nature, and in which they seemed to see the very image of rigid and unchanging law, the shadow of God's own Permanence, of His constant and enduring Immutability, has been broken up under the keen insight of the new criticism. It has felt the sway and swing of motion: the activities of a living process have been seen to shoot along all the inner passages of its huge bulk: it has become in our eyes no fixed embodiment of law, but a moving, growing, changing mass, building itself up by slow and laborious pressure, by endless transformation: its very rocks, the type of all solid immobility, have been watched at their growth, have been detected in their silent changes: the whole round world has been set moving; it has been in motion from the first, and still its movements proceed; from hour to hour it ceases to be what once it was, it passes on towards new arrangements and novel combinations.

Nor is it otherwise with that other world in which

man loved to find the reflex of eternal Fixity. The world of spirit, of reason, of intuition, offers us no more, apparently, the picture of a Median kingdom, ordered from end to end, whose laws and institutions never know the weakness of change. Our eye no longer falls upon a table of unalterable commandments, set up in the thoughts of savage and civilized alike, pre-suppositions, decrees, assumptions, to which all rational beings instinctively conform. Here, too, the light of criticism detects movement at work within all that seems most fixed: it exhibits growth and change in operation upon the mind itself, forming its first intuitions, building up its premisses, shaping its gradual action. More than this, the very emotions themselves,—the primary efforts of sensation at the root of all our being,—have known the slow process of formation and transformation. Man does not feel as once he felt, any more than he thinks as once he thought.

It may, indeed, well be doubted whether the detection of movement in all worlds can conceivably represent the final or absolute aspect of things; but it at least carries us a long way; it is obviously true over an immense field of fact. And I have ventured therefore to recall, without discussion, its larger significance before noticing its results in one peculiar direction.

All things, then, are undergoing a process of shift or change,—that is anyhow what we learn: within as well as without, a deep and silent movement is everywhere at work, altering, transposing, correcting, enlarging. We hardly feel it, or hear, except that now and again there is a sudden and awful shake, as some ponderous mass heaves or tumbles: for a moment we stop, and strain our ears to listen to its hollow thunder, its dim reverberation; but that is all: only that soon, upon the surface of life, results appear that were not there before: we are startled to encounter strange evidences of those deep, unknown convulsions: something has occurred, we see, that alters the face of things: we note down a change.

Now, one such change we can certainly all observe in the nature of modern argument. Men nowadays dislike deduction; they distrust all positive reasoning: they are not overcome by logical proof: and naturally. For it was one thing to argue, when reason was regarded as possessed of a scheme of abiding and irresistible rules, without which it could not act, and with which it advanced to new ground, by a certain process of its own, a process over which it possessed entire control, which it dominated from end to end, and by which it reached results which its own innate criticism could ascertain, test, overhaul, ratify: it was one thing for men to meet each other in the tournament of Dialectic, when each was supposed to possess the same identical weapon as any other, the same reasoning faculty, in the same condition of use, obeying the same stipulations, wielded with perfectly equal facility. But argument becomes quite another thing, when the means of argument is not so much a tool as an organ, a function, the constitution of which is no necessary and unalterable scheme, with certain uses and characteristics of its own, from all eternity; but rather a living formation, moulded by long and slow efforts, determined, more or less, by experience and habit, susceptible of a thousand influences from external conditions, itself a living, fluid, moving substance, capable of infinite variety, changing as the years change, possessed, it may be, of a peculiar unity and identity of type which it preserves throughout all its changes, but still, for all that, capable of a thousand different degrees of development, so that its action in one man may differ indefinitely from its action in another, its force and effectiveness depending always on the stage of development obtained. This is reason, this the mind, as many men now fancy it: and if so, they naturally and instinctively recoil from the claims of an infallible and universal logic, to the convincing necessities of which all must bow. Such logic may but represent the momentary structure that your mind has taken at this particular stage of human history: it has force to you to-day: but once it would have been a sheer impossibility, and to-morrow will already have affected its validity, and have begun to turn it into idle antiquarianism.

Such a point of view has limitation, which I will not now discuss. But, at any rate, while taking it, we do not much heed, or need, the force of final and positive arguments. These pass us by: they sound thin and unreal; we do not know what to make of them: they may seem as convincing, as unanswerable, as ever, but we do not somehow care to take the trouble to answer them: we do not believe in them; a syllogism, a dilemma, all the old apparatus, is accepted with respectful attention, but it does not persuade, it does not really move or influence; it has lost its compelling force. More especially is this true in the highest and fullest subjects. In politics it has long been proverbial. We learned there long ago that constitutions were not made, but grew; that there was no rigorous and imperative logical standard; that systems depended on the temper of the people, on the assumptions which were natural to the genius of one nation, but which, in another, you would look for in vain; that there was no forcing things down men's throats, no possibility of moving the masses by sheer, unalloyed reason, no security that an argument which availed with one class would equally affect another, or that an appeal to this or that motive could be counted upon as a constant quantity over all time and in all places. And Science, now, by its emphasis on experience, trains men to a like indifference to the force of abstract argument; indeed, it itself is almost as indifferent as common sense to the necessities of logical consistency. It is perfectly content, in most cases, to fall in with a philosophy which denies the validity of all those palmary hypotheses on which Science itself depends : yet it can only be sheer indifference to logic which makes it put up with a bedfellow so uncongenial and treacherous. In reality, what does it matter to Science if its assumption of permanent Causality be, according to its own chosen logic, unproven, unverified, absurd? It still goes on its way with robust assurance; for, at the bottom of its heart, it knows that it can dispense with an appeal to deductive consistency, so long as it has that far more convincing ally on its side, the alliance of its own inherent belief in itself—a belief warranted by the assent of all reasonable men to whom its assumptions have become the natural and undeniable facts, that Science assumes them to be. Not for a moment do we, or any one else who has once realised the scientific aspect of the world, doubt its reality, its trustworthiness, its sureness of foot. Whither it carries us, we follow: we may dispute its entire universality: we may believe that we see its limits: but, while we are on its ground, while we are moving within its dominion, we, if we have once understood its appeal, are sure to accept its arguments, and proofs, and conclusions; we feel it foolish to deny them: we should be attempting to fly from our own minds if we tried to avoid their persuasive force,—a force that retains its vigour undulled and undiminished in spite of the most obvious weakness of its speculative groundwork. I do not intend to imply that Science has no rational consistency, but only to notice this, that it can audaciously refuse the assistance of any logical certainty, without apparently loosening at all the binding power of its appeal, so sure is it of men's spontaneous assent.

And, if this attitude of mind is already recognised in Politics and in Science, we shall not be surprised to find it affecting the character of the arguments that avail in the still more complex fields of Religion.

Men do not care much for logical proofs of the being of God, or of the possibility of miracle. Reason may assert, perhaps unanswerably, the intellectual necessity for the existence of a single Supreme Creator; it may exhibit irresistibly that any logic, based on mere empiricism, is powerless to demonstrate the necessity of irreversible laws in Nature. Still men remain as doubting, as uneasy, as before; still the pressure of Science continues to drive steadily against the miraculous; still the creeping tide slides in almost like some blind and enormous fate, that has no ears for our voice to enter, and moves by some impulsion, alien to our cries, untouched by our endeavours.

We still carry on the war of argument; but the results of the conflict seem too distant to be taken into much account: and we have but little heart to throw into discussions, which, endless themselves, yet have no distinct end to attain, and achieve so little, and convince so few.

After all has been argued out, men throw over the argument: for behind the intellectual battle lies the region of conviction, that mental condition which is sensitive to one appeal and not to another,—that mental condition which cannot be gainsayed, cannot be upset or discomfited by any momentary difficulty,—that mental atmosphere which admits one impression and repels another by some instinctive method of its own,—that mental structure which the long years have laboriously built, and which nothing but the long years will ever unmake, or refashion. What is the need of struggling over this or that logical detail? At the end of it all, the man under attack will pass all argument by with a wave of his hand: miracle, for instance, he will say, cannot offer itself in any conceivable shape to my imagination; it is no good proving to me that it ought to appear perfectly probable: as a fact, its improbability increases every time I look at it.

Such is the state of things,—it exists as well for us as for those who differ from us: we have the same sense as they of hollowness and insufficiency and remoteness, as we listen to old abstract argumentation, while it deals with the living things of spirit and of God. True, we may still believe that that high metaphysic has its place, has its office, has its reality; but its force lies in some different plane; we are on lower levels: and on these lower levels we hardly know what to say to it, or where to rely upon it: we feel hazy and uncomfortable as it delivers its decrees: we seem to have so little grip upon its method, the words may sound strong as ever, yet the tale has but little meaning for us: it fails to make its entry good within the substance and fibres of our real life. This is our condition: and if this is so, it may be well to examine a few of the characteristics of such a state of mind; for only by understanding it can we control it; and only by retaining it in our control can we avoid sinking in irrational submission, under forces that may carry us whither we would not.

Suffer me to touch on one or two of its obvious principles and perils. This modern way of regarding things does not in reality suppose itself irrational, because it distrusts abstract argument: rather, it is the conception of reason itself which is modified. Reason is regarded, not in its isolated character as an engine with which every man starts equipped, capable of doing a certain job whenever required, with a definite and certain mode of action; but it is taken as a living and pliable process by and in which man brings himself into rational and intelligent relation with his surroundings, with his experience. As these press in upon him, and stir him, and move about and around him, he sets himself to introduce into his abounding and multitudinous impressions, something of order, and system, and settlement. He has got to act upon all this engirdling matter, and he must discover how action is most possible and most successful: he must watch, and consider, and arrange, and find accordance between his desires and their outward realisation: so it is that he names and classifies: so it is that he learns to expect, to foretell, to anticipate, to manage, to control: so it is that he rouses his curiosity to ever new efforts, and cannot rest content until he has got clearer and surer hold on the infinite intricacies that offer themselves to hand, and eye, and ear, and taste. Continually he re-shapes his anticipations, continually he corrects his judgments, continually he turns to new researches, continually he moulds and enlarges, and enriches, and fortifies, and advances, and improves the conceptions which he finds most cardinal and most effective. Undisturbed in his primary confidence that he has a rational hold upon the reality of the things which he feels and sees, he acts on the essential assumption that, in advancing the active effectiveness of his ideas, he is arriving at a more real apprehension of that world which he finds to move in increasing harmony with his own inner expectations. This effective and growing apprehension is what he calls his reason: and its final test lies in the actual harmony, which is found to result from its better endeavours, between the life at work within and the life at work without. Reason is the slowly formed power of harmonizing the world of facts: and its justification lies, not in its deductive certainty so much as in its capacity of *advance*. It proves its trustworthiness by its power to grow. It could not have come so far if it were not on the right road: it must be right, because ever, in front of it, it discovers the road continuing. Reason moves towards its place, its fulfilment, so far as it settles itself into responsive agreement with the facts covered by its activity, so far as its expectations encounter no jar or surprise, so far as its survey is baffled by no blank and unpenetrated barriers. Every step that tends to complete and achieve this successful response tends, in that same degree, to enforce its confident security in itself and in its method.

Such a position as this leaves the real problem of metaphysic untouched and unresolved; they are in the background, unattempted. But, on the other hand, it forces forward a new sense of our moral responsibility for the working of our Reason. In former days, the working of thought was regarded as beyond our control: it was a separate faculty, endowed with laws, principles, schemes, methods of its own: its announcements proceeded by some infallible and necessary rules, identical everywhere, identical in all: we had no more to do with its ways and customs than we had with the arrangement of heart or brain. It was a tool that had one use and no other. But now it appears that we have to do, more or less, with the actual construction and nature of the reasoning organ itself. This construction is alive, and every instant sees it change: it is no isolated faculty where workings can continue, or be watched "*in vacuo*," as we can watch the movements of a machine even when it has no material to work upon. Rather is it to be held in unbroken connection with the facts on which it works, for only in relation to them is its success, its truth, obvious, or verifiable, or intelligible. Its force, its persuasive potency over the man in whom it acts, lies in the manner in which it offers to group, and arrange, and present a certain body of fact. If it can so order the various and manifold facts before the man, as to make him feel them to be in harmony with the whole mass of his experience, so that he can move up and down the domain covered by his knowledge with ease, and regularity, and evenness, and fair consistency, then he accepts its work with secure and unhesitating peace. But, if so, everything depends on the character of the facts before him, and on the nature of his main experiences. The excellence of a piece of reasoning lies simply in its adaptive facility, in the response it evokes between those particular new impressions and the mass of older and habitual experiments. Change the facts, or the experience, and its excellence disappears,—it becomes unintelligible.

It is on our inner and actual life, then, that the action of our reasoning depends. Deep down in the long record of our past, far away in the ancient homes and habits of the soul, back, far back, in all that age-long experience which has nursed, and tended, and moulded the making of my manhood, lies the secret of that efficacy which reason exerts in me to-day. That efficacy has, through long pressure, become an imbedded habit, which, if I turn round upon it and suddenly inspect it, will appear to me inexplicable. Why this gigantic conclusion? Why this emphatic pronouncement? Why this array of dogmatic assumptions? I may take those assumptions up in my hands, and look them all over, and poke and probe them, and find no answer in them for their mysterious audacity. No, for they have no answer within themselves: their answer, their verification, their evidence, their very significance, can only be got by turning to, and introducing all that vast sum of ever-gathering facts which the generations before me, under the weight of the moving centuries, pressed into these formulæ, ordered under these categories, wielded by the efficacy of these instruments, harmonized, mastered, controlled in obedience to these judgments,—judgments which justified their reality and their power by the constant and unwavering welcome with which the advance of life unfailingly greeted their anticipations, and fulfilled their trust. I am, of necessity, blind to their force as long as I have no corresponding experience,—as long as that body of fact which they make explicable remains to me unverified and unexplored. What to me, for instance, can be the potency of the conception of Soul, if I have no soul-facts that require explication? I feel the need and necessity of a name only when there are certain phenomena before me which no other name suits or sorts. What need or necessity, then, can I see for the word Spirit, unless I have, within my experience, those spiritual activities which were to my forefathers so marked, so distinct, so unmistakable, so constant, that it became to them a mental impossibility to retain them under a material name, and a practical impossibility to carry on an intelligible common life without distinguishing those activities from the motions of their flesh? What sense or reason can I discover for the assumption of a God, unless I can repeat and re-enact in the abysses of my own hidden being those profound impressions, those ineradicable experiences, those awful and sublime ventures of faith to which the existence of God has been the sole clue, the sole necessity, the one and only interpretation, the irresistible response, the obvious evidence, the unceasing justification?

And yet how difficult is the matter to which these announcements apply! The complexities of the physical world make it hard enough, without persistent experience of the facts, to understand the full force of the intellectual expressions in which Science sums them together. But here, in the spiritual world, the experience must be yet more attentive and persistent, if it is ever to appreciate the proclamations made about Soul and Spirit and God. For, how far more intricate is the matter with which these expressions deal! How infinitely subtle! How many-sided! How quick, and changing, and complex! How swiftly its phenomena enter and pass! How multitudinous its operations! How far-reaching its activities! How profound its surprises! How confusing and startling, and dazzling, and astounding all its sudden and rapid transitions; all the fallings from us, vanishings, blank misgivings, all its high instincts, its first affections, its shadowy recollections! Who is it that is going to pronounce, at a glance, on the value of the formulæ, by which men have brought under intelligible order this vast and overwhelming world of spiritual impressions? No! Only in intimate and undivided communion with the facts which they express, have the announcements of the reason, on any field of knowledge, any intelligible value; and no one, therefore, who does not live, and move, and have his being, in constant intercourse with this spirit-life can enter into the deep necessities of its laws, any more than an untrained savage would be sensitive to the potency which an experimental proof exercises over the disciplined intelligence of a scientific explorer. We must live in no casual contact with spirit, if we ever intend to understand it. For Reason tells us nothing trustworthy of itself; it is in its applicability to fact that its surest test lies: it is by its sense of its steady advance in expressing the facts that it feels its true security: it is by long and active familiarity with the facts that it appreciates their ultimate necessities. This, which is the rule under which Reason has laboriously built up the facts of natural experience into an ordered world, must be the rule also of all its dealings with that large mass of spiritual facts out of which it learns, by patient experience, the form and fashion of supernatural life. Slowly the significance and the harmony of those spiritual events grow luminous; and their perspective reveals its steadier outlines. By touching, by handling, by tasting, by apprehending these spiritual facts, Reason forces its way along; it compels them to exhibit order, it shifts and moves and crosses them from place to place; it corrects, it extracts, it penetrates their significance, until the day breaks clearer and purer, and the strong powers that hold the spiritual fabric in adamantine chains stand out with visible, with undeniable insistence, and the great vision opens, and the large spaces become light, and the sun leaps out, and the vast heavens are aglow, and all about and around him a fresh life spreads, lordlier than the natural, in ordered and abundant wealth of colour, and splendour, and peace. It is a new and supernatural world that now at last lies in broad and solid expanse under his spiritual eyes, and it does so, because he has fed his rational experience with unfailing supplies of supernatural fact. This, and this alone, is the rule by which his reason can achieve its task or discover its justification: this is the sole law of its highest endeavours. Yea, for, in so doing, it obeys the law of that Divine Reason in Whose imag it is made,—of that Word, of Whom it is said, "the Word was *with* God."

The Word, the sole source and spring of all our intelligence, Who is the thought and reason of the Eternal, has never ceased to hold unbroken communion with that God, Whom it is His high privilege, His endless joy, to see, and know, and understand. The Word, now and ever, remains "*with* God." Away from God, apart from that resolute and enduring intimacy which knits Him by the bands and cords of unfailing love to the very heart and life of the Most High, there would be no possible intelligence of what God is, no perfect and absolute knowledge, no power of final revelation. In His Sonship lies the secret of all His knowledge: bound to the Father, turned ever to the Father, never alone, but for ever with the Father, for ever abiding in that endless intercourse, that loyal familiarity, that glory of the Father's nearness, of His presence, of His power, in that union which He had with God before the worlds were—so, and so only, can the Divine Reason fulfil its perfect work; so, and so only, can it penetrate, and achieve, and comprehend; so, and so only, can the Son know the Father, even as the Father knoweth the Son. Because the Word was ever *with* God, therefore He ever knew God. Because He abides constantly in that faultless love; therefore, and therefore only, does the Father show the Son whatsoever He doeth: and no man knoweth the Father but that one Eternal Son.

"The Word was with God." Communion with God is the secret of Divine wisdom: out of the abiding and familiar intimacy of the Son with the Father flows the wealth of the Word's high knowledge. He knows, because He abides in the bosom of the Father. This is the law of intellectual life in its highest conceivable expression, in that Word Who is the Thought and Reason of God Himself: this law, then, regulates the exercise of reason from end to end of its domain: in this lies the secret of its force, the condition of its success: and we, on our lower level, we, whose reason works in the image of the Word, in Whose light alone we see light, can win our intellectual way only through conformity to the primal conditions under which the Word of God moves forward to His victorious apprehension.

We can only understand that in which we abide, with which we have intimate union, to which we are ourselves conformed; that which we handle, and taste, and feel, and see. The closer our contact, the securer grows our knowledge; and only out of the growing pressure of familiar intercourse can our reason gain ever-quickening activity, ever-increasing assurance. Thought is our power of allying ourselves to facts, our power of acquiring consistency with them, so that the world within corresponds with the world without. It therefore shifts and changes its fashions and forms, its features and expression, according to the nature of the facts before it, according to the shaping of the world with which it deals. Its instinctive sympathies, its sense of security, its touches of persuasion, its effective pressure, all vary infinitely according to the character of its abiding habits, according to the range of its experiences.

This, then, it is which throws such awful reality into our intellectual responsibilities; this it is which makes its difficulties so anxious, so deep, so intense. We cannot estimate the judgments of reason from outside: we have no machine that will test and weigh them off-hand; we can never have one glimpse of their efficacy or their reality without entering ourselves within the circle of their proper fascination, without passing in within the range of the experiences of which it is their sole claim to be the supreme interpretation. How different, now, becomes the aspect of such arguments as those on which we have already touched!—such arguments as protested that every step of advanced familiarity with the methods of Historical Criticism, or with the presentations of Natural Science, made it seem harder to conceive the possibility of miracle or the rationality of prayer. Perfectly true! but what else would you expect? For what intimacy, what sympathy have these empirical sciences with those facts in relation to which alone prayer and miracle become conceivable? Such sciences classify and interpret our Past; but they have nothing to do with that tremendous world from which we win nerve and force to break with our Past, to throw off its hold, to shatter its fetters. Such powers as this they never profess to interpret; they abandon any claim to control or examine. With all that has been they can deal; but all that may be, all that ought to be—all the wide sea of possibilities that have never yet been—these they abandon to the unknown. And yet, are there no such possibilities to be seen or found in our lives? Is the influence of the Past the sole factor of importance in the shaping of our days? Have the possibilities of the Future no present and actual force within our souls to-day? Is there no world of spiritual fact ever grouping itself round about these possibilities that are alive and at work within us? Do we never feel or know the live and sensible energies of hopes, aspirations, ideals, regrets, remorse, repentance, absolutions, renewals? Are conversions, convulsions, spontaneities, resistances, revolts, revolutions, awakenings,—are such movements as these within the profound recesses of the soul all unreal, all fanciful, all unregarded? Nay, surely these are our realities, these are the master-light of all our seeing; and it is in face of realities such as these that Prayer and Miracles, which are the witnesses of a power to change the Present and transform the Past, assume intelligible validity. Often and often we have, surely, all of us found it so. It is after long and habitual neglect of the miraculous and spiritual elements that enter into the texture of our own existence that we find the formulæ of faith so perplexing, so irrational, so alien, so repellent. Only by constant and customary contact with those strange invisible powers that underlie our own sensible life, and move it so deeply, and enforce such superhuman demands,—only by abiding within the presence of these imperious mysteries, sensitive to their touch, responsive to their appeals, unstartled by their thrilling messages,—only so can the mind learn to admit within the lines of its possible experiences facts that claim to be miraculous. For only to such can miracle be welcome as a congenial ally, an expected and warranted guest whom they greet with ready ease; and this ease of entry, this congenial welcome, it is which constitutes rationality. Reason, whose whole aim it is to give unity and harmony to the whole round of life's experiences, is satisfied as long as her expectations feel no shock, as her harmony is unbroken; and no such break, no such shock, disturbs or discomforts her, if the miracle without finds an effective response in the daily miracle within. Its entry stirs no tumultuous repulsion in a world where its appearance is so familiar, and its advent so long looked for.

Deep down, then, in the dim recesses of each man's soul lie the secret springs of his logical thinking. His thought belongs to the very essence of his being, and with the innermost life of that being it, too, lives. Its exercise and use are inseparable from his mental habits and spiritual history; it works under the thousand influences of custom, of intercourse, of familiarity; and, if so, God Himself can only seem a rational solution to those who live in constant contact with the problems which His existence solves. The Incarnation can never be rational to any but those who know now what it is to have the Word of God alive and speaking within their souls. The Atonement can only appear rational to such as have sounded, in their own experience, the awful waters of remorse, or have been eaten by the devouring agonies of corruption, or have felt the horror of that gross darkness which settles down as a soundless night, without star or lamp, without any movement of hope, or joy, or love, upon those who find themselves, to their miserable dismay, to be sold unto sin.

Have we then known anything of this terrible drama? Have we wrestled and striven in this tremendous war? Have we moved about among these wonderful and surpassing powers that are alive within our life? Have we unlocked and entered these dark chambers? Have we groped with patient hands along the length of their dim walls? And if not, who are we, that we should be giving rapid and daring decisions about questions which, without this, cannot possibly to us have the slightest intelligible meaning? The time has come, it is true, for answers to be given to questions that press for solution in the realm of the supernatural; but no answer whatever will be possible to any but to those who have aided and trained their reason for the task by long habit and continual trial, by persistent watchfulness and intimate experience, by sober attention and practised handling, and the instincts that follow on patient experiment.

SERMON II.

THE VENTURE OF REASON.

"Through faith, we understand that the worlds were framed by the Word of God."—HEB. xi. 3.

As we look back and sift the conditions under which the childhood of the human race has made its advances into manhood, we habitually notice a double-sided character. First, we are met at the start by a whole world of *emotion*—impressions, feelings, affections, impulses; these move, and change, and shake, and compel the whole man. He is their creature; from them he derives all impetus; under their sway he is pushed along the pathways of life. His words, the lonely relics of an unrecorded story, are stamped with the superscription of this sensual dominion: they keep down on the low levels of physical imagery: they seem hardly more than the spontaneous and unthinking outcome of fleshly instincts. His whole being is cramped and confined in all its movements under the tight pressure of the physical network within which he lies meshed: the stress of physical needs, of physical passions, impels all his activities, and lends motive to all his desires. So we see him start; and yet out of that chaos of impulses, out of those blind motives of sense, a strange order mysteriously springs—a new life emerges, as a rainbow hovers, fresh and free, over the edges of the flying mist; and this new life does not pass and die with the mist out of which its beauty grew; it steadies itself down; it wins for itself, by slow and patient degrees, a solid settlement, a positive endurance: it orders all its ways, it sorts and places its materials: it fashions its chambers, and lays down its laws: it discloses increasing capacities of self-control: it adapts itself to novel arrangements: it extends the sway of its inventions: it discovers principle, and rule, and regularity there where all had been confusion. Under all the shocks of changing impressions, it presses forward its old and steady laws of combination, it builds up its unshaken walls. So, out of the tumult of passion, grows and develops the mysterious fabric of social order; and the greatest surprise is this, that all this process, as we read out its history, gives a reasonable explanation of itself. It is open to scientific exhibition; it commends itself to thought; and, by so commending itself, proves itself to have been fashioned under the control and direction of *reason*. For to be susceptible of historical treatment it must be rationally constituted; and if so, then we have to conclude that reason must have been at work from the first: a rational order cannot have been motived by irrational impulses. The passions, then the impressions, with which we began were never wholly what they seemed; they were from the very beginning the passions, the impressions, of a rational man, and so won for themselves a capacity which never lay in the correspondent affections of the animal. This capacity was not given them from outside, was not imposed; for the closer we probe history, the more obviously and undeniably do we find that this masterful supremacy in the ordering and making of life lies within the passions themselves. It is the instincts themselves that push nations into these novel social arrangements; it is the instinctive pressure of impulse that actually works the change. Affections, feelings, emotions, are the real and living agents who make history what it is; conscious and critical reason plays in the drama but a subordinate part. And yet the result is rational. It is not that irrational forces are made use of by reason to produce rational results, but the wonder is that these rational results issue out of the action of these very forces which appear so irrational. These forces, then, if they are the factors of society, of civilisation, must hold within themselves the secret of the issue; they cannot be empty of that reason, the existence of which their whole activity proves and exhibits. The passions of a man are themselves intelligent; they move under the motives of reason.

So we conclude from history, and so we find in ourselves. We each individually reveal a character built up out of feelings which, at first sight, we class with the instincts of the animal, or attribute to the blind influences of fleshly impressions. And yet, after all, it is out of these that our *rational* character emerges; it is out of these feelings that we elaborate a history which is perpetually advancing its problems, its needs, its solutions, its satisfactions; it is in these very feelings that we make manifest to all who have eyes to see, or ears to listen, the tokens of an enduring self, whose actions men can count upon and calculate, whose movements they can classify and connect, whose growth they can confidently anticipate. And still deeper down in our self-study, we discover strange effects in those impulses which at first we called animal. They are not content to lie back behind the narrow barriers within which the simple passions of that dim animal world run their unchanging round. They break through that ancient monotony; they take to themselves larger powers; they feel their way towards new possibilities; they increase the force and extend the range of their desires. The passions, in becoming human, are no longer animal. It is not that they are differently managed and treated; it is that they themselves are changed; they themselves desire what no animal desires; they themselves exceed, as no animal exceeds; they themselves disclose in their very excess a secret instinct of self-discipline, in which lies the seed of the new law, the law of Purity and Holiness. The appetite that is capable of self-assertion is driven by its own inner necessities to the task of self-control. Morality, as we look at it closely and carefully, is no system imposed on passion from without; it is itself the very heart of all desire, the very principle of all human impulse, the very inspiration of all passion. Out of the growth and increase of these vaster passions, righteousness springs like a flower to perfect, like a revelation to interpret, all that without its manifestation is left unfulfilled and unexplained. And if so, then these passions, these impulses, cannot be altogether blind and unpurposing. They have it in them to produce a rational order; they hold, hidden within their extravagance, the mystery of control; they inevitably tend towards temperance and chastity. They are, then, already rational; they are, from the very start, already moral.

All history, then, whether of ourselves or of nations, stands as a witness to the rational and moral necessities that underlie, and stir, and move, and invigorate, and propel the passionate instincts of our living humanity. Reason does not watch and rule from above, merely looking out from its high castle windows upon the surging and unruly mob that sweeps up and down the passages of the loud, unsteady city. It descends disguised often under some dark-hooded cloak, and mixes in with the loose and free tumult of the crowds; it lends its far-reaching skill to their uses; it sends up its voice into their cries; it lets them see, through its eyes, the larger horizon; it feeds, with its strength, their daring aspirations. The world of human passion feels, from end to end, the quickening movements of this infused and invigorating power.

So much it seems almost imperative to conclude.

But this recognition, so full of force, so rich with light, leads us inevitably to expect the truth of its counter proposition.

If man, as it appears, is no animal with reason attached, but rather is so entirely and perfectly one, that that which was most allied to the animal loses its sheer animality by contact with the new gift of thought, and itself is affected all through by a strange, transforming force, and becomes itself an advancing instead of a stationary kingdom, and exhibits novel effects, and wins unlooked-for range—if impulse is so changed by being advanced from association with instinct to association with that which, at least, is so different from instinct that we call it reason; then will it not also be most likely that reason, too, will be no entirely separable thing, isolated, removed from all direct hold on that which it so directly inspires? If the passions displayed in human action be indivisibly penetrated by reason, will man's reason so energize as to exclude the inter-action of passion? Will it not—does it not exhibit, throughout all its activity, the intimacy of its inner communion with those passions in which it so vigorously acts? If impulses are rational, is not reason impulsive? If feeling be instinct with reason, is not reason alive with feeling? If the one is so sensitive to its contact with the other, will the latter remain untouched by the same undivided contact? We may with ease distinguish the two, and the distinction we draw may be genuine and real: but yet, for all that, it need not be final; and indeed it cannot be final, if the man in whom both distinctions meet is himself indivisibly and inseparably *one*. He, the man, lives with the same self within either half of his life: he, the man, is as passionate as he is rational, and as rational as he is passionate: he recognises himself as readily, as entirely, on the one side as on the other of our distinction: in both he equally lives, moves, and acts, and with neither can he peculiarly or exclusively identify himself: in and out of both chambers he passes freely; in both, he knows himself at home; the passions are his and his only, such as none but he could have and feel. The reason is his, and his only, such as none but only he could accept, or use, or understand; from him both feelings and thoughts derive all their reality, all their character; divorced from him, they would be, both of them, shadowy and unintelligible. Bonded together in his indissoluble personality, they move together when they move at all; they are penetrable by each other's influences, they are touched by each other's infirmities, they respond to each other's invitations, they move under the pressure of mutual motives. Neither, in the final resort, would be explicable, except by the interpretation of the other. No single feeling that that one man feels could ever finally be conceivable as a feeling that might have occurred to any one else. It is intelligible only in its context with that one man's life: it is an expression of his being, of his character, of his thoughts, and of no one else's, in all the wide world. And again, no single thought that that same man thinks can ever finally set itself loose from the fibres that knit it up by infrangible bonds into that organic unity which is the self, and which feels as well as thinks.

The reason in man is human; that is all we mean. It does not act or live on its own account in abstract isolation: it does not work alone: it is not itself possessed of substantial and independent being; it belongs not to itself, but to another—to a man, to a being, that is, who is not only rational, but also imaginative, impulsive, sensitive, moral, spiritual. It is under this man's impulse that it argues and discusses; it is part and parcel of his corporate and complex existence. The whole long chain of its syllogisms is never mechanical:

it is alive along all its length, and feels at every joining the throbbing currents of his moving life. It is against the very law of reason's existence to separate it from all that, without which it would not be what it is. In such separation its energy dwindles, its leaps of advance cease, its bracing courage dies down, and all its potency disappears. We know not whence it drew its old force; we cannot entice it into its ancient audacities. Its rapid and intuitive connections, once so certain, so necessary, so imperious, all break up and vanish; the thread is cut, and the beads are all scattered.

Now, if so, what follows? Does it follow that, since reason derives its use and force from the particular man who works it, all thinking is therefore purely individual — the peculiar property of each separate rational soul? Does no one man think as any other man does? The answer to that question can surely be given only by turning to the results that follow the exercise of each man's reason. What is the issue of this exercise? Does he find himself, when he thinks, out of all accord with what other men are thinking? Are none of his arguments theirs? Are their conclusions never his? Amid all the intense variety of individual character which enters into the play of thought, are there no large and decisive unities that display themselves? Are there none that continually advance, and grow, and gain power, and enlarge their testimony, and establish confidence? Do men find that there follows, on the use of their reason, a sense of bitter loneliness, of horrible isolation? Do they, the more they think, hold ever more aloof from their fellows? Do they find themselves thrown back, shocked, jostled, when they utter their minds? Are they, when they try to argue or discuss, ever running their heads against hard walls? Or is it not exactly the contrary? Is it not in ignorance of each other's minds that men meet with rude rejections, and batter vainly against blind barriers? Is not the exercise of thought one long and delightful discovery of the identity that knits us up into the main body of mankind? If ever we do succeed in putting our thoughts into words that others understand, is it not a sure road to their hearts? Do they not run to greet us with open arms? Our sympathies, our hopes, our desires, do we not, when once we can find a language to express what they are to us, re-discover them all in the souls of our fellows? Is not all language one enduring and irresistible witness to the reality and depth of the communion which our thought arrives at, as soon as man touches man? And each new tongue or dialect brings with it new and delicious proof. There, in its forms, and assumptions, and ideals, and bonds, we read out what we within ourselves know and understand. It is our own mind that rises up reflected in this mirror. We enter into its most intricate ways with ready delight. Even its most surprising turns become intelligible as we watch them. Something in us wakes up from long slumber at the kiss of this strange arrival; something in us responds and welcomes and admits.

And history, again, at first so startling, so odd, so repellent, yet only requires study to open its secrets. The more we throw the light of careful thought upon its records, the more intelligible it becomes. We find

ourselves no longer repelled. Our minds mix freely
with the old fancies and doings. Here, too, we have
only to watch, and some familiar things emerge. The
confused babble steadies its voice into the harmonies of
a music that we feel and enjoy. The sense of nearness
and of intimacy grows stronger and firmer, and over all
there comes a look of friendliness and a touch of kindly
kinship. And, indeed, what is it that we intend to express
by that hard word "civilisation," that word which re-
minds us of such thronging miseries, and yet cheers us
always with a sense of inexhaustible promise, if it is not
this—that, in spite of all encumbering sorrows that burden
and trouble our way, in spite of the wide and desolating
cruelties that haunt and disfigure our advance, it is yet
worth all the pain to know, with increasing recognition,
that large fellowship of mind, and heart, and will, which
is for ever disclosing its untold resources, its unnumbered
delights, to those who dare to believe that "God hath
made man to be of one blood over all the face of the
earth"? Men are indeed of one heart and one mind,
and might have all things, if they would, in common.
This is the promise. And civilisation is the secured
discovery that this good news is true. It is the growing
acknowledgment how joyful and pleasant a thing it is
for brethren to dwell together in unity.

Reason, then, though exercised under the inspiration
of each varying and separate character, does yet testify,
by the social community in which its working inevitably
issues, that it is no isolated or isolating agency; that its
activities work in the mass, and signalize an irresistible
unity of law, and life, and movement. But if so, it

follows from what has been said that this unity must be looked for, not in the mere mechanism of reason—for reason is no mechanical instrument that any one who uses, inevitably uses in one way: reason, we say, is instinct with personal life throughout all its uses. And if it testifies to unity, then that unity must be looked for behind the formal rules and regulated motions of that abstraction which we call reason; it must be discoverable in the very heart-life of the personal character out of whose energy reason proceeds. There, far back in the deep recesses of our innermost being, in that last home of self-existence, even there, it would seem, we discover no separate, no lonely life; even there penetrates and prevails the sway of common movement, the strong influences that knit, and bind, and gather together. Unity is no accident made possible, to individuals essentially different, by the incidental exercise of a common reasoning faculty. Rather the use of the faculty gives steadfast proof that the individuals in whom it so essentially inheres are not divided and distinct, but are pervaded and possessed by ineffaceable unities, by ineradicable identities, which testify to their power and presence by every word that is spoken, by every deed that is done. It is we ourselves who are discovered in the common, the universal necessities of thought; it is we ourselves, and not merely our "laws of thought," who are then discovered to be at one with our fellow-men, to be bound up with them into a union so radical that we call it "necessary," so irrevocable that we call it "absolute." It is our very self that cannot act without revealing within itself those essential assumptions which all men instinctively adopt, and none can finally avoid.

To return, then, reassured, to our first point. At the roots of all reasoning lies the personal, the individual man: it is he from out of whom the reasoning issues: it is his living personality which endows it with motion, and being, and act. No wonder, then, if all reasoning starts with some primary assumptions: they are inevitable, since reason itself, the faculty of thought, has no independent existence of its own, but assumes always, behind it and in it, a living person, from whom it derives its existence, by whom it is set in action, in whom it finds its home, in whose energy it works, in whose service it is alive. Here, then, is reason's assumption. It is not complete in itself; it assumes a life which is not thought nor feeling, but is a single man, who both thinks and feels at once; who never altogether ceases either to think all the time that he is feeling, or to feel all the time that he thinks. Without such assumption, reason cannot begin: without it, it has no intelligible force, no valid security, no confidence in itself. It cannot find reasons to justify its root-principles. No; how should it? Its roots are imbedded in the man from whom it wins its life, and draws its succours and supplies. In his existence lies its sole justification: in the light of his character alone can its working be seen and understood: to him all its quick motions, all its rapid transitions, are intelligible, are logical, are irresistible, are necessary, *for they are himself.*

And, if it appears that these primary principles, which all reasoning assumes are not private and peculiar, but

The Venture of Reason. 33

large, common, universal, then we are driven, not to drop our first conclusion, but to believe a second; to believe that each single human being, who is himself the ground and justification of all the reasoning that he puts in action, testifies as he reasons to that binding fellowship which enters into, and penetrates, and possesses all his inward personal life—testifies to the intense and over-mastering reality of that common blood and brotherhood which encompasses and embraces all mankind, sealing on each soul its irrevocable stamp, animating each with its exhaustless breath, fashioning each to the liking of its dominant and imperial will.

Reason begins, then, with an assumption, an assumption that abides with it from the beginning to the end of its unceasing process; an assumption that all its action continually asserts, and continually verifies. It assumes the life by which it lives, the personality which it unwaveringly expresses. Without this assumption it cannot start, and that first assumption it never abandons: all its after-success, all its advances, are but a continuous disclosure of the full significance which that initial act included and involved.

Slowly man discovers the rich wealth of meaning with which an enlarged experience abundantly fills the simple and naked assumption, which his own free action constituted at the first to be the rule and scheme of all his thinking. Every touch, every sight, every sound, bring in to him their delightful confirmation, and ratify, with unfaltering faithfulness, those earliest movements in which his intelligence first asserted itself, that primary act of courageous anticipation, which leapt out from the dark silence of his spirit at the first moment in which he felt the greeting of a world outside himself. In that initiating act he has anticipated the whole round of knowledge; every motion forward is but a new discovery of the marvels that lay hidden in that bold claim with which he demanded the submission of all experiences to the conditions which he, without warrant, seemingly, and without a prospect of proof, asserted his right to impose upon them. The right was asserted without its proofs; the claim was, indeed, made without sanction or warrant. Who could say that man had the right to believe himself in possession of the power to know and grasp the real principles of things? But he had the courage to enforce his claim, to anticipate his warrants, and, ever since that daring self-assertion, the proofs have been pouring in with overwhelming abundance to justify and sustain it.

In what, then, does reason begin? How should we describe the act from which it issues?

It is an act, a movement, by which the inner man, that soul and substance of all the thoughts and all the feelings that express him, steps forward, at the touch of an outward world, and asserts his kinship, his alliance, his union, his communion, with that which has advanced to meet him from without. He recognises it, he welcomes it, he runs out, to fall, as it were, into the ready embraces of a brother: he lets himself go in confidence and security, as a bird that drops from branch or tower upon the large and steady spaces of the enfolding air: he leaps with a free spirit into these moving waters of encircling life, and, lo! as with hands they receive him,

The Venture of Reason. 35

as with arms they uplift him, and in the hollows of their deep bosom he finds himself carried, and at peace.

Now, what word have we by which to describe an act at once so presumptuous and yet so trustful; what word, if it be not the word "Faith"?

Faith is just such a movement forward of the entire being, under the compelling impulse of its own inward daring, to greet the advent of a novel visitant, who is at once strange, and yet instinctively familiar. Faith is that act of prophetic anticipation which risks everything on a venture, which nothing but the results can ever justify. Faith is that which lies shut up and asleep until the wakening touch of this incoming guest approaches, and stirs, and arouses; and then, at the first moment of the contact, does not so much think, or feel, as *will* that a future for itself should spring out of that momentary union. It wills in the power of some instinctive sympathy; it wills to trust itself to the fascination that draws it forward; it wills to rely upon the kinship that it assumes; it wills itself to be one with the arriving life. At the back of all the impressions of feeling, at the back of all the spontaneities of thought, lies the deep strength of energetic self-assertion which men call will; a self-assertion that presumes so far, not out of the blindness of pride, but out of the brave freedom of a childlike trust. It pushes out, it presses forward, it puts forth its force, because it is so true to the calls that summon it into action, because its innocent simplicity relies so readily on the genuineness and reality of all that it encounters. Such energy flows out into its wishes, that it seems to compel their realisation; so actively does it desire to know, that it seems to enforce things to conform to the conditions of its knowledge: they bend to the sway of its strong and effectual desires; it imposes upon them, as we say, its categories; and yet this imposition is, after all, nothing but its own natural and willing conformity to the conditions of that outward existence with which it so resolutely intends to unite itself, and so passionately believes itself to be akin. This is the paradox of knowledge; and this strange combination of passive submission with victorious activity is surely an exact repetition, on lower levels, of the characteristic working of that spiritual faith which we know better as it meets us in the highest walks of life—that faith which relies so ardently upon another, so desperately disbelieves in its own powers, that it itself acquires the force to achieve that which it asks for from another, and, in answer to its loud appeal for help and deliverance, is told that its own inherent energy has obtained the good result, "Thy faith hath made thee whole!"

Reason, then, dates its birth from some act in which it at once received from without, and yet assumed, and asserted, and presumed, from within; some act in which it both accepted impressions and yet imposed categories. And such an act corresponds to the nature of faith,—faith which is at once receptive, yet assertive: the extreme of passivity, and yet the extreme of activity.

Reason starts with an act which assumes and anticipates all that it afterwards discovers, and faith is that in us which is prophetic. It antedates its results:

it pronounces all done from the moment that all has begun: it seals to us in one momentary act that which a long and complicated process will afterwards realize and fulfil; a process that could not begin except by assuming its own possibility, by which assumption it is indeed made possible. By believing that it has, it does verily receive.

Once more, reason must begin in a movement of the entire man; and such a movement is faith; faith which carries the whole being along in despite of feelings, and in defiance of proof, by an energetic exertion of its living will, which leaps forward, and lays hold of, and clings close, and cleaves fast to, an object to which it becomes, by the very force of that vivifying impulse, assimilated, and united, and akin. That prime movement forward to salute the approach of a message from elsewhere, that first grip on the incoming life that meets it from outside, is an inspiration of the will preceding reason; yet not for that irrational, since it issues in reason, which spreads its powers in perpetual and enduring witness to the rational rightness of that act of trust from which it wins all its sanction and all its authenticity.

And can it be, then, that even in the barest exercise of reason we have stepped out into such deep waters? Is it indeed true that, in every motion of thought, we have already let go of all ropes and stakes that could give us a hold on the solid and steady earth, and can feel the ground no longer under our feet, but are being lifted and borne along by strange waves, in which we float suspended and amazed? Is it impossible even to think without abandoning ourselves to a movement, of which we can have but doubtful experience, and know not at all the issue? Is it contrary to reason's own law, that we should desire to secure certainty before we dare to act? Does reason itself refuse to exist, except to those who venture with no faint heart to follow the fascination of hope? Is it impossible to be rational without passing beyond the bounds of reason, without surrendering reason itself to the compulsion of a prophetic inspiration? Does all thinking hang on an act of faith? Can it be true that we can never attain to intellectual apprehension unless the entire man in us throws his spirit forward, with a willing confidence, with an unfaltering trust, into an adventurous movement; unless the entire man can bring himself to respond to a summons from without, which appeals to him by some instinctive touch of strange and unknown kinship to rely on its attraction, to risk all on the assumption of its reality?

A touch of kinship! Yes, kinship alone could so stir faith: and the call, therefore, to which it responds must issue from a Will as living, as personal, as itself. Ah! surely, then, "God is in this place, and I knew it not." From the first dawn of our earliest intelligent activity we move under the mighty breath of One higher and lordlier than we wot of: we walk in the high places, we are carried we know not whither. Not for one instant may we remain within the narrow security of our private domain; not for one moment may we claim to be self-possessed, self-contained, self-centred, self-controlled. Every action carries us out-

The Venture of Reason. 39

side ourselves; every thought that we can think is a revelation of powers that draw us forward, of influences that lift us out of the safety of self-control. To reason is to have abandoned the quiet haven of self-possession; for already in its first acts we feel the big waters move under us, and the great winds blow. We live by trust: life in its most rational and experimental form is still a venture, a hope which only justifies itself by its success. We can never escape the risks of faith, can never hold back and refuse to move till we are sure of our footing: so to hold back is never to begin. Everywhere faith makes its awful demand: everywhere we walk, not in the flesh, not in ourselves, but in the Spirit; in all things, we must believe that we have, in order to receive. Not even reason itself can shirk the imperative call. It, too, must make its leap into the dark. It, too, must surrender itself to the violence of an irresistible hope. It was no new law to which our Lord appealed when He bade His beloved "Have faith in God." His appeal only called forward into new energy that which was already the profoundest secret of all our life, the base and substance of our being. All our whole nature stirred and awoke at the great summons, just because there is nothing in us which does not know and obey the inspirations of faith. The very first moment of our experience had felt its motive and followed its impulse. "Whither, then, O my God, can I fly from Thy presence? If I ascend up to heaven, Thou art there: if I go down to hell, Thou art there also! If I take the wings of the morning, and dwell in the uttermost parts of the sea, even there shall Thy hand lead me, and Thy right hand shall hold me." Not only in the high places of Thy revelation do I find Thy tokens! Not only at the close of my long pilgrimage do I throw myself upon Thy heart, or fall before Thy feet! Not only there, but from afar I greet Thee; from the lowest levels of my rational soul! In Thy name, even there, I move forward! By faith in Thee, from the first hour, I set out! Upon Thee I did cast myself when first my thought stirred itself into life! Thine arms, even then, were under me! In Thee did I put my trust! Oh suffer not that earliest faith to fail until it carries us up to that nobler faith which they exercise, who, in that they have believed in God, believe also in His Son! "Leave us not, neither forsake us, O Lord God of our salvation!"

SERMON III.

THE SPIRIT, AND ITS INTERPRETATION.

"What man knoweth the things of a man, save the spirit of man which is in him? Even so the things of God knoweth no man, but the Spirit of God."—1 COR. ii. 11.

"A MAN who would write the history of a religion must believe it no longer, but must have believed it once." So pronounces the great French critic; and yet, in what a dilemma are we landed by this incisive epigram! How, then, are we to prepare ourselves for historical and critical treatment of religion? How can we be sure of securing the fit conditions? Can we believe experimentally merely for the purposes of discovery? Can we be certain of being able to cease from our belief at the moment at which we propose to begin our critical examination? Or must all then be left to happy chance? Must the historical study of religions be confined to those who have happened by good luck to fall outside the faiths which once they held? It is an awkward test to have to apply to candidates for the study. And, again, are we to consider them fortunate or unfortunate to find themselves so qualified? Which is the healthier condition of mind,—the earlier, or the later? If the later is the more natural and the more perfect, how can the earlier be at all sound or entire? And, if not sound, how can it be the essential groundwork of the critical temper? It can hardly be that the later temper is a product of the earlier,—that the natural evolution of uncritical faith is into critical doubt. For what happens in the loss of the temper of faith is, that we abandon the attempt to develop our faith. We call upon other and alien forces to fructify within us: we move under other influences; motives, once unfelt or disregarded, now stir us strongly; the old powers that once lifted us are withdrawn: we are in a different road, travelling along a different line. Once we tried one road, now we are trying another. It is not merely that we have spiritualized old ways of conceiving our religious aims; but what we now require for our present purpose of unbiassed criticism is, that we should have passed out of that temper which moves by some inspiration of faith, into that which no longer knows the witchery of such attractions: and such a temper cannot be the normal product of the earlier mood; and, if not its normal product, when and how can it be normal to break with the old and adopt the new? Is it a matter of regret, or of victory? These questions seem as endless, perhaps, as they are frivolous; and yet surely it is just such questions as these which M. Renan leaves us to the last in doubt whether he has ever clearly faced and answered. He loves, for instance, the high Roman ideal,—the Petrine Legend. You can read his picture of the early Christian centuries without discovering any more trace of the Eastern Church than you would find in the Forged Decretals. He enjoys the

The Spirit, and its Interpretation. 43

flavour of this bold conception; but is this enjoyment, we keep asking ourselves as we read, so piquant, *because* the conception is so unreal, so legendary? Or, again, he bids us cherish the brave and beautiful defiance which the religions have hurled at the inevitable doom of Death: but are we to cherish them because the doom is inevitable? Does the bravery of the defiance, then, lie in its hopelessness? Does the beauty of the dream lie in our knowledge that it will vanish away? Is the glory of a faith, that glad glory which bewitches, to be found in the splendid daring with which it lies? Are we to regret the falsehood of the "sweet Galilean Vision," or to rejoice in it?

Such are the puzzles in which he leaves us; and I would ask, is not this the paradox which haunts so much of the sympathetic modern criticism,—the paradox which lies at the heart of the delicious joy with which we enter into and revive the very charm which dead things once exercised; a joy which has in it the pride of successfully proving our capacity to embrace within the range of our sympathies that which is not ours, as well as the sense of freedom from the fearful anxiety which would belong to any passionate belief that the charm was real; and, moreover, carries with it also the pathos which distils from all memorials of buried delights.

We are, many of us, I think, brought into a certain confusion of mind by the very variety of our emotional exercises. We idealize the Past instead of the Future; we throw ourselves into the feelings and passions of a hundred dead generations. But such idealization works upon us with less practical force than an imaginary future; for its very charm, if we would confess it, is often the laziness with which we can afford to regard ideals which, fair and enthralling as once they were, have this additional fascination now, that their day is over, and they are perished for evermore. There they lie, all at peace, in their white shrouds; sweet visions that once drove hearts this way and that! How gracious were those eyes, now closed to us! how swift those limbs, now cold and still! Pleasant it is to stay or watch by their silent tombs, and picture their lovely life, and dimly feel the ancient sway; and yet, for all that, know that we have not got to do and die, as those once did, whom these visions drew into pain, and anguish, and heroic graves! We seem, as we revive the lost scenery, to be admitted to enjoy what those of old once saw, and felt, and followed; and yet we have in the background the proud confidence that we are free from the tyranny of that bewitchment by which they were mastered. We can see its limit; we can trace out the story of its fall; we are not captured in its bondage, to be persuaded, as they were, that there was no vision that could fascinate as this, which maddened them with such strong desire. No! When we have done with this of theirs, we have a hundred others as good, to which we can turn, which we can revive, to which we can give ourselves, until we are tired again with that, and ready to try the power of another. We are free from all, because we can criticise them all: but, then, do we really think that we know what they meant to the men who pursued them? Nay, surely! for to them each of these fair visions seemed the one and only victory for which it was well worth while to give up all else and die. It was the entire singleness, the utter supremacy of that one vision over all others, that gave it its power, that accounted for its marvellous sway: unless you see it in its masterful, and energetic, and compelling predominance, you do not see it as they saw it, nor understand it as they understood it. To them it was not one among many. For in it they believed; and to believe, what is it but to be subdued by the apparent predominance of one aim over all others? And we are shut out from understanding this subdual which is belief, so long as to us the aim is one which moves us indeed, but moves us only as many other ideals move us.

M. Renan himself sees further than this. To criticise a religion, to know it, to appreciate its history, you must, he allows, have *once* genuinely believed it; you must have passed under the mastery with which it swept up the whole of your manhood into its single dominion; you must have known how it filled, with its one imperial impulse, the heavens, and the earth, and the sky, and the sea, and the wind, and the fire, and all the silent spaces, the unseen movements, of those deep abysses where God and the Spirit touch, and mingle, and speak.

And yet strongly as he asserts this necessity, he still protests that all this must have ceased before the critical understanding can undertake its proper work: the sympathetic appreciation of its object, which is imperatively required in order that the criticism may be thorough and vital, must yet be but that melancholy and pathetic tribute which the living pay to the mighty dead.

Can this be an intelligible position? Does not the double demand betray to the light, by its epigrammatic vigour, a confusion which is continually troubling us, with a dark sense of perplexity, in ways more subtly concealed? For instance, we travel along with the general and obvious theorizing about the freedom from preconception which must signalize the perfect historian, until we find ourselves slowly and surely shut out from any power to measure or gauge the forces that build up history: for these forces are passions,—the passionate clinging to the right; the passionate loathing of wrong; the strong pressure of national cravings; the tempestuous rush of young movements towards new ideals; and how can the cool indifferent reason, that cares not which way the battle goes, propose to weigh, and sift, and estimate such forces as these? By what standard can it judge them? What balances has *indifference* by which it can test the fury of warring opposites? Without some living interest in the issue, history looks to us as the wild medley of madmen, whose rage, and anxieties, and designs fill us with a painful distress at their reckless exaggeration, at their ungentle obstinacy. Something is wrong, then; the historian must have a cue by which to disentangle this disorder: he must see, and make for, a right and a wrong: he must compel us to pass under the anxieties that harass the onward movements of the good: he must fill us with indignant wrath at the terrible working of the wrong.

So we are pulled up, yet without making quite clear

to ourselves how far or in what sense we are limiting our original position, that the historian is to be free from all partiality.

Or again, in theology, we go on pretty freely with those who plead that if truth be the sole aim, the searcher must surely be loose from all presuppositions that bind him to a particular conclusion, until it is at last provokingly suggested that the possession of a belief is a positive disqualification for a theologian.

Here we draw up again. An absurdity has come about; yet where exactly is the flaw in the argument? It is not so easy to say; only we feel that, somewhere or other, there is a limitation to our first position; but where it falls, is left to our private common-sense to determine; and each of us roughly places it there, where he himself habitually happens to arrive at assumptions which, to his mind, may fairly be considered final.

It is this difficulty, underlying and troubling our common discussion, which is brought to a head in the formula I have quoted from M. Renan; and I would ask you to consider for a few moments whether the truth of the first half of the statement will not, of necessity, turn the second half into paradox: whether it be not a bit of grim humour to suggest that the critic, in the field of religious belief, requires for his task the use of two inconsistent and divorced tempers.

To give the adequate history of a religion, then, you must first have believed it. This is our primary datum: and this means surely that the elements of that rational intelligibility, which comes to the surface under the action of the critical reason, are to be found *within* the living material of the belief itself.

Reason does not find its ground, its justification, its credibility, its evidence in itself, in its own separate and distinct working; it goes for these to that on which it works. *There* lies all its intelligibility. The gain achieved by the reason is simply the disclosure that the belief was already rational. All that it discloses was already the life and substance of that effort which we call Faith. Reason does but parallel within its own region, on its own conditions, that temper of mind which held secreted within it all that which now emerges into intelligible form. It offers an equivalent to what has before been felt: and if so, then the man who knows both sides can alone appreciate the value of the equivalence. To him, indeed, the living agent in both fields, this equivalence is no arbitrary and inexplicable symbolism: for he comes to himself in each: he is the same being in each: he is sure of his own identity throughout, and cannot, therefore, treat the two fields of his life as if they were sundered by a blind gulf: but still his ultimate consciousness is simply the direct consciousness of the reality of this parallelism between the matter of his thought and the form which thought gives it. And any process of reasoning, therefore, any structure of thought, is only really intelligible to him when it conveys to him something more than it actually says; when it suggests that of which it offers an image; when it enables him to assume all that it embodies, and reflects, and refashions, and exhibits.

And what an immense task has reason undertaken, then, when it attempts the critical portrayal of a spiritual faith!

The Spirit, and its Interpretation. 49

A task genuine, indeed justifiable, fruitful, progressive; but yet how vast, how complicated, how delicate ! It has undertaken to offer and present an intellectual parallel that will answer and correspond, in all its parts and proportions, to that huge emotional movement which expresses itself in an entire religion. It proposes to carry this whole body of spiritual activity across from one region of life into another, that it may make it intelligible by the very fact of giving it its double, of presenting to it its adequate equivalent. To appreciate such a task, we must recall to mind the depth and subtlety of that with which its reason has to deal. How can we measure its wonder, its overwhelming profundity ?

Let us example it by that other mode, by which we attempt the measure of our emotions, the mode of Art. Art, as well as thought, offers to explain our inner movements of soul by repeating them in a new region, and by the aid of a new material; and the complexities of the arts, therefore, are but an effort to gauge complexities of spirit.

A piece of orchestral music, with its web of interwoven melodies, its mazes of winding sound, its concourse of respondent instruments, its rhythmic sequences, its intricate variety of repetition, its rises and falls and balanced counterparts, its pauses, its refrains, its quadruple movements, that meet, and sunder, and return, and retire, its long and linked sweetness, its storm of gathered forces, its full and flowing wealth of multitudinous harmonies,—all this most subtle and powerful fabric of our invention, almost infinite in its manifold appliances, is but the machinery by which we attempt to embody and represent one small portion of that enormous world of spiritual life, which is alive within the range and compass of any single human soul. Not all the utmost elaboration of that marvellous musical skill can go beyond the limits of those passions which we hold, every one of us, within ourselves; and can use, and exercise, and enjoy, whenever the quickening touch of some sympathetic motion flashes out upon us from within or from without. Not all the tremulous voices of the flutes, not all the swift sighings of the violins, not all the noise of clanging trumpets or of shuddering drums, can equal or exhaust the splendour of our daily human joys, the throbbings of our loves, the quick pulsations of our fears, the nerveless sinking of our stricken hearts. The lovers that move on still evenings along the sheltering lanes, the mourners that creep back from a silent grave to a sullen and desolate home, these know more than all that storm of sound will ever say. As we listen to high music, rapt and uplifted, we learn what it is that we ourselves have been, what it is that we have felt, what it is that we could be, if the call came, if the blow struck, if the light broke in, if the darkness swept down. We are surprised, it may be, to discover all that is possible. We are carried forward to explore new regions of our souls as yet untouched and untrodden: there is much, we see, to open out, much to free, much to expose and expand: fresh springs of feeling are set loose: the doors and windows of all hidden chambers are flung open: at the kiss of this sweet music, all that had slept in frozen silence leaps upward into movement, startled by the touch of joy, or the sudden quickening of some tender thrill. We are surprised: yes! but we are not surpassed, we are not outdone, we are not dismayed or disappointed: still we have it in us, we are assured, to be all that the music can ever tell. That huge and intricate life, whose long story it is imagining, is ours, is shut up within our souls: we have felt it stirring, we recognise it all, we understand. This is why it speaks home to us, speaks with such familiar voices, with such intelligible pathos, with such illuminating eloquence; and far as the musician's ingenuity may ever reach, still all he can ever achieve will but continue to reveal the untold depths, and height, and length, and breadth of those emotions, under whose sway we now are moving,—of those impulses which we ourselves can, even now, in strong and passionate hours, both touch, and taste, and handle.

Here, then, in those mazes of musical writings, with all their elaborate and bewildering symbols, their endless intricacy of mechanism, we see some sample of the measurement demanded by the play, and motion, and variation of that spiritual stuff which makes our original and essential life.

We might example it again in the familiar instance of a people's literature. How huge is the effort there embodied! The very grammar itself of each separate tongue is a marvel of ingenious and manifold devices by which every shade of changing significance may find its expression. And yet this is but the beginning. That language, already in its barest grammatical form, a most intricate structure, is taken up, and turned and twisted this way and that, with a thousand thousand minutely different transpositions, into periods subtly varied, modulated by ever-shifting intonations, with unwearied persistence, with infinite pains, that at last it may succeed in giving some slight gradation of sentiment which no single expression had yet adequately conveyed. This or that feeling remains hidden and lost, restless and uneasy, until some tiny transference of phrases, some curious change, indescribable and unanticipated, in the sequence of the words, attains victorious utterance through some prophetic lips: we recognise it in an instant. That is what we waited for: that is the word: no other but that. A hundred poets had striven to say it, but no one till now could exactly seize what we felt and knew. So delicate are the balances, so minute the scales with which we test our inner life!

And if this is so, if this is true of all that stuff of human passions which music and literature attempt to parallel and measure; if each separate emotion of the heart be capable of such consummate and minute intricacy of difference, what, then, must be the power, and fulness, and depth of that supreme spiritual movement in which the entire man, gathering up into a single effort all that builds up his humanity, all his aspirations of love, all his passion of desire, all his vehemence of curiosity, all his indignation at wrong, all his desperate horror of remorse, all his bitterness of desolation, all his hunger for help, all his straining after righteousness, all his inspiration of hope, all his terror of death, all his searching of soul, all his agony of sin, all his audacity of faith,—summoning the whole body of emotional impulses to his succour, throws himself forward with indomitable devotion, with unutterable effort, into the arms of God?

This is religion : this is the supreme moment which crowns that strange and secret life which all the powers of art have for so long striven to test, and weigh, and sift, and sort, and distinguish, and arrange. They have spent their strength again and again in giving some echo, some reflection of that gladness which any man and maiden feel when first they know the response of love ; and, lo ! here is a love, dominant and high, under the pressure of which men have cast to the winds all the treasures of that lower human love in which art has found so inexhaustible, so unutterable a theme ! Here is a sorrow which all the pangs and pains of earthly desolation do but faintly portray, the sorrow of an eternal love ! Here is a death whose horror and woe the bodily corruption does but seal and confirm ! Who can tell, then, the immensity of this huge world into which we have entered ? Who can penetrate or number its spaces, its secrecies, its maze of marvellous chambers, its halls, its towers, its ways, and paths, and wanderings ? If the lower emotions demanded all that subtle and delicate handling, then the highest emotion will be yet more sensitive than they. It will hold a richer abundance of mysterious charms ; it will repel, far more than they, imperfect and unworthy expressions : it will appreciate yet stronger differences and yet more rigorous distinctions.

Nor is this all. The sum of the difficulty is yet to come. This peculiar sublimation of the entire man, which crowns his emotional and spiritual activity, and which we name religion, wins for itself strange and novel conditions. Here, at the summit of fleshly life, we pass over the fleshly limits; the whole movement upward, which has tended throughout to surpass itself, to overstep its natural boundaries, to generate fresh motions as fast as it completes them, to reach out after discoveries of wider range and larger meaning than any yet attained—this movement does here, at last, in religion arrive at that transcendence after which it has strained from the first. Here, at last, it does not merely push out feelers into an unknown beyond, but is conscious of a response that meets it from without, of a fulfilment which enters in to answer its efforts, of a correspondence between its inward dreams and its outward experience. For long it has pushed and thrust into the dark; it has known only the dim stir of flying cries that spoke and flew away. Now there are hands that touch, there are arms that uphold, there is a voice that abides, there are words that greet it with effectual welcome. Powers from afar mix and mingle with its endeavours: an unknown glory dazzles it with sudden consecration : blessings move down from above charged with the grace of abounding consolation. That mystery of the unseen, in all other fields vague and insecure, has now in the region of religion become steady, and certain, and persistent. The supernatural has discovered itself, has set loose its forces so long restrained: it puts out its strength and works.

The Spirit, and its Interpretation. 55

And under this strong working that now interweaves its motion into the intricacy of human efforts, man's impulses receive their transfiguration. They win for themselves solidity, consistency, security. They no longer grope, they touch; they no longer feel, they grasp; they no longer waver, they make for their aim, they go forward with glad confidence; they have found the path which no fowl knoweth; they pass in within the golden doors; they are raised from tentative emotions into assured beliefs; they have transcended their former hesitations, their loose and irregular movements; they have been shot through by a new fire, the flame of the spirit; they are uplifted into a *faith*. Now, for them, that which they report, that which they touch, that with which they hold communion, asserts undoubted dominance over all the lesser motives of the heart and of the spirit. It is not made known, except as supreme, alone, victorious, worth more than silver, or rubies, or coral. This is the peculiar significance of a faith. It cannot be held as one emotion among many. It leaps into some strange solitude of power. It lays triumphant and masterful pressure upon the swarming desires, upon the struggling will. Its strangeness lies in this mastery : it is not significant, if it is not imperious. Yet, whence comes this royal rigour, unless we may assume the entry in upon the scenery of human wishes of that mysterious Power, invisible, eternal, of whóse action we have just spoken —that action which breaks in from some world beyond upon the drama of our passions and our prayers?

This is religion. It is the crowning and transcendent

movement which reason undertakes to rationalize, *ana rightly undertakes*. It is not the right that we are questioning. If religion is the expression, the act of the entire man, and not merely of some peculiar and isolated organ in his being, it is inevitable that reason, which is part and parcel of that wholeness which is the man, should have its say about that action in which it itself, in its corporate capacity, as bound up with the unity of spirit, has already borne its share. It is inevitable; it cannot be excluded from that which is its own. Who, indeed, would desire its exclusion? Such office of rational interpretation is thought's highest and noblest labour, without which the spiritual movements themselves would work in oppressive and discouraging darkness, without freedom, without joy. They would miss their natural fruit, the blessed fruit of intelligent self-discovery; they would lack their true and perfect development.

Nay, it is just because the entire activity of faith is so eminently and intimately related to reason that the difficulty of which I speak is so pressing. For it is not from outside or incidentally that thought touches the works of faith: it penetrates the whole mass: it is woven into the fabric itself: it is inherent in the structure, in the constitution, in the material. Its office is to disclose this, its pre-existent presence; to unfold its secret prevalence, that prevalence in virtue of which it finds itself now enabled to bring forward, to estimate, to manipulate, to define the whole articulated scheme, allotting the due balance, the fit proportion of part to part, of part to whole, rendering account of the distinc-

The Spirit, and its Interpretation. 57

tions, distributing the gradations of force, justifying the fluctuations, and changes, and advances of the spiritual momentum.

This is its labour; and no wonder, then, that such a work can only be attempted with success by those whose reason has, at least once, enjoyed a living and energetic contact with that which it proposes to unravel. No wonder, perhaps, if it should be found impossible to ensure positive advance, unless this contact be still preserved fresh, and effective, and inspiring.

For can it be believed that thought can afford to permit this fortifying, interpretative touch to become a fading memory, already past and gone? Can it work securely on the basis of an inspiration which has already, for it, ceased to be justifiable, and therefore rational? Even if it can recall something of its lost emotion, yet the very fact that that emotion is now an impossibility turns all its niceties of difference into empty and frivolous distinctions: the edge is taken off its subtle varieties of flavour: they no longer possess this ancient significance. Can we ever efficiently recall them, any more than we can requicken into actual revival the quiver and sting of any other vivid sensation long dead and gone? Surely they slumber in remembrance, they touch us with the unreal doubtfulness of dreams; and yet it is in their vividness, their sharpness, their unmistakable effect, that their rationality lies. They are susceptible of intelligible distinctions—these spiritual sensations—only because they are so sensitively different, only when they are experimentally distinct.

And if it be hard to recall the varied impress of these

abandoned spiritual emotions, how much harder yet to recover and revive that which can never be again; that peculiar emphasis which raised them from a feeling into a faith; that touch of mastery, of supremacy, which gave them a dominance such as no other emotions conveyed or contained; that prophetic power which turned them from passing impressions into permanent symbols, into secure revelations, into sacramental moments such as seal us to themselves, moments not possessed but possessing, not our own but come from afar, not accidental but of eternal validity?

Does this mean that no religious criticism is possible except to those in full belief?

Who would venture to assert what facts would so obviously gainsay? We are far too mindful of all the brilliant and suggestive gains won out of the critical struggles of the last fifty years to make such a limitation possible to us. The movements of the human spirit are indeed too complicated and varied to be covered adequately by any one rule, or formula: or, again, a principle may be valid, a formula absolute, and yet the traces of its working may lie hidden amid all the manifold intricacies of the material with which it deals, and often it will appear to be contradicted as a law by the very effects it produces. The lights, for instance, that in our time come flashing in upon the Christian problem, from a hundred opposing points, may be but witnesses that the very intensity of partial and one-sided belief may enable it to penetrate more deeply into this or that recess of the faith, and to drag out the intimate secrets there lurking into clearer

The Spirit, and its Interpretation. 59

intelligibility than had ever been possible to a more balanced and entire belief.

So, again, there are differences in the degree in which the presence of faith will affect the various fields of study. The examination of the documents, of their origin, of their production, differs widely from the elucidation of dogma, as every one would admit. It is more difficult to detect, what I would especially notice this morning, how widely the HISTORICAL criticism of a religion depends for its results on the spiritual temper, on the spiritual apprehension of the critic. Yet his estimate of what is probable, of what is possible in the past, his calculation of motives, of forces, his interpretation of conduct, must all turn on his capacity of vivid and experimental insight into the nature of those Presences and Powers, whose effects he is measuring, and whose significance he professes to declare. It is at once rational and inevitable that a difference of belief as to the character of the forces engaged in the making of human history should involve our distrust of any historian, between whom and ourselves such difference lies: it is natural that any emphatic difference of the kind should issue in a collision of interpretations: and it is rational and inevitable, therefore, that, without presuming to limit the right of others to judge and weigh the story of the Past after their own mode and by their own standards, a Church which has a faith about life should yet endeavour to secure for itself a succession of students, who will come to the interpretation of her history with a spirit that is sensitive to all the forces which she believes to have been at work ; a spirit that feels and knows as its own the aims and the inspirations that, as she believes, have moved men and women in the days that are dead; a spirit that applies her standards to the motives of conduct, and calculates probabilities according to her estimate of the chances, and weighs out profit and loss by her rule and balance; a spirit that instinctively hopes what she hopes, trusts what she trusts, ignores what she ignores.

"To write the history of a religion a man must have believed it *once.*" Yes! and if it be needful once, then —if the criticism is ever to be other than fragmentary, if it is ever to be vital, and fruitful, and entire—it cannot but be needful always: for to have lost the belief is, as the formula confesses, to have lost the key to its history. It is, surely, only in sad irony, in bitter mistrust, that it is added, "he must have believed it once, but he must believe it no longer."

Has belief, then, by its own faithlessness, incurred this taunt against its honesty, its uprightness, its courage? Has it, indeed, feared to face its own problems with the reality and the singleness of heart which unbelief can bring to their unravelling? Has its sincerity, then, fallen so low that it cannot be trusted to use an equal scale? Has it had to appeal to those who have not enjoyed its good chances, nor possess its excellent tools, to assist it in the task for which it alone is adequately equipped?

These are solemn questions for us. They cannot be dismissed by a brave word of frank denial: they arouse in us shameful and humiliating doubts. We ought to have seen for ourselves long ago much that now we are

The Spirit, and its Interpretation.

shown by others' guidance. We ought to have learned to correct our blundering misapprehensions, without having had to undergo such late and painful schooling.

It is for us to bow our heads in confession and penitence before a God of truth, a God Who mightily secures us against all those perils which we so dreaded to face, and to ask ourselves, one and all, in the light of His instructing Spirit, what faithless fears we have allowed to hinder us, what mistrust of His power yet corrupts our honesty, what sloth yet blinds our eyes to that new dawn which is smiling in at this hour upon our night of dreams, illuminating our languor, and reproaching our unready sleep.

SERMON IV.

THE COST OF MORAL MOVEMENT.

"Unto whomsoever much is given, of him shall be much required: and to whom men have committed much, of him they will ask the more."—
ST. LUKE xii. 48.

LENT cannot but enter into this life that we lead at Oxford with the sharp shock of a surprise. It is a time that asks for strong lines, and downright colours, and clear-cut forms. It supposes that we can mark out our days according to the needs of the moral life: that we know undoubtingly what good is, and what evil is; what we aim at, and what we lack: that we can define our habits, and can set to work at shaping our tone and temper by a rigid canon and with decisive tests. It assumes, above all, that there will be already in us such a fervent desire for holiness, such a horror at the corruption of sin, that we shall be ready by a certain hour, at a certain day, to give especial emphasis to our search for the one, to our strife against the other. So Lent thrusts itself in, rough and abrupt, and how does it find us? It finds us mingled together, Christian and unchristian, good and bad, sinner and saint, all engaged in the same work, fashioned in the same mould, moving amid the same interests, mixing in the same crowd, clothed in the same garb, sensitive to the same feelings, talking the same talk. Nor does this outward appearance belie the inward condition of things. We look within ourselves, and still the same confused uniformity puzzles us with its indistinguishable sameness. Within, as well as without, no sharp dividing lines start out into distinction: no rigid black clashes against as rigid a white: a thousand influences cross, and intermingle, and intertwine, and each of them seems to come equally from faith or unbelief, from Christianity or paganism, from good or from evil, from heaven or from hell. We cannot analyze their elements; we cannot sever their kind; we cannot fix their origin, cannot tell, with any precision, whence they come, nor whither they go: they meet, and move, and part again, and reappear in strange shapes and shifting scenes, at one moment greeting us as angels of light, at another we seem to catch sight in them of the devil's leer, and to hear echoes of some sudden shout of demon-laughter. One feeling is fair, yet as we look at it, it dwindles, and withers, and grows old: another strikes in upon us, at first forbidding and uncouth, yet under our very eyes it changes, it stirs with hidden powers, it is transfigured with light and loveliness. Which are we to believe? Which are we to follow? Lent puts the knife into our hands; but what are we to cut out of our lives? Which is the evil that is to be hacked and hewn? Which is the good that we must die to preserve? Nothing comes to supply us with a clear answer. None of us are put to searching proof. It is, for instance, action that forces strong decisions: it is action that sharpens trials, and reveals flaws: it is then that the leak breaks out, that the weak planks start. But we, we are shut out from much action: we are not forced into difficult situations, nor driven to stake all on perplexed issues, nor dared to test all the practical thoroughness of our convictions.

Nor, again, do violent temptations often lay brutal hands upon us. These come to those who have hard work and little satisfaction, to men who find few pleasures at hand, few and meagre interests to absorb them, narrow and mean surroundings, without refreshments and without ease. But we are whipped by no such scorpions. We have no such compelling hunger. We have endless vents for excitement; we can spend ourselves in infinite directions; we can feed our emotions; we can expand our sympathies; we are nursed along softly; we feast on fat things, on wines of the lees well refined; our sensibilities are not imprisoned or unregarded; things about us are full of grace, of gentleness, of fair delight. We may indeed fret amid all this easy wealth, we may waste ourselves in the littleness of discontent, but such tempers as this do not lead to great and awful sins. There is no flow of unrealized passion to be gathered up behind huge and silent barriers, until the main bulk of our being hurls itself down evil channels in some vast and thunderous outbreak.

There is nothing, therefore, to produce any violent and startling difference between man and man, between one act of our own and another: varieties of faith exhibit no bold contrasts in practice. If we have a creed, we seem no better than another: if we have none, we seem no worse. Materialism is not coarse, nor idealism extravagant. The common culture which fashions us all ensures to us all the same sensitiveness to ugliness, to absurdity; and, since violent sin is both absurd and ugly, we all have a horror against it. We have all of us, too, the same duties towards younger men than ourselves: we are responsible for our example: we are held back, by the necessities of our position, from any perilous break with traditional codes, from any offensive affront to principles, or standards that we ourselves do not happen to hold. We live very near each other: our life is in public: it is open to all men to see what we do: we are discussed, criticised, observed, by young and old, by parents and pupils, by authorities and followers, by enemies and friends. We cannot be heedless; we dare not be secret. Everything conspires to check all that outrages, all that shocks. It is almost impossible for any of us to sin hard and broad. And the result is that the lines between good and evil are difficult to seize: they float vaguely in this large atmosphere: they vanish as we try to fix them: they slip from under our hands as we feel after them: subtle, shadowy, impalpable, they come to seem, at last, but light and airy distinctions to which it is hard not to be indifferent, and it is into such a dreamy, indistinguishable, hazy world as this, that Lent abruptly thrusts its rigid and imperative demand. It does not politely refrain from introducing itself into such an ordered and gentle place. Still it presses in: still it seems to be confident of work to be done: still it talks hard words, and lays down rules of austere defiance. Sackcloth and ashes, fasting and contrition, penance and judgment, God and devil. These are phrases, it insists, of real meaning to us as to all; for through us, too, the lines of distinction are in reality being run, sharp, vivid, decisive as ever. The judgment is sundering good and evil with unwavering sureness. Clear through all this thick and misty air, amid the close and matted trees of the luxuriant garden, the voice of God is forcing its way, resistless as the sound of a trumpet, steadfast as an arrow, piercing as a two-edged sword. We cannot escape it: we know this too well. Forget it as we will, conceal it as we may, there is, we dimly feel, a trespass in our tent, there is sin in our clothes: somewhere, hid in the earth, in the secret places of our lives, there lies buried some goodly Babylonish garment, some wedge of Canaanite gold. It is little, it is nothing, it is unperceived, it is hardly worth noticing. We ourselves do not understand or recognise its shame, its corrupting influence; yet the eternal issues of right and wrong are working themselves out upon it, are involved in it. To us, too, as surely as to the drunkard or the adulterer, the charge is made, "There is an accursed thing in the midst of thee, O Israel!" "Thou canst not stand before thine enemies, except ye destroy the accursed thing from among you."

How can we discover our curse? How can we rend this veil which hides our sins from us?

The very means and instrument of our confusion are surely the means and instrument of our escape.

This culture, this intellect, this power of subtle analysis which can break up so much in that present life before us, that once stood out rough and distinct, can also, by extending our vision far beyond this present, exhibit the immense and awful import of those minute differences in thought and act which it has reduced to such slight and momentary bulk. It can recover for us in the gross that solid evidence, that sure footing, which it seemed to dissipate in the particular. It can carry us down long centuries of history, it can move us freely up and down huge layers of social life, and there can manifest, "writ large," the steady laws that are energizing within our small and fragmentary existence. Here, in history, it offers us a canon by which, at least, to estimate the reality and force of that which we are required to do. It may not answer all our questions of what is to be done; but, at least, it will measure for us what has been the nature and extent of the task which is laid on us, as it once lay on our forefathers.

What standard, then, does the scientific study of history reveal by which we may have our eyes opened to the intensity and the reality of the eternal judgment that is being enacted now in the moral sphere of our daily life?

Let us consider the change, the progress with which we are concerned, in which we are bearing our part, *i.e.* the spiritual advance of the human race. What is this change? How has it been accomplished?

Placed individually in the presence of the uncivilized man, and comparing ourselves with him, we find the same vagueness often creeping over us, the same timid uncertainty, when we attempt to compare ourselves with other men in Oxford. He is shrewd, shrewder perhaps than we are; he is dignified, polite often, eloquent perhaps, loyal, with a noble simplicity, with a quick and high imagination. We are staggered, we wonder for a moment where all the difference lies; and indeed it is hard to tell, until we place this savage within the circle of conditions which we call civilization. Then there suddenly reveals itself a tremendous lack. That which we carry easily and unconcernedly as the air in which we move is to him a frightful nightmare, an impossible, an unintelligible burden. The self-restraint, the steady control, the unfailing purpose, the large and delicate discernment, which we exercise almost without an effort, and by which we manipulate our forces and maintain our course, are out of his range, are beyond his faculties. They are to him mysterious powers, before whose presence he is instinctively prepared to bow. Something there is which a white man holds in hand and wields; something which is not cleverness, nor force, nor courage, for all these he himself possesses; but which, whatever it be, fascinates him, subdues him, commands him. This power it is which enables the white man to deal with the infinite complexity of a complete society with ease and assurance, while the savage, in the face of the same social circumstance, loses his head, loses his will, loses his self-control. He cannot fix his aims, cannot bend his energies, cannot retain his steadiness. He becomes the careless prey of all the shifting and unruly impulses which the stern discipline of his primitive necessities had kept under and mastered. His simplicity breaks up; his vigour dies down; his dignity and self-respect sink back into effeteness. If he would save himself from becoming the prey of a vile sloth, or of viler vices, he must fly far from this bewildering chaos, which confuses, and baffles, and paralyzes, and terrifies him. And not only when introduced into our ordinary life does the savage reveal his difference from us; when we look at his own ways and manners the same shock meets us. This very man, who, at first sight, seemed so like ourselves, so intelligent, so tender, so noble-minded, shows himself suddenly capable of brutal cruelties, which he can laugh at and chuckle over, while our very blood turns cold with unspeakable horror. He can allow and enjoy customs, low, foul, loathsome with filth and impurity. There are frightful possibilities of rage, of barbarity, of reckless, extravagant evil, lying latent there within him. He may at any moment break loose from all restraints; at any moment he may be whirled by his passion far out of the ken of our expectations. Or again, as we look still closer into him, a strange incapacity to keep at a fixed level begins to show itself. He cannot sustain himself up to the rigour of the demands which we think natural between man and man: he is false, he fails to keep his purpose: he drops back so swiftly from that standard up to which our presence had drawn him: he is unsteady, we cannot count on him: the movement within him is too restless and fitful: and, moreover, below its changing surface, there is a deep-seated content which we are powerless to stir, a content which keeps his life down at the same dead level through all the dragging centuries without any permanent aspiration, without any laborious curiosity, without growth, or change, or novelty, or hope of better things, or sense of "stepping westward." There is then a gap between us and him—a gap not caused by any vital difference of faculties, for his whole nature corresponds so closely to ours that it is difficult to detect at first any disunion; but rather a gap made evident by some difference in capacity to put those faculties to full use, by some lack of scope and extension in their exercise, by a lack of resolution, of solid insistence, of steady grasp, of unswerving will, a lack, that is, of all the qualities that could deal successfully with a formal and civilized society. It is in all this that the change is felt: it is here that the advance is made evident: and history is our record of the forces which it has taken to work that change, of the effort which that advance has cost.

Those forces have been terrific, that effort has been supreme. The record points us back, beyond itself, to periods whose meaning we may read in the primitive people of to-day: periods in which the ever-shifting, yet ever-unchanging populations of the nameless days first felt the strong action of the forces that were to fashion them anew, under the hand, we would believe, of some remorseless power such as we see now sweeping men together into some rough and ready system of order in Dahomey or Ashantee. It is might in its most murderous aspect: yet, at least, it arrests that unresting movement under which the endless generations of savage life gathered, and grouped, and parted asunder, without purpose and without issue, as clouds of driving sand that rise and fall in empty uncertitude under the barren breath of desert winds. Bound up with this earliest pressure, there is slaughter, there are often fiendish rites of bloody sacrifice; but there is also solidity, and there is something of aspiration. The advance has begun.

We know not how many such efforts may have arisen, and then died away in failure, before the might of some prevailing conquests has succeeded in securing a permanence. Only dim hints and glimpses are left us of all the long and unrecorded strife by which, through slow and patient struggles, man disentangled himself from the necessities of the mere hunt for food, and found strength to spare for the larger issues, in which lay the beginnings of a formal society. We can but guess at the pangs of those huge births which set vast hordes of men moving with something of compactness, something of fixed intent, across our earth from out of the dark heart of the mysterious East. Only we are sure that such immense impulses can never have been begun or fulfilled without throes and agonies, without slaughter and misery, without hunger and tears; and when, at last, their wanderings found a goal, and they succeeded in attaining to what we should recognise as a civilization, how unutterably awful were their swift and terrible failures! Again and again mankind appears to have attained to social power, to city life, to wealth, to ease, and then to have broken down miserably, helplessly under the strain: the feat was still beyond the measure of his powers, he could not sustain the needful, the imperative self-mastery: he sank, exhausted by his own exertions, into deplorable weakness, he drained away his strength under the sapping fever of maddening vices, he relapsed into a hideous and sickening corruption. One such failure of man's earliest efforts, it may be, is revealed to us, below layer after layer of the after lives that rose up upon its ashes, in the burnt and wasted citadel of Troy; and another had to perish, root and branch, under the unsparing sword of Israel that hewed its hosts to pieces, hip and thigh, at the going down to Bethhoron, and by the waters of Merom; and yet another lies hidden, we know, under the dreary darkness of the Dead Sea waters; for God had looked down and seen that the wickedness of man was very great; and the Lord rained upon Sodom and Gomorrah fire from the Lord out of heaven; and Abraham rose early on that morning on which Lot hasted for his life into Zoar, and behold the smoke of the country went up as the smoke of a furnace.

So enormous, so terrible was the cost that had to be paid before the effort after an ordered life could attain a steady foothold and secure the possibility of advance. It was done, at last, in the realization of those gigantic empires—Egyptian, Assyrian, Babylonian, Persian—in which the far-seeing prophets of Israel recognised the elements at last of a continuous and unceasing historical process—a process which should no longer die down utterly at the ending of each separate attempt, but one which would pass on from one stage to another, unexhausted and unshattered, until it gathered itself into the larger fulfilment, the final and perfected triumph of the empire of God. Yet for the accomplishment and the sustenance of this orderly progress what untiring struggles, what dauntless energy, what infinite love! It is appalling merely to let the imagination faintly recollect the multitudinous hosts that sweep hither and thither in endless battles across the scenes of those old stories, the fragments of which we find scattered up and

The Cost of Moral Movement. 73

down the pages of our Old Testament; stories in which all the slaughters and destructions of Jerusalem must have formed but brief samples of the work that was continually proceeding; stories whose frightful vastness still astounds us, as it reflects its terror in the long lines carved or drawn on the memorial palaces of Nineveh and Babylon. Line upon line of soldiers marching in eternal wars; line upon line of captains pointing ever forward from their advancing chariots to new scenes of carnage; line upon line of captives— men, women, and children—dragged weeping in chains from home to desolate exile; line upon line of tortured prisoners, of massacred populations, of sacked cities, of bloody and remorseless victories. There, written in letters that burn, we read the awful record of the Titanic forces which built up those empires, out of which our own civilization first established its foundations, first achieved its solidity. I need not recall all the misery and the pain, the tumult and the shouting, the blood, and fire, and vapour of smoke that had to accompany the uplifting of all this old-world life into the purer and freer air of Greek and Roman civilization. The step up which the human spirit then mounted was not won, we know well, without the payment of its full price; and still the debt was uncancelled. Still, long after the Cæsars had ceased from their labour, the framework of Roman law, so slowly and painfully reared, trembled and tottered, threatening again and again some disastrous collapse. Still it was only sustained against assault by dint of some strenuous effort which mastered the assaulting power, and subdued it to the higher service, at the risk of fearful loss, and with a daring disregard of all that it might cost. I can but hint at a few instances. It is with a burden of humiliating disgust that we can venture to remember the unspeakable brutalities, the sickening tortures, that crowd the annals of the Middle Ages, and bear witness to the severity of the struggle by which the savagery that found a vantage for itself in Teuton feudalism had to be tamed into conformity with the needs of fixed justice and the demands of the moral code. Or again, there are dark passages of history in which we dimly perceive through the darkness the martyrdom of those nameless thousands, who, amid the chaos of the Renaissance, first asserted the protest of the peasant against his dreary and forlorn exclusion from those circles of public right and social life. Once more, we ourselves have known, have almost tasted, the bitterness of the fight by which the cruel pride and careless indifference of dominant classes have been broken and avenged, and by which the large freedom and massive movements of an entire humanity have become at last actual possibilities, definite factors of society, real elements in our spiritual growth.

And even at this very hour[1] the removal of deadening and unassisting matter from our civilized life, the introduction of new and capable material, the extension of the sovereignty of social and moral right over a fresh area, can only be accomplished at the old cost and with still unslackened efforts, by the thunder of battle, by the sweat, and the blood, and the wounds,

[1] 1878.

by the weeping, the hunger, the despair of the widow, and the orphan, and the destitute.

Such are the forces, such the deeds, which, while attesting and measuring the burden of our sin, do also attest and measure that pressure and strain which the Word of the Lord has brought to bear upon the spirit of man, driving, compelling, uplifting him to stronger action, to quicker motion, to wider command.

And within, the upward stirring of the soul to meet and grapple with the force that bore down upon him from without, has been not less vigorous and not less intense. Continuously, unweariedly, unflaggingly, the energies of the inward man have pressed forward, have strained, and battled, and striven, and so alone have kept themselves level with their work, have won their way to the requisite expansion and power. They have made their effort in a thousand strange and fantastic forms; but still the effort was made, and by that effort the day was saved. That upward effort we encounter at its first start, in the mad excitement of devil-dancing, in the phrenzy of Shamanism. We shudder at its sterner passion in the Red Indian medicine-man, who can hang by ropes fastened through his flesh from sunrise to sunset, with his eyes ever fixed on the moving glory of the sunlight, that by this masterful exhibition of the spirit's strength he may win control over the minds of his fellows. In all this the soul is alive and stirring. It is testing itself, stretching its wings, feeling after an increase of power, breaking down the barriers that hinder and cramp its freer action. We find its handiwork, its method, again in finer and steadier form in the austere disciplines of India; in the marvellous endurance and relentless audacity with which the fakir can give his body over to unceasing pain, to unutterable torture. In that torn flesh and wasted frame we surely have no doubtful evidence of the fury with which the spirit of man beats against the bars of its prison, of the intensity with which it pushes its claims for a larger field, for a fuller vision. Higher still, and not less vigorous has the effort become, in the nobler passion, the desperate self-sacrifice of Sakya-Mouni. The standard of heroic devotion is fast rising. Buddhism has carried it forward, has set it high. The spirit begins to understand the full significance of its work: its ideal has begun to disentangle itself from its early grotesqueness: it has gained shape, and charity, and truth. Yet the clearness of the issue does not diminish the struggle, and the pains of attaining it; the cost is sharp and severe as ever. We have but to turn to the language of those who knew clearest of all ancient peoples the direction of man's upward movement, in order to estimate the hard and painful strife through which alone the higher spirit forces its advance. There, from the Jews, we learn that the tortures of the flesh with which we began the tale of man's aspirations have not ceased their rigour by their passage upward into the regions of the soul. The scorn, and hatred, and shame through which man's rising effort after holiness has to burst its way, are not less bitter than the wildest bodily agonies with which they mingle their assaults.

"I am poured out like water, and all my bones are out

of joint: my heart is like melting wax." " My strength is dried up like a potsherd; my tongue cleaveth to my gums: I am brought into the dust of death." "The waters are come in, even unto my soul. I stick fast in the deep mire: I am come into deep waters, so that the floods run over me. I am weary of crying; my throat is dry: my sight faileth me for waiting so long upon my God." "Thy rebuke hath broken my heart; I am full of heaviness: I looked for some to have pity on me, but there was no man, neither found I any to comfort me." "There is no health in my flesh, neither is there any rest in my bones." "My wounds stink, and are corrupt." "My loins are filled with a sore disease: there is no whole part in my body. I am feeble and sore smitten: I have roared for the very disquietness of my heart." "My heart panteth, my strength faileth me: the sight of mine eyes is gone from me." Such are the voices sounding through the storms of the long centuries behind us, telling of the torments and of the pangs under the sharpness of which man's soul has been quickened into a diviner sense of the worth of righteousness, and under the discipline of which he has mastered, with a fuller consciousness, the power of that image of God that lives and is astir within his being.

And still, as the standard of spiritual life rises, it raises with it the measure of intensity by which man's soul must press forward to fulfil it. The uplifted cross towards which all men are drawn with an infinite passion of desire has not lowered, but heightened, the rigour of the strain, the austerity of the struggle. It is now no longer, a wonder or a puzzle, but it is the very mark of a chief Apostle of Righteousness that "he should be a fool, be weak, be despised; that he should hunger and thirst, and be naked and buffeted, and have no certain home: be reviled, persecuted, defamed, the filth of the world, the off-scouring of all things: troubled, distressed, perplexed, cast down, always bearing in his body the dying of the Lord Jesus: in afflictions, in necessities, in distresses, in stripes, in imprisonment, in tumults, in labours, in watchings, in fastings, as dying, as chastened, as sorrowful, as having nothing." This is the discipline through which they pass, who fully know the meaning of God's secrets: through this they perfect the new creature. Nor has humanity been false to the standard given in Christ and realized in St. Paul. From that hour to this, its devotion has been set in this high key; its morality has clung to this uplifted aim. This enthusiasm for righteousness it was, this burning horror of evil, which threw Augustine down under the fig-tree in the Lombard garden, when he "gave the rein to his tears, and the floods of his eyes broke out, God's acceptable sacrifice, and he cried aloud in pitiable cries, How long, O Lord, how long? And he rolled on the ground, and wept in the bitter contrition of his soul." This it was which crowded the cells of Antony, of Bernard, of Francis, and of Dominic; this which drove the spirit of Bunyan out on its passionate pilgrimage; this which has moulded the devotions of and inspired the deeds of countless Christian souls.

But I do not want to stop and tell what is familiar to you as to me; only I would insist here in Oxford, on this first Sunday in Lent, by all the memories of the Saints of

The Cost of Moral Movement.

God, on the immense cost, the appalling severity of the effort which has been spent on lifting man's spiritual faculties from the state of the savage to the condition in which we find them in ourselves to-day. That difference when we stood face to face with him was not so easy to distinguish: only in actions, in dealing with facts, in moving amid the vast detail of an ordered civilization, we found a lack of grasp in him, a lack of moral steadiness, a lack of delicate spiritual perception. This grasp, this steadiness, this delicate perception is what we instinctively possess, and we have won it at the cost of all the struggle that I have described. *We* are the result, the fruit of all this weary toil, this tremendous strain, this age-long conflict. Through wars without, through tumults within, the deed has been done, and the fight has been fought. Still humanity has pressed forward, through the smoke, the ruin, the disaster, torn, scarred, battered, and bloodstained; and small and meagre as the prize of victory seems to us, it is one that we have no choice but to accept as worth all the cost. We have no choice, for to that humanity we already belong, body and soul. That struggle has made us what we are; that pressure is behind us; that strain has drawn us to where we now stand; that fiery discipline, that passion for right, those desperate aspirations, have moulded and fashioned our souls. They are all still alive without and within us: in them we are carried along; on them we are uplifted; by them our whole being is fostered and fed. They have passed into our very blood; they have penetrated our every fibre and nerve; they are the very stuff of our lives. And since it is the moral necessity of our being that we should raise into conscious realization the force to whose secret working we owe our creation and sustenance, it is therefore our imperative duty that we should enter with a full and thorough will into the lists of this hard fighting. We may not stand outside; we may not be content to run the eyes of our intelligence over the episodes of this battle, and mark down its critical moments, and analyze its issues; for that battle is ours: its issues are even now astir in our veins: we are ourselves implicated in the agonies of its crisis. Not alone, then, may the intelligence scan the field, but the will must bow down, and enter into the terror and the tumult of the onset. Are we alone in Oxford to be free from the labour and the pain of that spiritual upheaval by which the world has moved forward? May we sit here in comfortable ease, and suck dry the fruits of a well-ordered life, which the desperate conflicts of a thousand generations have won for us? Surely the water of those clear and delicate habits which seem to us so natural and so facile is "the blood of men that went in jeopardy of their lives" long ago, and we may not lightly slake our thirst with it. Surely on us, too, as literally, as severely as on the millions who toil and struggle against the blackness of evil things in our dark and cruel cities, the shadow of the primal curse has fallen, "In the sweat of thy brow shalt thou eat bread."

SERMON V.

CHRIST, THE JUSTIFICATION OF A SUFFERING WORLD.

"Having made known unto us the mystery of His will, according to His good pleasure which He hath purposed in Himself: that in the dispensation of the fulness of times He might gather together in one all things in Christ. In Whom also we have obtained an inheritance."—
EPH. i. 9-11.

SUCH words as these of St. Paul spring out of that first bewilderment of joy which belongs to the sense of discovery. Christ is still a newly discovered wonder, and the wonder of the newness still fascinates, still overwhelms. The secret of God has broken out of the silence of the eternal counsels, swift, sudden, and unforeseen. The night has fled away as a dream, the sun has leapt at a bound into high heaven: the mystery kept hidden from the foundation of the world has in the twinkling of an eye been made known, and behold all things are become new. The eyes, so long sad with blindness, are, even in a moment, gazing on the things into which angels have desired to look, the things which prophets and kings have for age after age longed to see and have not seen.

To us all it is so different, to us all this new joy of the discovery is so strange, so unfelt. We have grown up all our lives in the very midst of the revealed counsel: it has been familiar to us as air, and sky, and trees: we have breathed it, fed on it, drunk of it, consciously or unconsciously, every year, and day, and hour: we have belonged to it from our mother's womb. We have never known what it is to live outside it or without it. The Christian interpretation of life has intertwined itself with our very lives. Our thoughts, our feelings, our very senses have long been moulded by it. Grace is our nature, and this naturalness of grace becomes often itself an argument against grace. We seem so easily, so naturally what we are, that we cannot recognise the immense effort that it has required to make us what we have become; and when once we have lost sight of the need of this effort, we have lost the cue to all the counsels of God. We can see no need for this laborious machinery; no significance in these elaborate dogmas; the whole scheme of redemption seems useless, unnecessary, too big for its work, unnaturally extravagant: and at last the birth of a God-Man appears to us an immense call upon our faith, with but little meaning to our experience; it seems to have but little relation to fact, to reality, and so at last the question begins to creep forward, why this enormous strain upon our reason, in order to accomplish so little result? It is a mere dogma, a scheme that hangs in the air; it has no foothold. So we suspect, so perhaps we begin to say to ourselves, or even, some of us, aloud to others; and therefore it is most necessary at Christmas time, especially now[1] that the first hearty enjoyment of the happy season is passing, to reflect

[1] Sunday after Christmas.

of a Suffering World.

seriously and with pains on the long labour of the centuries behind us, on the inconceivable effort which it has cost to make our life what it is. For only if we realize this labour and effort, can we estimate the reality or the amount of forces required for the task; and only when we have done something to measure the forces required, can we learn what the Incarnation has accomplished, or make God's scheme intelligible.

What, then, is the mystery of God's will in gathering together all in one in Christ? Why was the Incarnation the true and only secret, the fit and only instrument? What did it actually do? Why was it such an immense relief to St. Paul?

Let me take it very broadly. What is the primary plan of God, as we see it in Nature? For this is the plan that Christ came to fulfil. Science tells it us in language that surprises us by its consistency with what we look for. Science takes to pieces this fresh, fair world of ordered and harmonious life, which floods us with the rich splendour of its beauty; it breaks it up, it leads us through the veil behind the scenes, and there we are stunned and bewildered as we gaze on the endless, infinite, unceasing struggle which sustains the outer frame of things. We look back through countless ages, and listen to the rough roaring of the fiery furnace, out of whose stormy chaos the chilled fragments of harder matter slowly coalesce: we are told that it is by the gradual dearth of heat that the colder shell of the world grows stiff, by death and decay of its first life of fire that the very shape of the world masses itself into outline and substance: the law of surrender, of self-sacrifice, has already begun to work. We are shown a wild chaos of heaving stuffs, cracking, tumbling, rent, shattered, and yet, out of it all, a sweet rhythm of order continually shaping itself, continually becoming stronger and more imperative, even as valley and river, mountain and sea, part off into distinct and established arrangement. And yet this order is not something alien to the chaotic matter; not something forced upon it in spite of it, as the old philosophers fancied; but is itself the result of the very same forces which make the noise and turmoil of the chaos; the very principles which dash the particles of our earth together in confusion, also, and at the same moment, sort, and select, and separate them into order. The very law which shrivels the earth's surface into rents, and freezes it into a deadly stiffness, so shrivels and so freezes that the ordained purpose of a habitable world is fulfilled.

Such are the features of this first period. We look on and it is the same. For a thousand ages the rains and storms beat down over the desolate hills, the ice grinds and sends them to powder; and, lo! the very decay of the hills is itself the law by which broad lands spread and grow deep and rich. Or, again, hidden swarms of living things in silent seas perish for myriads of generations, and yet the very constancy, the very unchangeableness of their waste lays the even layers of man's home. It is not that there is one law of death and quite another of life, but that the very principle of death is turned into being the principle of a fuller and richer life. We look on to the animal creation; still we meet the same awful law of destruction, of endless struggle.

Strange dragons and monstrous serpents fight, and rend, and devour in dreary marshes, and at last die out unlamented and forgotten before the advent of a newer and stronger generation. Vast floods sweep over the globe, wiping out its teeming life that another race may enter into the heritage : the whole of earth and sea is full of deadly hunt and of cruel capture, of breathless escape, of haunting fear : fish follows hard after fish, bird flies from bird, beast preys on beast, and yet the very eagerness of the hunt itself works ever new wonders of order and beauty: out of this very whirl of death, still the higher life rises and prevails—rises under the very pressure of the need, prevails by the very necessities of weakness. It is not one law that allows slaughter and another that produces strength : not one law that says, " Devour," and another that says, " Be beautiful;" but out of the very conditions of the combat arises the fair glory of strength; the very voice which ordained the decree " Be fruitful and multiply " seems to have said also, " Slay and eat." I do not ask now by what act of evil this law of suffering may have made itself a necessity. I only say that God has consented to work out His scheme in it and by it; and that, if so, then He must have seen and prepared some issue, the worth of which would render all the means used tolerable, intelligible, justifiable.

We gaze and wonder at this terrific process of creation; and if we ask in awe and amazement what is the end of all this, what is the purpose to be achieved, we are told " *Man.*" Man is the final achievement in which all this preparation issues. Man· is worth all this infinite toil, this age-long effort, this endless struggle, this thousand-fold death. He is its justification: it all is very good since it all rises up into his crowning endowment. We turn to look at man, then, man as this world's fulfilment; what has he done to be worth it all?

Man offers himself, to our first gaze, as did Nature, robed in the majesty of his gifts, rich in the multitudinous array of his powers. He has subdued the earth; he has reaped its wealth; he has surrounded himself with a fair garden of fruits and of flowers; he has reared large fabrics of law; he has guided and controlled kingdoms into the sweet and ordered ways of peace; he has prepared for himself lovely works of grace; he has won for himself gold, and jewels, and pleasant odours, and all delicious things. He has sent his spirit abroad to sift, and to weigh, and to understand and to measure, and to describe all sights, and all thoughts, and all imaginations: his handiwork, as did Nature's, forms a wonderful and exquisite vision. But once more the deeper knowledge lifts the veil: we look behind, and here, as before, we see no rest and satisfaction; here, as before, we discover behind the outward result all the fearful and tremendous straining by which alone this order lives. Man has no appearance of being the perfect and complete crown of creation; nay, rather, he toils and wins his way forward by the same laborious pains as the rest of the animal and vegetable worlds. He, too, slowly, blindly, confusedly, struggles forward towards a goal that he knows not of: by continual effort, through ruinous disasters, through scars, and tumult, and fightings, beating his way along against buffeting winds and swallowing waves, in sorrow, sickness, and woe unspeakable, he wins by hard degrees the higher life. Indeed, with man the gloom thickens yet deeper: for in him, first, we discover plainly a wilful aggravation of the perils and the pains. He infuses into his life wasteful disorder; he spoils and degrades his power of movement; he struggles, savagely, against the good of his fellows. He creates for himself a history, that tells, in dreary records, of miserable infamies, and bloody shame. This it tells; and it suggests what it cannot tell of the hundred times ten thousand who have fallen in the red carnage of uncounted wars, or have starved pitiably under freezing skies, or have been swallowed up, after wild thirsting for each other's blood, by lonely and remorseless seas; and still, shudder as we will at the ghastly story, history compels us to confess that even this long agony has been turned to the higher use: out of it has grown an ordered life; the disobedience itself has been made to do service: out of his weakness man has been made strong. These suffering generations have been controlled by a purpose to which they were blind; they have served their turn; they have by their disasters advantaged those who came after. Out of the chaos of struggling and blinding agony, the fair framework of our everyday present lives has reared itself: men have fought, and starved, and miserably perished, for ambition, for luxury, for causes dimly guessed, and beliefs that could never be expressed: yet the very shock of their ignorant armies has, in spite of itself, established and strengthened the sanctuary of social life. So it has ever been, so it is still. Man has not yet entered into his rest: still the same rule of woe, of poverty, hunger, famine, disease, holds good: still our civilization rests on this vast under-world of terrible ruin: still, alas! it fails to win its way forward from an evil state to a better, except by the old familiar road of war,—war, with all its terrific slaughter, its wounds, sad cries and groans, its nameless cruelties, its broken hearts, its weeping women, its horrible terror, its helpless, hopeless despair. We close our eyes: we dare not look into the awful nightmare of pain and loss: we cry aloud, " O Lord God ! O God most merciful, most mighty ! what can it be that is worth all this cost ? What precious thing can it be for which such a price may well be paid ?"

Many a nation has tried to answer this question. Some have said, "I sit as a Queen for ever, in the midst of the seas: and these have become a terror and a hissing, in the blindness of their fall." The nobler have said, "Freedom and law, these are worth it all; to win them we are content to die." Such people have had their reward; they have lifted the banner, and men have borne witness to its truth by flocking to greet it: we have all lived by their light, but something still has been wanting: man missed something yet, he was restless, he overthrew each system of free law that he had found: for still he hungered, still he dared not say, "Here I may rest, here in this my earthly freedom I am worth the woe of the world." No; this answer has *of a Suffering World.* 89

never wholly satisfied, never has fully justified itself; the bargain is felt to be a bad one, the price paid is extravagant. Man cannot find in himself the worth of all this age-long sacrifice.

One nation only kept its head clear, and seized the clue. Its history told it the same tale as other histories: for the Old Testament is no dream of some fancy world that a God of our imagining might have made, but is a real story of this very earth we live in; and therefore it, too, told its tale of murder, of floods that destroyed, of generations that went down to the dust of a disastrous death, of cities swept into fearful ruin by fire and brimstone: it told of plagues and weepings, and of slaughter; of armies engulfed in mighty waters; of wandering peoples that leave their bones to whiten the dreary wildernesses; of wicked populations sunk in sin that have to be rooted out and hewn to pieces, man, and woman, and child; of fallen enemies smitten through the temples by the hammer and the nail; of adulterous queens trodden under the feet of horses, and devoured by the teeth of dogs; of kings slain in high places of the field; of people that fall under pestilence and famine. Such was this nation's history, and yet it never became wholly bewildered: it looked all the terrific story in the face, and still proclaimed that God held its life in His hands, nor had He ever fainted, nor grown weary: through all it pressed forward, until out of the very midst of carnage it slowly raised the ideal that God had planted in its heart,—the temple that God had shown its great leader in the Mount. In all the disasters it saw sin punished, and the right chastened and directed; and, more than this, it detected and announced that a single purpose of God was slowly being achieved. Nor did it stop even there, but, when it sadly recognised that this achievement was far off from the present generation, nor was to be found by it in a present land of milk and honey, it failed not, but rose to the height of its great argument: it was content to forego it for itself, to lie down and die, if only in the end this purpose should be accomplished in its children's children: it was prepared to live by promise, and not by sight, to see the promise afar off. It was enough for this people that all their present bitterness was yet working towards that which should be, but which it would never see: God would bring something to pass worth all the cost: it would come: for He, the Eternal, could not fail. Enough for them that it should be hereafter, that God in His own good time would bring in His salvation: enough for them this hope, even though their holy kingdom was split into fragments, even though the very fragments were broken in pieces like a potter's vessel, even though the Egyptian, the Assyrian, the Babylonian, the Greek, the Roman, swept over their desolated fatherland, and defiled the beauty of their sanctuary. Still, more confidently, more proudly, more defiantly than ever, their prophets proclaimed that the Lord was yet, even in this, working out His salvation, was bringing in His holy day. Yea, let Rachel refrain her voice from weeping, and her eyes from tears, though she gazes on the slaughter of her children in bloody Ramah; for "there is hope in thy end, saith the Lord."

of a Suffering World. 91

What hope? What was this end? The lines of the Jew's answer are distinct. Wisdom, righteousness, knowledge of God in the heart and in the head of man, this was most certainly the end for which he hoped. This would be the comfort to Jerusalem, this would repay her for all her pangs—"*Holiness unto the Lord,*"—Spiritual Holiness that knows God, and lives in His image. This, if this could be obtained, would be worth all the pains that had been paid. To win this, the Jew would be content to see Jerusalem a heap of stones, and all her pleasant palaces as ruinous heaps: to win this, he could endure to be carried away beyond Babylon, to be an outcast among the people, the off-scouring of the nations. Let him only at last attain to the favour of God, the light of His presence, the delight of His peace, and this would be, indeed, to give him double for all his evil. This would make all the trouble of the captivity but a very little thing.

Here, then, is our guiding clue,—the one nation in all the world which discovered a permanent purpose of God in history; the one nation which succeeded in finding a path through its own disasters, so that its own ruin only threw into still clearer light the principles of God's ordained fulfilment—this unique nation pronounced that this fulfilment, this justifying purpose, was to be found in *holiness of spirit*, the union of man with God, Whose image he is. Accept this as man's end, and no destruction appals, no despair overwhelms; for this is the higher life, which is worth all the deaths that the lower can die; this is the new birth, which would make all the anguish of the travailing be remembered no more.

That the Jew was right, experience has made certain; the historical facts bear their unwavering witness. The Jewish people *did* live by the power of this faith, through such ruin and peril as no other people have succeeded in conquering or enduring; and what is more, the books of the prophets are an indisputable proof that the clue which they had discovered grew steadier, clearer, and stronger, the more bitter and perilous the test. By this testimony of facts, then, they were shown to be in possession of the secret which overcometh the world, the secret which reconciles this carnage with the will of a gracious and merciful God, Who desireth not that any should perish.

But to know the secret was one thing, to achieve its fulfilment was another. It was good to recognise that all suffering would be worth enduring, if, at last, the righteousness of the law should be revealed in a people in whom the Lord, the Holy One, delighteth; but where was to be the appearing of the holy people? Was Israel, the chosen, the beloved, was it able to achieve this fulfilment of all men's labour? God is ready; is man prepared? "Behold, the Lord's hand is not shortened," cried the prophets to Israel, "but, alas, your iniquities have separated between you and your God; your sins have hid His face from you; your hands are defiled with blood, your fingers with iniquity; your lips have spoken lies; none calleth for justice, nor any pleadeth for truth."

So it was. The one possible end—the achievement

of holiness—was itself become impossible to the only people who recognised it as their end. And the Lord saw it, and it displeased Him that there was no judgment; and He saw that there was no man, and wondered that there was no intercessor. " Therefore He Himself put on righteousness as a breastplate, and an helmet of salvation upon His head, and was clad with zeal as with a cloak." There, at last, on Christmas Day, in the very midst of the toiling generations, on the blood-stained earth, at the world's darkest hour, with trouble behind and terror before, between the sword of Herod and the iron heel of Rome, amid the oxen that had perished age after age that man might be fed, and the asses that had bowed for centuries to blows and burdens that man might be at ease, in the very flesh that had for so long endured bruises and stripes, the scourge and sword and spear, with the very human soul which had wept and mourned under the chastisement of sin, under the tyranny of the oppressor, a little Babe lay in the stable of an inn, born of a pure Virgin, Himself free from all spot and taint of sin, a beloved Son of the Most High and Holy, Who inhabiteth eternity; a Man after God's own heart; a Man in whom He is well pleased; a Man who will love righteousness and hate iniquity as no man has ever had the spirit to love and hate them before; and Whom therefore God will anoint with the oil of gladness above His fellows; and in that anointing of gladness, that Christ of holy joy, all the sorrowful sighing of the poor will at last and for ever be done away.

My brethren, we announce our belief in a great, a

tremendous fact at Christmas; but is it a little thing that the day demands? God incarnate in the flesh! a God-Man! It is a serious, a perilous dogma to assert; our faith quails and trembles. But, then, remember what it is which we assert it to fulfil,—nothing less than the justification of a suffering world. We say that we believe in a Divine order; that life, that history, are to be made rational, made intelligible in Christ; and not some other life, some other history than what has been; not some pleasant, easy fairy facts, but such actual life, such actual history, as is, for instance, now being enacted on the frozen hills of Kars,[1] in the butcheries of Bulgaria, in the slaughters that have heaped with the crowded dead the passes of the Balkans and the fields of Plevna. We have got to justify dealings such as these that fill the long vista of human history. We have got to supply ourselves with something that is worth all this, worth all the blood that God has left men free to shed; worth all the tears that God has had to see women weep; worth all the pain that God has allowed the animal creation to endure; worth all the process of unceasing sacrifice by which God has permitted this earth, with all that is therein, to rescue itself from sin, and rise to the higher life.

Is the long roll of toil and anguish to find its rest, its satisfaction in man as he is? Can the law of sacrifice be arrested in him? Are we, we civilized Englishmen, worth all this cost? Can we offer ourselves to this labouring, suffering world as its rational justification, as God's perfected work? Can we cry to the

[1] 1876.

of a Suffering World. 95

millions upon millions who have perished in nameless woes, "Rejoice, forget all the pangs of your world long travail; for I, a man, an educated Englishman, am born into the world?" Surely, surely, if we measure history carefully and soberly, without Christ there is no rational God; without Christ the whole fabric of the world shatters into ruinous fragments, or stands only as a slaughter-house in which men tear each other down into unavailing misery, into meaningless deaths.

But if the Jew was right, and Holiness is worth all the struggle and all the agony, then we, too, to-day, who feel the terrible insufficiency of our own holiness to repay God for all the ruin of the Past; we, who know too bitterly our own utter and foul wickedness, our ugly lusts, our cruel vanities, our pitiful weakness, our horrible selfishness, our greed, our jealousy, our anger, our impatience, our idleness, our malice, our unkindness, our worldliness, our shame and hypocrisy; we, who are bowed down under the bondage of horrible sin; we can leap up into the vast joy of belief which filled the soul of St. Paul, as he saw the mystery of God's purpose accomplished in Christ.

The Holiness of God incarnate in the flesh of this labouring humanity, the holy Image of God's perfect righteousness taking upon Himself the whole agony of man, accepting on His shoulders the burden of all this awful woe, resigning His spotless Spirit to the grief of all this bitter desolation, dying the death which justifies all death, in that it turns death itself, by the honourable way of sacrifice, into the instrument of the higher inheritance, into the sacrament of righteousness, into the mystery of holiness, into the pledge of perfect peace; this, and this only, makes a consummation by which the effort of God's creation achieves an end; this, and this only, is a secret and a victory worthy of the merciful God in Whom we trust.

I need not spend many words on the practical application of this. It is practical enough sometimes just to draw out and study God's Truth; and if we meditate on it, it will enforce on us its own applications. Only I would implore you to realize that we are saved only by being well-pleasing to God; and we are well-pleasing only if He can recognise in us the fruit and crown of all this long travailing, the satisfaction of all this immense effort of creation; and that is, the Holiness of Christ.

Our salvation, then, is no light, easy task. Alas, for those who think that a prayer or two of their own, and a few good-natured acts of their own genial kindness, will satisfy this terrific demand!

Alas, for those who cannot offer to God at the great Day of Decision a worthy compensation for all the iniquity, all the pain, all the toil that He has been compelled to allow!

Alas, for those who insult the reason of God by dreaming that a decent and delicate idleness will serve to repay the cost of all this laborious patience!

Alas, above all, for those who complain and murmur because the agonies and weariness of a thousand generations have not secured them easy, pleasant days without a loss and without a sorrow, as if the blood and its holy and hidden abode in Himself, and to become active, and strong, and substantial in the establishment of a life which, however proceeding out of God, was yet other than God's own, distinct from God, a thing to be looked at apart from God. God, as it were, would enjoy the joy of the artist,—the joy of standing off from the product of His will, the joy of contemplating from a distance, from outside, that which His hands had fashioned, and His heart conceived. There it lay, outspread before His eyes, a living thing, suspended, indeed (if you will), in the breath of His eternal will, as a feather is borne in the moving impulse of a wind, but yet, for all that, a living reality, whole and entire, held together unto enduring unity by the energy of its own laws; no mere dream which would vanish as any airy phantom of the imagination, but a solid, self-possessed, and actual creature, the movement of whose life shook its full and free pulsations along all the quivering channels of its organic frame. There it rolled along, this earth of ours, before the unslumbering eyes of the mighty Watcher,—His own work, His own achievement, the expression of His purpose, the shadow of His beauty, the witness to His love, having its entire consistency in Him, yet itself, in itself, instinct with marvellous forces and powers, which had passed into it, and had become inherent in it, and upheld it, and embraced it, and penetrated its recesses, and moved hither and thither, creeping, pushing, driving, moulding, quickening, animating, so that it was made no dead, cold, blind mechanism, but a warm and breathing animal, with life tingling throughout its entire bulk,—

life teeming in the moving air, and flying light, and ever-rolling sea,—life breaking upwards into the endless wealth of bud, and blossom, and flower,—life straining and outpouring into the swarming growth of fish and fly, and bird,—life gathering together the full energies of its splendid freedom into the self-directed activities of that brave animal world which has, at last in man, its crown, possessed itself, so to speak, of its own life,—possessed itself of *flesh—flesh*, which feels for itself, and has its own hungers, its own desires, its own passions, its own pains, its own delights, and lives its own life, making its own way, aiming at its own aims, deliberating on its own satisfactions, imagining its own fulfilments, collecting its own experience, sensitive to its own vibrations, fashioning its own joys, watching its own movement, reasoning out its own conclusions, creating its own future, ever severing itself from its own past, and from all that pressure that arrives to it from without, ever starting forward toward new ends in the gladness of fulfilling a self-chosen impulse.

Here, then, at last, is something like freedom—something like a life that could distinguish itself from God.

Creation crowns itself in man, because, in man, it most nearly attains to exhibiting before the eyes of God, a life self-directed, substantial, positive, real, the image of His own self-government, His own freedom, His own substantiality.

But yet, for all that, this free, deliberative life of man was only man's own, in the same sense, though in a nobler degree, as the movement of water downward is the water's tears of millions might well be shed, in order that they themselves might enjoy comfort and ease!

Alas, for those who trifle frivolously and selfishly in the face of those stern, unchanging laws which, in the terrible tumult of living history, display before our eyes the awful character of the crisis in which we stand.

We cannot mistake it. The God before Whose Judgment Bar we look to appear hereafter is one, Whose Mercy sees it possible to permit all this horror of war and blood, wherewith we fill His earth, if only, at the last, He may attain in us that which He desires. So dear, so precious, to Him is the Hope towards which He toils.

What, then, can avail to please Him, on that day, when He counts up the gains of all His long husbandry? What can avail if it be not Christ Himself, Christ the Blessed, the Holy, the Beloved, in Whom God is for ever well pleased?

O Jesu, in Whom we all may be made desirable! O Lord, Redeemer and Saviour, Prince of all Holiness and Peace! We have sinned, we have done amiss, we have fallen, we have gone astray, we are not worthy so much as to gather up the crumbs under the table of God! Enter Thou, therefore, into our souls. Possess our spirits with Thy Spirit, our body with Thy Body, our blood with Thy Blood. Feed us with Thyself, Who art perfect Righteousness. Lay hold of us by Thy Grace, Who art the Truth and the Life. Uplift us, mould us, transform us by Thy own power into Thyself, into the image of the Holy and the Eternal. We will shrink from no suffering, we will endure all, in the energy of Thy broken Body and outpoured Blood, if only we may be drawn upward into the Likeness of Thyself, into the Joy of Thy Holiness! Fill us with sorrow, if so only Thou canst fill us with Thyself: for only by abiding in Thee, only by eating Thy Flesh and drinking Thy Blood, only by fastening on the Grace of Thy perfect, holy, and sufficient Oblation, can we hope to pass from Death into Life, and to be raised up at the Last Day from the lowliness of the grave to the Holiness of Heaven!

SERMON VI.

THE SACRIFICE OF INNOCENCE.

"That I may go unto the altar of God, even unto the God of my joy and gladness."—Ps. xliii. 4.

THE contemplation of sin, which has filled the spare moments of Lent,[1] is drawing fast to its close in that great act of death, in the dark silence of which our Lord Christ, working in hidden and mysterious ways, unloosed the bands of hell. More and more, as the sense of our vileness intensifies within us, do we turn our eyes forward to that uplifted Cross; its anguish, its horrible sorrow, its bitter pangs, its appealing patience, even though our minds fail to enter into the secrecies of its justification, yet, at least, present themselves to the instinctive passion of our hearts, as the alone adequate solution of a world's desperate failure. We dare not, perhaps, argue about it; but we feel as we fall back, staggered and appalled, from the study of that vast and ghastly wickedness, which despoils all human life of its fairness and its joy—wickedness so foul, so sickening, so relentless, so devouring, with its unutterable pains and maddening despair, such wickedness as chokes our cities with corruption, and eats into our blood, and fills our veins with fire, and drags all the sweetness of our

[1] This and the three following Sermons were given, as mid-day addresses, during Holy Week in St. Paul's Cathedral.

souls into infamy and pollution—we feel, as we turn from this to the enduring Cross and Passion of Christ, that its horror is, at least, on a level with that which it redeems—that here is no bathos, no unworthy close. It may be hard to trace the threads that bind the world's sin to the world's salvation; but, at any rate, the one has a look of kindred with the other; we pass easily across from the one to the other without a shock. They touch hands; a sympathy works between them both; they seem each to know and understand the other. The more intense our appreciation of the dreadful reality of the sin, the more assuring, and familiar, and needful becomes the vision of the Crucified. We may let our minds wonder, still, at the necessity that decreed the biting nails and shuddering fear; but our hearts feel no surprise. No: they demand some such end, some such crowning act; they spring to the recognition of its consistency with its surroundings and antecedents; they are even comforted to acknowledge an effect that is commensurate with its cause. Here, they feel, is no dream, no mocking vision, coming with cold and shadowy comfort, to offer its misty thinness for the food of a pain-burdened race of worn and suffering men. Here, rather, is a *reality*, vivid, actual, solid, with the vivid solidity of fact. A wounded and bleeding humanity knows what to make of a bleeding and a wounded God. God's justification of Himself on the Cross plants itself down with a substantial and undeniable plainness, such as makes it at home in a world like ours, where evil is actually rending and tearing the flesh of man,—a world where worn women are withering to death with hunger in naked garrets, and men's lusts are savage, and their passions cruel, and a mob of devils work out their rage with whip, and scourge, and sting. "Yea, O my God, we lay hold of Thy Cross, as of a staff that can stand unshaken, when the floods run high. The tale told us is no fairy story of some far-away land: it is this world, and not another, —this world with all its miseries and its slaughter and its ruin,—that Thou hast entered to redeem, by Thine Agony and bloody Sweat."

Let us attempt, under the gathering shadow of this most merciful death, to touch on some of the possible principles which make it felt to be the one and only solution of man's grief, that our hearts could admit. No such rational account of the mysterious efficacy of the Passion will ever, perhaps, give the significance of the whole; but, under the control of the Holy Spirit, we may venture to take up this or that thread of thought, and follow it home to the moment when it vanishes into the gloom that shrouds the awful hour when the sun withdrew his light and there was darkness over the face of the earth.

The Cross of our Lord Jesus Christ is no isolated event; nor is it the first, but the last and final moment of God's unfolding of Himself. It closes a long drama; it is the crisis up to which whole histories were working through a thousand centuries. It cannot be interpreted, therefore, in and by itself. It is by such abstract and unreal severance of the Passion from all its conditions and antecedents, that it has been made to seem "foolishness to the Greeks:" these antecedents, these conditions are its justifying causes; for they are history, and the Cross is historical: they are the facts, and it is to the facts that the action of God on Calvary applies itself. To remove them, therefore, is to remove all possibility of its explanation. Rather, by the word of the Lord, we are to confess that, from the hour of that great Sabbath in which God first allowed Himself the joy of repose, up to the day when the Jews first determined to slay Him who called God His own Father,—from end to end of that enormous and protracted development, " My Father worketh, and I work." They worked unceasingly a work of which the Cross was the one absolute result: and only by following the long order of the untiring work, can we ever lay hold of the motives and issues which make that Cross the clear and intelligible close of the Divine Revelation.

To do this, now, in four brief addresses is impossible: but, at least, I may attempt to recall the general premisses which govern that argument which concludes itself in the Cross of Christ.

What was it, then, that had happened, and which, in its final stage, Christ died to rectify?

We must go back to the primary premiss of all, back to that first Sabbath Day on which God justified His creation, pronouncing it very good: for it is this justification which was recovered on the day when, once more, God looked, and beheld, and pronounced, "This is My beloved Son, in Him I am well pleased."

God had created: He had, that is, allowed a work to take form and substance away and apart from Himself: He had suffered His almighty power to go forth out of and all that he is, to be in no sense his own, but entirely and altogether a created thing, existent in and by another.

This created thing, which is himself, his whole self, his whole body, his whole passions, his whole force, his whole mind, his whole will, his whole soul—the whole of it—he, by the power of the Spirit which is in him, can lay hold of, can embrace all round, can take up in his hands, and lift and raise on high before God, and offer, and present. He is himself the offering: he is, by the Divine Spirit in him, himself the priest.

This is religion; this is its root-life. Religion is man's recognition that he himself, with all that he possesses, is entirely and absolutely the *possession* of God. Hence religion is, primarily, an act of homage, an act of dedication, a sacrifice—not of blood, or agony, or overwhelming dismay, but the sacrifice of a delighted and exultant confession in the glad lordship of God— the thrilling confession which is felt stirring half blindly in all those thousand forms of heathen offering, whether of fruit or flower or rice or bread or lamb, which startle us by their constancy amid all the varieties of so many heathen faiths. The thought is obscure, and darkly hid. Often it works underground, and the signs of its movement are, it may be, low, and strange, and coarse, and mean; it manifests itself in fear rather than in love; in self-will, instead of in self-abandonment. But it is there, and it prompts, always, the offering and the sacrifice; for, always, the root-spring of all religion lies in the intense joy of the discovery: "I am not mine own. I have nothing of myself. O my God, I am altogether Thine! Receive what is mine, in symbol of myself."

And observe;

Sacrifice, in this sense, carries us back behind and beyond all pain, and sin, and suffering. It is, in its primary premiss, not the sad means of recovering a lost state, but the delightful recognition of what actually is, and has never ceased to be.

It is the symbolic act of a discovery; the discovery by the creature of its Creator. Even if no dividing sin had ever severed man and God, still religion would consist in the joy of self-dedication, the joy of homage, the joy of an offering, the joy of a sacrifice. There would still be the altar, and still the priest; an altar of joy, and gladness, and thanksgiving, and praise; a High Priest, royal, enthroned, wonderful in blessing, after the order of Melchisedec, ever living and supreme.

So might man have continued to this day, active, vigorous, enterprising, as we ourselves, yet without a lie, without a lust, without a crime, without a doubt, presenting himself, in perpetual confidence, to proffer to God his willing and natural service.

Is such sinlessness incredible? Is it unreal? Yet surely evil is not our real, natural life. Surely it works, for every one of us, as a vast and hideous blunder. We have that in us, even now, which would be pure, and upright, and holy, only that it has lost its chance.

Ah! our lost and forgotten innocence!

Ah! our Paradise, the garden of our irrevocable joy!

How good, even now, from amid the black shadows of our pollutions, from amid the grime, and filth, and squalor of our dreary decay,—how good to recall, with tears of tender remembrance, what faith might have been without a fall! What worship might have been before a sin! What the gladness of God's approach might have meant, before ever we had had need to hide ourselves among the trees of the garden!

And what if, as some suppose, He, the Perfect God and Perfect Man, the dear Lord we love, would have at last entered in upon that blessed and sinless human life, to make, in it, the pure sacrifice of unalloyed, unchecked, untainted praise, Himself the one and only Priest, moving to the altar of that delightful offering, without a wound, without a pang, without a tear, without a sorrow, in the fulness of an exultant love which rose in joy to meet the unbroken joy with which God for ever pronounced all to be very good!

O Lord Jesus! Thou, Whom we, by our sins, have robbed of that good gift of joy, which might have been Thine! Thou, Whom we have forbidden to partake of flesh and blood, except at the bitter cost of that agony and blood-sweat! O holy, merciful, all-forgiving Redeemer, teach us more worthily to repent of the terror and horror of our fall, by the memory of that innocent gladness with which we should have gone with Thee to the altar of God, to offer there, no sorrow-stricken, death-stained, sin-worn sacrifice, but the unshrinking homage of a spotless heart!

SERMON VII.

THE SACRIFICE OF THE FALLEN.

"Then said I, Lo, I come!"—Ps. xl. 7.

THE Cross of Christ presupposes an original innocence before the Fall: and we can, therefore, win an insight, in its full significance, only by going back behind all the unrighteousness which has spread its evil power like a vast and devouring disease over our earth and our own hearts, and by starting with a thoughtful recognition of the conditions which constitute the state of purity in which the union between God and man first sealed itself with joy,—a union, a purity, a joy which we *can* still, even though it be through tears of vain regret, recall and interpret, because that, even now, the conditions of its innocence lie at the base of all our being, broken, fragmentary, disordered, yet still living, still stirred by old memories of a lost holiness, still sensitive to high impulses, still mindful of, still moved by, the sad fragrance of happier and purer days, those sweet familiarities, that tender intercourse, when, on fair cool evenings, God walked and spoke with man, as a man speaketh with his friend, among the trees of the garden.

There, far back in the depths of history, in the depths of our own souls, we seem to detect a living worship which would still, even then, take the shape of sacrifice, the sacrifice of a loyal allegiance, the offer of a delighted homage, the sacrifice that expresses the simple gladness of the discovery that there is nothing in us which is not God's very own, our Lord and Master and Maker.

Now, that root-idea of worship remains, from the first till to-day, unshaken, unruined: it expresses the formal and essential relation of man to God, and, since the primal essence of our humanity, however marred, overclouded, defiled, has retained, through all, its first identity, never wholly divorced from its first estate, therefore, too, the ground of its primal attachment to its Creator holds on unchanged. Man remains to this hour the one created being whose main office it is to recognise, confess, fulfil the allegiance of creation to its Maker.

Still, then, that act of holy homage has got to be rendered. Still that altar stands, and still God waits for man's priestly ministry, to respond to and return His Sabbath rejoicing. For God to miss this response would indeed be to let failure cancel the purpose with which He fashioned man out of the dust of the earth. Such failure may not be. The act of homage is still due, still demanded, still imperative; any change that events may carry into it, cannot abolish the demand; it can only affect the mode of its accomplishment.

What change, then, is it that has intervened? The change, the terrible, the marring change of sin. The whisper of the evil one has crept along under the leaves of the garden, as a wind, with sudden stealth, ruffles and discolours the clear loveliness of sleeping waters: the simple heart of the woman has let the wonder of curiosity work within the blood: the hand has slid out, she hardly knows how, to touch, and feel, and take, and hold, the pleasant dream of an idle and forgetful soul: the lips have tasted, the evil is sucked in; it is taken into the veins, and into the brain; its subtle poison has penetrated, with rapid secrecy, into all the deep corners and hidden recesses of her being; in a moment, its activity has passed out from her to her companion. The flame is alive: it has got its hold: it leaps out to new victories: it catches up all it can get near: its volume swells and rolls and roars with ever-gathering force, with ever-triumphant fury: the world is wrapped in the fire and in the smoke.

We understand, now, the depth, the awful seriousness of the change. Sin has traversed the primal, the essential service that man is made to render to his God: for is not sin just this, a lack of loyalty, a failure in allegiance? The heart, whose only delight, as a created thing, was to know itself another's, has been deceived into deeming its impulses to be its own; its freedom has seemed to it to be, not what it actually is, freedom to do freely another's will, but freedom to make a will and a way for itself: its desires, its imagination, its curiosity—these have made good their claim to their own satisfaction, instead of joying to discover all their satisfaction in the satisfaction of Him Who made them to be what they are, and in Whom alone they possess any true being.

The change, then, has cut right into the heart of man's worship: his homage is no longer true.

The Sacrifice of Innocence.   105

own. He is the highest moment of physical creation, the nearest approach it can make towards self-existence: but he is still only a part of that creation. He is as entirely and completely dependent on God's sole sustaining will as the veriest atom of blind matter. He is no more his own than that atom is. Not one hair's breadth more than it can he pass outside the limits of that dependence which is the essential law of all created things: and it is by this very fact that he enters on his peculiar office for the fulfilment of which he was made. Creation has this peculiar charm—this is its especial delight before God—that, while seeming to live in and for itself, it is, all the time, only living in and by and for God. For this, God rejoices over it—it is His own, His very own, even as it moves along in its own free gladness. For this—because in it all He sees Himself—for this alone He pronounces it "*very good.*"

Creation, then, enters into the joy of God, the joy of that great Sabbath, the joy of its own eternal repose, just according to its power of realizing that all its life is not its own, but issues out of, and returns into, the God in Whom it for ever and uninterruptedly subsists. And man—man in whom its self-possession, its self-movement attains its supreme movement—man alone, of all that vast world of varied life, has the capacity to supply, to creation, this, its Sabbath-joy. Without him it moves along before the All-seeing, in dumb and deathlike silence. Noises there are, but none that echo the voice of that gladness which pronounces them all very good; eyes and ears and mouths there are, but the eyes are blinded and the ears are deafened; they cannot see or hear, beyond the narrow bounds of their own small animal lives, into the infinite splendour of that from which they came, and to which they belong.

Man alone can speak and see, can give sight, and sound, and hearing to that which, without him, remains with its joy unattained, unfulfilled, unknown. He alone is gifted with the double character, by which he not only exists, as creatures exist, with power, capacities, strengths, movements of their own, but also distinguishes what he is, and whence he is, and how he is, and, if so, cannot but distinguish that his life is not his own, but entirely and for ever Another's, to recognise Whom is his supremest joy. He alone is the world's high priest, who, made one with it by a like nature, by a common kinship, by closest ties of creaturely being, passes up from and before the eyes of that waiting world, within the veil, outside which it remains bowed in silent awe, and in earnest expectation—passes in, and up the steps of neighbourhood to God, the steps of thought, and meditation, and reflection, and memory, and fear, and love—until, within the Holy of Holies itself, in the name of all God's creatures, he does the things of God, he swings the censer of praise, he carries the offering, he stands and bows himself before that high altar, and ministers the service of praise and thanksgiving.

What, then, is man's offering? What his holy service? Surely this, the offering of himself.

Man has the power to contemplate, to lay hold of himself: he looks himself all over, and sees himself,

His disloyalty has disturbed the direction of his desires, the even flow of his emotion: he knows, and remembers, and enjoys the memory of, a counter-delight to that of owing his being wholly to God. He can come no more to the altar with his old straightforward gladness of an undivided heart.

Yet the homage is still due: God still looks for it. How can it be given?

Let us think what sin has signified.

Allegiance to God is man's sole life: the created lives solely and entirely in and by God. Man's personal self, with its personal hungers, and personal thoughts, no more belongs to itself, or exists in itself, than a stone in the road does. His very existence is only intelligible and only possible, so far as God exists in him, and he in God. There is no point at which man's analysis of himself can stop, and lay its finger, and say, "Here ends all that I derive from God; here ends the Divine assistance; here I and I alone begin, and am." Not one tiniest atom of his flesh, not one swiftest moment of his will, can be wholly severed off from God into self-existence. His whole life, from sheer start to sheer finish, in every muscle, fibre, nerve, emotion, sensation, impression, perception, memory, thought, will, hope, fear, affection, aspiration, faith—all collapses, if God withdraws His hand. Separation from God, even the slightest, means, then, absolute and entire collapse, and that is DEATH.

There it is: we have touched the great word: "Death."

Allegiance to Him in Whom alone we have any being—this is *life*: and the recognition of this, in acts of loyal homage, is the perpetual renewal and preservation of life. The loss of loyalty, the fall from allegiance, the inclination to live in self, and for self, in self-will—this is to lose hold on life—this is, necessarily, to die. Death is the horrible break-up of all that makes us man, which follows the loss of our hold on God: death is the shudder that shatters our being, as it first misses God. This is death, sin's inevitable issue.

But still, I insist, in spite of sin's fatal entry, God demands homage. He has made man, that he may offer up the sacrifice of a true heart to Him. He cannot be disappointed: His omnipotence is pledged to the attainment of His hope.

Man must even yet offer his sacrifice—what sacrifice can it be?

The sacrifice can only be now, not a *discovery*, but a *recovery*, of allegiance: and a recovery of allegiance must start, then, not from the old primal joyful sense of finding oneself in God, but from the sad and ruinous sense of finding oneself outside God.

But to be outside God, disloyal to God, to be claiming self-existence—this is sheer death: to start with the sense, then, of severance from God is to start with a sense of death.

Man, then, comes to the altar of sacrifice, burdened and crushed with a bitter, a destroying sense of death upon his soul; and still God cries to him, "Bring up thine offering; fulfil thy ministry; testify thy fealty."

What may he offer? What has he to bring?

Surely, one offering, and one only,—the offering of that very sense of death, which loads and drags downward into ruin all his life.

For consider, may not that sense of death itself be made the proof that man owns himself to be a very nothing outside God? In feeling disloyalty to be a very death, he confesses where his true allegiance lies. He finds himself fast dying down into hideous corruption; he recognises, in this horrible state, the natural issue of a self-willed life: let him gladly, then, accept the issue; let him welcome into himself the very horror that devours him; let him take it into the arms of his soul, and lift it up, in all its ugly and disastrous deformity, before the eyes of the Most High! Let him cry aloud, "Behold, O my God, Lord of the spirits of all flesh, Behold, I know myself, now in the pangs of the death which has caught me in its toils, I know myself to be dead when I fall from Thee. I have tasted the bitter anguish of severance from Thy service. I feel it to be death. I have endured it, and confess it to be torment; and now, I bring before Thee my acceptance, my recognition of this inevitable law. I lay out, I hold up, I plead, I offer, I sacrifice to Thee my own sense of this death, my own intense unutterable abhorrence of this separation, into whose unmerciful gulf I sink. I die, O God, in severing myself from Thy living name. Yet lo! I abhor the death I die. And my abhorrence of this sin in which I perish, is the measure of my sense of the allegiance due to Thee alone." So let him cry; so let him plead; and the offering of his death would itself become a pledge that the true loyalty of heart had been refound. Allegiance would be recovered; the act of homage would be made once more complete.

But alas! who of men can make that offering?

The allegiance is only recovered wholly when the horror that belongs to death is felt entirely, in all its awful force, as the expression of that ruin which severance from God works in the soul. Only when that separation is felt to be the dissolution that it actually is, can the willing fealty of a loyal heart be, by the ready endurance of that death, indeed expressed and renewed.

But here lies the crucial difficulty.

Such a resolute and utter horror, which is to be commensurate with the ruin which severance from God works in the soul, can only be known by one who feels sin to be a very death. Its touch must feel to him as an alien, repulsive, loathsome thing: its breath must be as the breath of a vile and terrible plague. Only then could he plead before God, as a pledge of his continual loyalty, his dire sense of what sin signifies.

But the man who has sinned, feels now no such horror in sinning: the sin itself blunts his sensitiveness; his shame loses its acuteness; that sin, even while he professes to hate it, has its charm for him: he cannot but confess its delight, even while he repudiates it. He may come before God, with the lamb in his hands, to be the witness of this confession that sin is death: but his heart is itself impregnated with the poison: it lusts after the fleshpots it has left behind in Egypt; its perceptions of the infinite holiness, of which it has once risked the loss, are dulled, and cramped; its love for itself, for its own desires, carries division, disruption, into its offer of allegiance. The will cannot retain its secure and unimperilled freedom of choice, the security of a passion that had never wandered from its aim. Its imagination can no longer measure the gulf which yawns between God and evil, for the vision of God has become hazy and obscure, and the mists thrown up by inward hungers have risen to becloud it.

Do we not know it?

This is no far-off history, hidden away in the forgotten past,—no tale, left to be pictured out of dead records, by our uncertain and unsteady fancy.

No! Its story, recorded once for all in Scripture, lives its life, repeats its issues, over and over again in every soul that breathes in this great church to-day.

We have fallen—we know it—fallen from the primal innocence, which *might* be, even now, if our truest self but had the power to put out its life and assert its purity of will. The sonship of God—which is in us—at times wakes up and weeps. It weeps for its lost whiteness of will, now so stained, so polluted—for its gladness that leapt up of old to greet the bright glory of the near-drawing God—its gladness now so depressed, and burdened, and worn.

It weeps, but ah! who of us can now weep the tears that we would wish to weep! the tears of abasement, of agonizing penitence, which would be worthy of the ruin that has overtaken our soiled souls! worthy of the offence that we have flung at the Most High and Holy!

This is the very misery of our most miserable fall, that, knowing the healing and purifying energy of penitential sorrow, we yet grope blindly, seeking to obtain a sorrow that we cannot feel; we clamour out vain words of appealing grief to God, and yet know them to be vain—know that we cannot put our soul into them—know that they must come up before God, cursed with the curse of hypocrisy.

"The sacrifice of God is a troubled spirit; a broken and contrite heart, O God, Thou wilt not despise."

Yes! but your and my spirit! your and my heart! dare we call them for one moment contrite? Dare we call upon God to witness that they are troubled and broken?

Our very words acknowledge, that anything short of a "broken" heart, God may well despise. And yet, a "broken heart"! Whose is this broken heart? Dare you call your spirit troubled, or your heart contrite—that spirit, which moves along so lightly and easily under its curse, that heart which is still pricked by many a fond desire, many a fleshly appetite? Are you the one to plead before God the sacrifice of a "broken and a contrite heart"? Are you? O my God, am I? Am I at all the one to cry before Thee, "Lo, I have seen Thee with mine eyes, and I abhor myself in dust and ashes"?

Where is our abhorrence? Where are our tears? Where is our sense of horror and death? Where in our faces, or in our hearts would God learn, that we feel the loss of His presence as a shadow of great darkness, as a terrible collapse, as a very stroke of death?

Yet, unless He is given this, He wins no offering from us. He receives no proof of recovered allegiance. He obtains no filial response to His own infinite joy.

Without this, man's altar stands unhallowed and desolate, his ministry fails, his sacrifice is an abomination. For if he knew the Father as He is, if he saw His Majesty, if he felt the thrill of His love, then the sorrow unto death would pierce his soul with its seven wounding swords, at the thought of having ceased to dedicate his being to his God.

In vain, in vain to proffer dead kids and goats! In vain to leap and cut ourselves with knives! In vain, for still sin has taken the sharpness off the edge of our penitence! Deep in our heart of hearts, there dogs and haunts us the cloying love of the very sin we bewail. Its memory rises up, and, fly as we will, its memory still half fascinates; enticing voices call after us, clinging hands are laid about us, and we are half unwilling to throw them off. We may strain to break away—strain longing eyes towards the hope of God's awful purity—but we have not now the moral grasp to hold it fast. Its image is blotted, and confused, and shifting; it fades, it passes away; we fall back powerless, exhausted, discouraged; we cannot see God—we cannot grieve the holy grief that comes only to the pure in heart.

No; and if not, then we have no offering to bring Him; no sacrifice to lay on His altar; no sealing sign of fealty to plead. Our whole service is impotent and barren.

Unless it may be that there shall stand one day upon our earth One, clothed in our flesh, a man with blood, and bones, and body, such as we ourselves have, a man, with all the fulness of human passion, unswerving, and invincible, and true, that it would feel any severance of its bond to be the very torture of death. Such an appeal witnesses that any such severance is for ever an impossibility to a soul so intimately conscious of what severance would involve. Such an appeal, then, is in God's ears the pledge of perfect homage, the recovery of a renewed allegiance, by a humanity which, since it had once fallen into disloyalty, could only recover itself through a recognition, that it felt such disloyalty to be its ruin, its despair.

In that bitter cry, the sacrifice that man has to offer is once more renewed. That Cross has become his altar. The communion of the creature with the Creator is once again recovered; the joy of the Creator in a loyal and true-hearted creation, renews itself into its old Sabbath gladness, the gladness of a God who can repose, since the crown of His labour is achieved. Worship has begun anew: the victim is there to make victorious appeal; the priest is there, lifting once more holy hands. The incense of praise and thanksgiving once again ascends as of old. The temple of God is filled with the smoke, and shakes with the tremendous Presence, as once more the voice of man goes up to mingle with the cry of the seraphim, "Holy, holy, holy, Lord God of Hosts! Earth as well as Heaven is full of Thy glory. Glory be to Thee, O Lord most High."

Let us venture to contemplate still nearer the nature of this our recovered sacrifice: by doing so, I think we may realize that it is no abstract theological dogma, but is endued with that real actuality which fits it to become a factor, a power, in a world of flesh and blood.

For consider how the offering of a freewill was made: it was an actual physical death; and we know how startlingly vivid is the identification by St. Paul, nay, by our Lord, of the moral with the physical death,—" He who loses his life for My sake shall find it. Unless ye eat My flesh, ye shall die." " Dead with Christ." Who can trace any dividing line that keeps asunder the twin conceptions? The death *of* the body is the death *to* the body; no analysis can keep them finally apart. And so, too, the cry of the bereaved heart against that deadly abandonment of God is no mere spiritual act; it issues out of, it takes effect in, an actual perishing of the flesh.

How is this? In attempting to account for it, forgive me if I once more recall the conditions of man's allegiance.

He was possessed of a double character: on the one hand, he was a mere creature, a created thing, a bit of this visible creation, a complicated living organism, moving on its own lines, endowed with its own capacities; an embodiment of a certain fixed quantum of force, which God has, as it were, detached from Himself, and set moving, and supplied with energy, and continuance, and substantiality, to go its own way, under the control and limitation of its own laws and conditions. So far he was simply the subtlest and most elaborate instance of that delight which had moved God to allow creation to assume the character of a real self-supporting existence, the image of that absolute self-sustenance which constitutes His everlasting joy.

On the other hand, man was more than the mere creature: he had the additional gift of a spiritual capacity which could outstep its creaturely existence, could look it all round, take the measure of it; could recognise the unreality of that seeming self-existence, and in the might of that recognition could discover the God in Whom alone lay its right and its strength to exist at all; could look up to Him with joy, acknowledging its entire dependence, its entire dedication to His sustaining and sanctioning energy. So, as a spiritual priest, he offered himself and all creation, a glad and ready sacrafice, to God: and, in that worship, found his life.

Now, what is that which would be the due material for an offering made under such conditions? Is it not the flesh, the body? He is to offer to God his whole creaturely existence, all the powers that belong to him as a created thing; and the body—what is it but the organ and instrument and seal of all those living powers? The body is that particular portion of the earth's substance which man's spirit takes, and inhabits, and possesses, and indwells: in the body he plays his part, as a creature in the midst of a creation; through it, he belongs to earth, he deals with earth, he communicates with earth, he experiences earth. In it and by it, he possesses, he creates for himself, a solid and substantial life. Only through its quivering cords does he himself win his way to sensation, or movement; only in its fine and free activities does he himself become conscious of emotion, or desire, or joy; only through its delicate ministries and responsive service do his powers wake up from sleep, and obtain the delight of life, and motion, and display.

In his body, then, he knows himself alive: by his

body, he achieves such self-existence, such self-manifestation as belongs to his created nature.

But this apparent self-existence, this seeming power of self-manifestation, is just what he is enabled by his spirit to recognise as due to God, due to Him for all that it is, due to be dedicated to Him, due to make the one offering which he, the priest, has got to present on God's high altar.

The body, then, which is the instrument of his self-manifestation, is the due and proper instrument, also, of his self-sacrifice. It is the body, it is the full, manifested life of the creature, the organ of all its motions, affections, perceptions, intuitions, pleasures, needs, fancies, delights—it is himself as alive in the body, which he may lift in his hands, in glad discovery, to recognise and confess in it, his own entire consecration to his Maker.

And how when that primal allegiance has been lost? How was it lost?

Was not the body, that ministrant of creaturely life, just that which made man's inherent life seem to him so real, so intensely personal, so entirely his very own? In his flesh it was that he felt himself alive; that he knew what it was to enjoy, to feel, to move: through it, he could gain for himself pleasures; through it, he could feed his passions; in it he seemed most genuinely to possess something which he might use for his own purposes, put to serve his own needs, adapt to his own interests, make minister to his own imaginations and lusts.

The body, then, is that piece of nature which a man

occupies, and controls, and directs; his possession, his dwelling, his dominion; that private portion and lot set apart for him to do with as he will, that heritage allotted him by his Father: the body is the scene, and organ, and tool of man's peculiar temptation, the temptation to consider this creaturely life intrusted to him, to be his very own, to be used as he chooses, for his own delight. It is upon the body that man's eyes first fall as they look down from God to earth, and ask whence man may invent for himself pleasures.

And observe; the sinfulness hidden in man's secret will does not know itself, does not show itself, has not yet sinned its life away, until it has leapt out of its secrecy, and has moved the body into rebellious action. Man's will had only then committed the full sin, when the hand had been put out to take, and the mouth had tasted and enjoyed. For sin is an act: and the body is the organ of action.

Yes, and sacrifice. Sacrifice, also, is an act; and the body, the organ of all action, is the organ not only of sin, but also of sacrifice. God asked of man an act, a self-dedication, a dedication to be accomplished, therefore, in and with the body. And man, in spoiling and sullying, by selfish uses, the organ of activity, had, therefore, spoiled and sullied the instrument and fuel of his sacrifice, the sole material in which to render up the act of his offering. He had no pure offering any more which his will could carry in within the holy places. It is blood, with which the ministry of sanctification, of remission, is accomplished: it is blood, the life in the flesh, with which all the tabernacle of grace is to be sprinkled and purged. But in man's blood, now, hot fevers work, fierce passions run riot, angry lusts are stirring: he dare not carry and offer such wild blood as that, in within the cool quiet of the Holy of Holies.

And yet worse: in laying hold of the body for his private gratification and prize, man had not only fallen from loyalty, and sullied his sole offering, but what was the penalty, the necessary result of such spiritual severance from God?

Death: utter, ruinous death.

And how does that penal death touch the deathless spirit in man? How can it ever lay its loathsome fingers on that which is beyond its cruel clutch?

Nay, not entirely beyond!

That high spirit is netted into the delicate meshes of all-penetrative flesh; that flesh is the sole organ of all the spirit's feelings, passions, delights; and to that flesh it has turned as to its pleasure-house, to seek in the opportunities of the body, its joys, its desires.

How disastrous, how fatal a blunder!

"The wicked is trapped in the pit that he hath dug; in the net, that he set, is his foot taken." He has turned to the body to satisfy his lusts, and just through that body can death, the penal issue of lust, get at him; just through it can its foul working reach, and touch, and defile that which otherwise were beyond its grasp. Death operates upon his spirit through the body. The body is that which must be upheld by the continual in-breathing of God, or else it would sink into ruin, into corruption, into the jaws of hell: and, lo! man, by the very act of turning to the body, has withdrawn from him and it that essential inbreathing of God: the soul has ceased to draw in renewing supplies from God, and has identified its interests with those of the perishing flesh: and therefore, by that very act by which it spiritually died to God, it finds itself caught, tangled, snared in the horrible, clinging corruption and death of that body in which it sought its delight.

The wages of sin is death: and now those wages can be paid in full. For the spirit cannot attain the life, which belongs to it, except through that organ by which it lives: and that organ is now dying. Man's sin, in implicating him so fatally with the body, has made the payment of death possible. That death which he has died to God, can be paid out to him in the very coin in which he incurred it. It is paid out to his sinning spirit by virtue of its self-chosen implication in the ruin of the perishing flesh. There in the physical dissolution of its home and fabric, it reads, it feels, it is penetrated by, the sentence of its own helpless, hopeless fall out of life. The terrible collapse, the sickening horror of annihilation, the fearful sobs of an ebbing life, the torment and agony of God-abandonment,—these which eat into the soul through the channels of a decaying and collapsing body, are then known by it to be its very own: they impress upon it, with scathing letters of flame, its own inevitable doom: as it sinks into that devouring gulf which consumes its flesh, it can foresee for itself nothing but a death that yet, for it, can never reach that annihilation which is the refuge of the bodily frame; a death, then, which never ceases to be the death which now it experiences; a worm that gnaws, and never dies; a fire that consumes, and is never quenched; a torment of corruption, which has no need to reach a limit and have done.

The body, then, which we found to be the due instrument of sacrifice, and the due material and scene of man's temptation, is become, too, the instrument of his punishment, the scourge of his sin, the organ and material of death.

And now, how will that offering be renewed?

How will allegiance be fitly recovered?

It was to be renewed when man could re-dedicate, in proof of recovered loyalty, that very torment which he suffered in penalty for sin, the torment of that very death which, through the body, penetrates into, and massacres the spiritual life itself, which may not wholly die.

That pure and stainless will, then, in which man is to renew his offering, must experience that utter sense of collapse which touches the sinning spirit through the perishing fabric of its flesh: it must know it, as man knows it, in the actual pangs of a bodily death. It is in these pangs that man's fall is made actual, made intelligible to him: in these it is that he definitely knows what it is to be forsaken of God; and, therefore, it is just this sensible experience, known in physical sickness and death, of his utter and torturing failure, which he is to plead before God, in token of his re-recognised allegiance. He is to die to that death in which he finds himself implicated, by offering back to God that veritable agony which, by means of his attachment to flesh, does actually lay hold of him, and make him sensitive to its bitterness.

It is in the death-pangs of the body, therefore, that he finds the material of the renewed sacrifice; in them he discovers that peculiar act of re-dedication which will fitly and exactly cancel the act of his rebellion. It is these he should offer; it is these he should plead.

And now see what follows. These very death-pangs which he confesses, by that offering of a perfect will, to be the due issue of sin, its bitter punishment, its cruel and crushing and inevitable rebuke,—these become to Him Who, in the might of His sinlessness, can make them the instruments of His worthy confession, of His sufficing penitence, no longer what they would be in any other, no longer the expressions of God's wrath, the torment of despair, the merited pangs of remorse. No; Christ, our true Lord, was never tormented, never punished, as He thirsted with hot agony on the shameful Cross. God forbid! No; the very nature of those horrible pangs is changed as they touch that spotless and transforming innocence: they are changed wholly and altogether, from symbols of wrath into symbols of praise, as the most holy will bows itself to accept their awful fury, their desolating anguish, taking them into itself in unfaltering submission, as that which, with all their horror, it yet confesses to be far short of that horrible woe which it would be ever to swerve and fall from perfect loyalty to God. Yes; Christ's sacred courage will go right through with its task. He takes upon Him our flesh: that flesh which had been our ruin through its enticing pleasures, shall be turned to our salvation by its pains. Through the body we had known pleasure, and had laid greedy hands upon it, to feed our lusts with its delights. Through the body, now, we know what pain is; in the body's ruin we know now what the curse of death signifies. It is this bodily pain, then, this bodily death, which He, our Lord, will endure, that those very pains which now devour us with a sense of their justice may become the fuel of sacrifice, the proof of fealty, the tokens of victory, the symbols of our repose in God, the holy sacraments of a restored communion, of a recovered worship, of an unending thanksgiving.

So no purpose of the Most High has failed. The body is, once more, the instrument of praise. That which was the fuel of wrath is itself—that very body, and no other—transformed into the fuel of love.

"A body hast thou prepared me!"

"A body"—that very body, which we had dragged over the rough ways, and torn with the bitter thorns, of sin: that worn, wasted, beaten, battered, mangled, wearied body which we had filled with racking ills, and aches, and diseases; that very body in which pain and torture and death still in us to-day hold abode, and work their terrible will, in the free security that our fleshly lusts have allowed them: that poor, miserable, sickened, ruinous, perishing body He, the Pure and Holy, has entered; He has taken it, that He may make His very own all the agonies to which that flesh is heir; that in it He may be bruised for our offences, wounded for our iniquities, scourged for our healing; that He, too, may know what it is we suffer when the mouth is dry, and the lips parched, "and the tongue cleaveth to the gums: when the bones are burnt up as with a firebrand; and the heart is smitten down, and withered like grass: when wounds stink and are corrupt, and the loins are filled with a sore disease and there is no whole part in the body—when the heart panteth, and the strength faileth, and the sight of the eyes is gone from us."

That is what He would feel: this is what He took upon Himself, as He nailed that prepared body to the tree: and all this, felt in its full bitterness, felt to be, even then, only the image and symbol of that more awful anguish which desolated His purity of soul—all this He uplifted on high upon the Cross, with holy arms outstretched, and offered, in unshaken willingness, as the proof that not even then, amid all that tremendous horror, could He swerve for one moment from His allegiance to His God.

So, in that body, with that body, He appealed, He pleaded, He interceded with strong crying and tears: and was heard in that He feared, in that He endured, in that with that body He died. The victory was won: man, in Christ, had conquered: He had an offering once more to offer, the Holy Body and Blood which had been broken and shed, in the might of an invincible will, on Calvary. "Consummatum est"—"It is finished." Now, for evermore, there stands in highest heaven, in the holiest of holy places, a Lamb with wounded body, a Lamb as it had been slain. The closed seals are broken, the book is at last opened. Weep no more, O dear disciple whom Jesus loved; for in heaven, and in earth, and under the earth, are heard voices, and thunderings and lightnings, and through the thunderings the sound of a great hymn—"Worthy is the Lamb that was slain, and has redeemed us by His blood, to receive power, and riches, and wisdom, and strength, and honour, and glory, and blessing."

SERMON IX.

THE SACRIFICE OF THE REDEEMED.

"Unto you it is given in the behalf of Christ, not only to believe on Him, but also to suffer for His sake."—PHIL. i. 29.

CHRIST offered the one true sacrifice of His Body and Blood, in our stead; for our sakes He was buried. He took our place under the scourge, and the thorns, and the spear, and the nails. It was done for us, and not by us, because none but a spotless and unblemished will, none but an entirely innocent heart, could, by its own inner force, turn and transform the pangs, which had been our condemnation, into the instruments of a higher allegiance. He alone, our Samson, could use the very pillars which carried the house of sin, as the tools with which to work its fall. He, and no other, could be so perfected through suffering; He, and He alone, could so become the Man of sorrows, that the sorrows themselves were made the means and tokens of a purer holiness.

For us, then, He died; Christ, our Passover, was sacrificed for us.

But this vicarious assumption of our sorrows and pains has issues, not only towards the Most High and Holy God (Who, in His almighty love for us, had endured to see His only Son tortured, despised, and stabbed to death, in blood and agony, in our stead, and Who accepted the offering for the sake of the blameless will of the Son, which proved by those vicarious griefs, the unconquerable love that He and the Father together bore us), but it has issues, too, towards us.

The sacrifice is vicarious; but that vicariousness does not shut us off, like a wall, from our suffering Redeemer. God forbid! Rather, it is that very vicariousness which exercises a binding, a uniting power upon us. For by what can our love be drawn out more vividly, more victoriously, than by the offer of a life made most willingly for us? By that strong and stirring attraction, we are drawn by the cords of a man: we have a new hold on God the Father, Who is now known to us as one Who will give up His own Son to death for us. We have a new and irresistible sense of the longing desire with which He thirsts for our souls, as we watch and weep over those cruel wounds, that bleeding brow, that pierced side, as we shudder in the darkness under the anguish of that loud and exceeding bitter cry. No, surely, we do not stand outside, shut out from that absorbing act: the fearful twelve who knew not the undying passion of love which was working its way to them from that terrific Cross, they indeed might be far off—might forsake Him in His sorrow, and flee; but even then the instinctive love of the holy Mother and beloved John, and the clinging hearts of a few faithful women, could not endure to be far off from a grief that they, as yet, misunderstood: and we, we, who know all, we, to whom those gaping wounds are red lips that speak of unquenchable love, we, who, through that bleeding side,

The Sacrifice of the Redeemed.

can see a heart that beats as no human heart ever beat, in the intense fire of its desire to save—we cannot, surely, be less close to Him than they: we cannot but draw even nearer than weeping Magdalene: we cannot rest until we be one in love with Him Who so loved us —until He take us to Himself, our souls to His, our life into His own life, lifting us, by the out-streaming energy of His own power of love, up on to that Cross on which He hangs; lifting us in the strength of His unfailing promise, " I, if I be lifted up from the earth, will draw all men unto Me."

Christ's sacrifice is no far-away fact, to be shown and gazed upon. It draws *us* also into itself. For consider what exactly it was.

Where does its vicarious efficiency for us lie?

Surely, in this; that Christ made His offering out of our very flesh.

He laid hold of no foreign thing to offer; He looked not elsewhere for a gift. He looked at this world we live in: He took of its substance for His gift. He laid hold of its present nature, and offered that. Forasmuch as the children partook of flesh and blood, Christ also partook of the same. As of old, on the Galilean hills, so now, He took just that which we had in our hands, five poor loaves and two small fishes; and, with these, just as they were, He looked up to heaven and gave thanks. That flesh and blood, which He took, He found to be covered with wounds and putrifying sores. He found it subject to pain, wasted with illness. He found it liable to be crushed and trampled to death, if it attempted to hold itself pure and undefiled, in a world that violently hated both Him and His Father. As He found it, so He took it; just it, and no other: this, and just this, is that in which He would accomplish His priestly work.

But these are the very conditions in which we, to this day, live: that flesh which He took, we still wear: still it is full charged with ache and torment: still it wastes and sickens: still the dominion of sin keeps its corrupting grip upon our passions: still we are open to a thousand murderous assaults which beat down, and rend, and massacre all the purity and uprightness that we have it in us to put forth. We, then, hold in our hands the very gifts which Christ, our Master, offered. It was just these very human sorrows that He turned into sacraments of allegiance.

Are we blinded to our opportunities by the fact that they fall upon us by natural laws; or that they seem entirely accidental; or that they are brought upon us unjustly by wicked hands?

But consider the offering of Christ.

What can possibly be more unlike a pleasing sacrifice to God, than His death? What sign of its being a High Priest's offering, broke through the shadow of this world's darkness? It differed, in no degree whatever, from any common disaster that happens to us. It came upon Him by simply natural means; it looked, to the outsider, as a most cruel, and unfortunate, and bloody accident. It came upon Him by no casual choice of His own: He did not choose to select His own time, or way, or manner of suffering: He let it happen, as it would. No power is put forth to check or hinder the natural course that things took with Him. No; He will not benefit

The Sacrifice of the Redeemed.

Himself by any twelve legions of angels: He will, in no sense, repudiate the conditions of the flesh in which He had come to dwell: it is man's hour, and the hour of darkness: He is in their hands for a time: and let them wreak their hate as they will. He will raise no protest, He will set no limit, He will refuse nothing. "So, as a lamb was He led to the slaughter; so, as a sheep before the shearers, He never opened His mouth."

He never opened His mouth: but, throughout those awful hours, in the secrecy of His most holy silence, that stainless and unfaltering Will worked in and beneath the miseries of shame and spitting, the biting scorn and savage thorns; throughout it all, it lived as a flame, quickening the whole, yet not consuming; throughout it all, it rose, as a fountain, leaping up towards the eternal throne; throughout it all, it ceaselessly upraised before the Father's eyes, the pains that smote it, and the wounds that bled; throughout it all, from dreary sunrise to that last hour of blinding swoon, the lips of His Spirit pleaded, in unbroken patience, the liturgy of that tremendous consecration.

He offered, then, and saved by offering, just that human life which still is ours to-day; and if so, His sacrifice is not only a vicarious act, but, also, a revelation of the true use to which we may put this very world in which we stand; a revelation of the manner by which even it, with all its confusions, and disappointments, and sickness, and weariness, and anguish, and death, may be justified, may be hallowed, may be transformed into the fuel of that one sacrifice which alone can reconcile the world to God.

We are drawn into the circle in which Christ's eternal energies work: the love of Christ lays hands upon us and constrains us: we, as we are uplifted by the power of His passion, we, too, recover our priesthood; we may lift the offering of this our flesh to God, since that day when Christ died in the likeness of our flesh, and sanctified it to become an offering to God.

We may do it, now, though we are severed from that great day by eighteen hundred long and weary years: for still, to-day, Christ, the ever-living Priest, pleads within that Holy Place, into which He has passed before us, that holy Blood, once poured out in love for us, which makes Him still bone of our bone, flesh of our flesh; and still, to-day, as the Father looks upon that Blood, there breaks from His eyes, ever and again, the splendour of an unappeasable and exhaustless love, which hastens from afar, to greet our poor and pitiful gift of ourselves to Him, kissing us, and rejoicing, as God the mighty Forgiver can alone rejoice, that this His Son "was dead, and is alive again; was lost, and is found."

What is it that we can now hold back?

We are invited, by the example of Christ's Cross, to offer up our bodies to God: our bodies, because it is in them that we are what we are, as living creatures, men born on this earth, of flesh and blood.

We are to bring our bodies; not some imaginary, speculative, airy-natured offering, but just those very loaves, those two fishes that we hold in our hands. There is nothing else in our baskets, nothing else we can buy for God's use on these windy and desolate hills.

No; our bodies, our very selves, in the actual conditions that enclose us, and that knit themselves into our very being; our bodies, all the emotions, impulses, affections, ties, desires, hopes, fears, anxieties, troubles, diseases, losses, griefs, pains, that build up our real and moving earthly life, these are our offering, these the gift Christ authorizes us to bring. It is these, the interests of our bodily selves, which we were once tempted to believe our own, to claim for ourselves; it is in these that we once found pleasure for ourselves, and sought our delight; these to which we once clung; these on which we angrily rejected all attack; these the loss of which we so grievously regretted; these which we could not endure to imagine stolen from us. Our bodies, with all their attachments, and needs, and joys, have been the scene of our sin, of our forgetfulness of God: these same bodies are now to be the scene of our redemptive action, of our recovered fealty, that they be laid up as memorials before the Lord for ever. Our bodies we must give: we have no other gift. We may not come empty-handed; and the gift is laid in our hands by God: we cannot repudiate or deny it; we cannot plead that we have nothing to offer. The offering is ourselves, ourselves in our actual, present, physical estate. That is what Christ offered: that is what we, by His grace, may offer to-day.

How wonderful! This breathing frame, this living network in which I feel myself alive, this sensible, warm motion, this quickening flow of impulses, this swelling flood of aspiration, this tingling quiver of joy, this stir of sensitive passion, this delicious movement,—

all this which I know to be myself, and name by my own name, and belong to, and am,—all this, so close, so familiar, so intimate, is a holy thing, acceptable to God, that peculiar offering in which He finds Himself well pleased. This is what He asks for; this He loves to receive; for this is that which Jesus Christ took, and blessed, when He looked up to heaven, and gave thanks. All this!—ah! and far more than this!

All that I feel of bitter remorse, when sin has defiled the flesh, I owe to God; all the sadness, and the indignation, which chills, or fires, me with horrible dread, as one by one my earthly delights fall away from me; all the dreariness and the weariness which settle down upon my heart, as life's novelty dies down, and the world grows grey, and flat, and stale, and unprofitable; all the sobs that suck out my life's strength, as I stand by the open grave into which the creaking cords are lowering one whose smile will never more at all on earth greet me with its old, tender, endearing welcome, whose voice will never more again be heard in the old places and paths where we walked and laughed and talked together so many and many a happy hour in merry days gone by;—all this I may bring and offer. Yes, and the blinding tears, and the aching void, and the desolate loneliness, and the voiceless gloom; all this and more. The pain of unrequited love, of lost hopes, of cramping disappointment, of all the cold and nakedness and hunger, in which I am left to wander along the hard and barren roads of a niggardly world; all the anguish, with which the accumulated vileness and foulness of man's horrible sinfulness load and weigh down my soul, itself, alas! only too akin to the sins which it loathes; all the crushing trouble of injustice and infamy; all the hateful pressure of swarming lusts that crawl and climb within; all the coming agony when my soul shall wrestle with the dark foe, at the gathering of the night of death; all the torture that may then rack me, all the miserable sense of abandonment, all the fearful sinking of heart as the black waters close over my head; all the shudder, as the flesh falls away to corruption and loathsome abomination; all the parching thirst of that last dread struggle in which my soul and body shall break asunder, shattered and dismayed;—all this that seems only made to torture, and bruise, and condemn me, so ruthless, so useless, so blind, so unmerciful, is, after all, no horrible accident, no pitiless blunder, no victory of some dark and monstrous law of fruitless pain. No; this is just the very thing, that I may uplift and plead before God. All this is the very offering, the token of true and loving homage, by which I can prove myself loyal-hearted, and so become, in Christ, well pleasing to God.

O most wonderful, most holy privilege! How is it that I have so long overlooked the gift that God had placed in my hands to offer?

Can it, indeed, be true that that which was to me as the shadow of despair, is the moment of my priestly service within the holy places?

Yes, now; now is the moment of your call to the ministry of Christ. Now, when the loss of friends is bitter; now, when the agony of suffering is intense; now, when the light of your eyes is gone from you, now is the acceptable time; behold! now is the day of salvation.

Be strong; be strong and of a good courage. It has come to you; it has been put into your hands, your gift, your sacrifice. That suffering, that loss—that *is* it—that is your offering; your own death, that is your opportunity. Now is your time to show yourself the follower of Him, Who carried His own Blood in within the holy places.

Offer up to God your life; your anguish; your blood. Offer it; be not afraid. It is a consecrated, a holy thing, the one worthy sacrifice that man can offer.

It is true, *you* are powerless. You cannot make that offering aright. You have not the heart, nor the will. You sink down oppressed. You dare not plead before God sufferings so unwillingly accepted, so wearily endured.

No—but it is not you that offer, but Christ that offers in you. Christ, the mighty Interceder, leaves you not comfortless, leaves you not alone, in the midst of a world of tribulation. He comes to you, to make His abode in you, in the power of that Holy Spirit, the Comforter, Who, from within our ignorant prayers, sends up His strong and prevailing supplication.

He comes—most wonderful, most gracious, most blessed of all His many mercies—He comes to you, in the very might and reality of His own perfect sacrifice, to quicken your dull will by the marvellous efficacy of His own Body and Blood—that Body and that Blood, in which He bore all your weaknesses and all your groaning sins, and laid them, purified and sanctified, on the altar of His holy Cross, that by their everlasting strength and consolation, we, who eat of that flesh and drink of that saving Blood, may indeed be baptized with the baptism wherewith He was baptized.

There, He comes, to that upper chamber, where His Church has made ready the passover: comes at all hours, when the world, that hated Him, turns its hatred upon us; and our friends betray us; and we ourselves are only too ready to deny Him: comes, when, against us, evil gathers with its swords and its staves, and our soul is exceeding sorrowful even unto death. Thither He comes; He enters in; He abides; He sups with us; that we, His friends, may have peace. Peace ! not from trouble, and anguish, and death; not the peace of easy safety; not the peace that the world longs after; but peace in Him, Who amid all trouble has pledged to us the victory; peace in that we possess within us Him Who is stronger than all that can be against us. "Let not your hearts be troubled, neither let them be afraid. In the world ye shall have tribulation. But be of good cheer; I have overcome the world."

SERMON X.

THE SPIRITUAL EYE.

"They are not of the world, even as I am not of the world. . . . As Thou hast sent me into the world, even so have I also sent them into the world."—St. John xvii. 16, 18.

THERE are two aspects in which the world presents itself to all of us, and these two are so utterly different in outline and temper, that most of us can but stare helplessly from one to the other, and wonder what possible thread of connection can ever bring them together into that harmony which constitutes reality, into that union which binds them the one to the other with the living energy of God. In the one, the eye falls, wherever it looks, upon a steady, enduring, substantial world, spreading out far and wide around us its serried array of facts—unending, unbroken, unceasing. We have before us, it may be, a lovely landscape; we look up into the sky, and above us rolls the great sun, and all around us glistens and quivers the quickening breath of air; and at our feet the vast sea spreads its plain of moving waters, and away behind us lies the infinite, varied distance of wood, and field, and heaving hill; and through the fields run for ever and ever the movement of the rivers and the rustling of the brooks, and, far above, the clouds hang patient and slow, and the rooks pass by, pressing intently towards some distant

The Spiritual Eye.

home, and the sheep feed unceasingly, and the bees come buzzing about the wild-flowers, and all the air is alive with the incessant murmur of tiny life. There it is, the great life of Nature, moving along in its steady and strong magnificence, large, resistless, self-contented. And man—man is borne along in the mighty, massive whole, part and parcel with it; his presence hardly perceptible but for a touch or two of blue smoke in the fields; his world of thought and religion just marked here and there by a faint church tower, half hidden among the trees: and we, too, as we lie on our back on the hill-side, we, too, have almost disappeared, are almost forgotten; we are but an accident in the great scenic display, carried along with it, melted into it. What are we to the rhythm of its giant march? What disturbance would there be if we dropped out of the picture? Whether we were there or not, that sun would still be shining, the sea still gleaming, the butterflies still flitting along in endless rise and fall, not a quiver would cease in the leaves, not a ripple would be changed on the waters. Such is this aspect of physical nature; and Science comes in to aid in spreading out the limits of this vision of Nature far back into the limitless Past, far forward into the endless Future. It exhibits all this, that enters at eye and ear, as but one moment of an infinite process, one chain in an unalterable sequence. It unrolls the long and awful histories of ages upon ages, and through all of them it shows us that sun still rising and setting, those waters still moving, those clouds still gathering and vanishing, those winds still creeping along the grass; and as we look, and read, and listen, man has vanished out of the drama. It matters not whether the human race be yet brought into existence: still the huge formation continues its ceaseless coalescence: still the vegetable growths rise and wither and decay, and rise again: still the waters wear and mould the cleaving rocks. Careless of us, the silent impenetrable years labour, in solemn and tremendous stillness, at their fateful work. We—we are to them as the smoke that vanisheth away. " We look, and behold we are gone, and our place can no more be found."

Or, again, we rise from our dreams and our studies, and pass out into the hurry and crowd of our city streets. Here, at least, we shall find the reality of humankind: and what do we see? We see men, eager and intent, hastening hither and thither, with all that hurry of business which we watch going on round any nest of ants, or in any toiling bee-hives. We watch the unresting labour, the terrible seriousness with which they are at work: and all this toil, and all this intricate machinery, is just to carry on this human life of ours. Round us swells the roar and clamour of the struggle, the multitudinous detail of the docks and the merchandise, the elaborate mechanism, the wearisome rush and tumult of the railways, the vast noise of our arsenals, the clanging of our mines and of our mills; and men, in the midst of all this, as they hasten by us, as we see them swarming, and jostling, and shouting, what are they to us more than the bees or the ants? What are they to us but ingenious pieces of nervous living mechanism, things of flesh and blood; like the animals, only a little cleverer, capable of larger stretches of reason and sharper calculations; but still nothing more than what we *see* them to be; nothing more than can be shut up within the walls of the body; beings whom we can sift and analyze by experiment and observation, whom we can classify according to their obvious habits and tempers, whom we can sum up into statistics, so as to examine and predict the amount or degree of their disorder, their drunkenness, their crime, the general laws under which they are blindly pursuing each his own interest: and in all this, again, what is it to us who this or that individual may be, who passes before our eyes, or is swept up into our statistics? Labourer, merchant, beggar, he is but a specimen of his class. To our generalizations it is absolutely indifferent who form the particular cases. If all those men before us died to-day, and others of a like class stepped into their places, it would be all the same to us who look on: our formula would be as true of the new as of the old; nor, again, would it affect one atom of this swarming life before us, that we were there, we were watching, classifying, criticising them.

Such is nature, such is science, such is human life, as they appear to the fleshly eye of man: the fleshly eye, observe, because, wide and elastic as may seem the scope covered by the sensuous imagination and the scientific understanding, they do but extend the horizon given by the eye of flesh, they cannot outstrip its bounds; they can but describe to you what the eye *would* see if it were present; and, therefore, they only serve to widen the compass of the physical sight; and, therefore, all that they give you is still subject to those conditions which make the *flesh* to be, not sin, but the symbol, and the sphere of sin. These conditions are not evil in themselves, as abstractions, any more than the lovely mechanism of the flesh is evil, as exhibited by the physiologist, severed from the soul that lived in and through it. But, still, they are only *abstractions*—abstractions useful or picturesque of the letter from the spirit, of the body from the life, of the creature from its Creator; and if they lose their abstract character, and become presented to our spirit as the *real* sphere in which it lives and moves, as the actual, substantial, concrete world in which it has to find its place and work, then at once these abstractions become the poetry, the science, the commonplaces of Materialism; and, the materialistic attitude once reached, then the logical confession passes into a moral disturbance, as St. Paul draws out in the great First Chapter of the Romans. We have lost hold on the true significance of this earthly fabric, the glory and power of God, and God gives it and us over to a reprobate mind: it becomes then the ground, the possession, the material, and the food of sin—the body of death; and therefore it is, my brethren, that to us who believe, this aspect of things which I have tried to sketch is inscribed with the evil name of *"the World"*—the world, the flesh, that which the carnal mind can understand: not that the object before it, on which its eye falls, is itself anything but good, but that the aspect itself, with all that is given us in it, is removed, changed, transferred out of the conditions which hold it in communion with God, in dependence on His spiritual life.

We are presented by it with a world professing to live its own life, to be itself real, self-sufficient, independent: a system of things standing there before us complete, actual, palpably substantial, supporting, sustaining, animating itself on its own principles, its own grounds: a concrete fact of itself, to be judged, and tested, and gauged by the sure line and plummet of the senses, or of the general rules educed from sensible experience by the safe steady guidance of common sense. This is the World! "The World!" Ah! which of us does not know the horrible reality with which it can clip us round! Often and often, as we feel ourselves talking its light talk, passing its easy judgments, acting our part as if there were no other existence but it: often and often, as we look on at men who meet, and bow, and eat, and smile in front of us: often and often, again, as we glance along the glib classifications of history, the laborious analysis of political economy, the passionless abstractions of astronomy or geology, there suddenly flashes across us the swift memory of our old familiar religious language,—language about God, and the soul, and the activity of the spirit; language that sounds no longer real in the face of this world of solid flesh and blood, of linked and serried facts, which shuts us in on every side; language become vague, floating, dreamy, fanciful, startling us like some guilty thing, surprised by the fearful haunting sense of far-away, which has come over it; language which we know ought to be ours, but yet which we cannot adapt to the conditions before us, cannot fix, cannot find a place for; language which we dare not produce just now, dare not apply to the life we are looking at, dare not touch on to the man with whom we are talking; ashamed, baffled, confused, we creep home from this or that social gathering, false, we are dimly conscious, to our best and highest profession, yet uncomfortably doubtful as to where our mistake lies.

Doubtful, I say, and yet we,[1] who are prepared to be sent by Christ to be as lights in the world, testifying to the reality of God's action, witnesses to the Resurrection,—we cannot afford to be doubtful about these primary, these elemental issues of faith. No; we cannot have laid upon us the High Priesthood of God, until we have known how to face, and measure, and forswear the kingdom of the world; until we have been verily assured that the kingdom of God has come amongst us. And I have only ventured to dwell so long this morning on this world-kingdom, in order that you may recognize, in all its size, and force, and influences, what it is you pledge yourselves at ordination to strip off, and lay aside, and throw behind you, and abandon for ever—what is that scheme, that entangling system of things, that glamour of circumstance, that mode of looking at life, which you undertake to hate, and to fight, and to overcome, with all the might, and strength, and courage, and spirit that you can give to Christ to-day! "If ye were of the world, the world would love its own: but because ye are not of the world, but I have chosen you out of the world, therefore the world hateth you." So our dear Lord says to me and you, to all His Church, and most directly to all His Priests. To be chosen by Him is to

---

[1] Preached at an Ordination Service in Salisbury Cathedral.

pass out of this carnal temper. It is to feel that the world and the fashion of the world are an enemy warring against the life; and, therefore, let me attempt to tell you a little of that other aspect into which He chooses us, and from out of which we can look back on our old falsity, on the treacherous service we have forsworn as a realized foe.

"As the Father hath sent Me, even so send I you:" we are *sent* as Christ was sent from God. Our mission, my beloved, has God, and God alone, as its starting-point. A direct *act* of God, in Christ, upon us: the full and abiding recognition of an immediate contact between our souls and God's Life: the known and felt actuality of His Personal choice, mission, ordination of us for His work—with this we begin; from this we date our life; by this we know ourselves to be born again; in this we have our being. We, who are servants of Christ, we cannot, we dare not, set out on our task unless we feel, as it were, God's expressed and living energy of will at our back; until we can feel that for God to withdraw for one moment that living breath with which He spoke our name, and appointed and sent us forth, would be to feel all our support, and sustenance, and force broken down and departed. "My soul hangeth still upon God." That is our primary fact. To confess that we live only by the force of that spiritual activity which flows out of God, and begets, and uplifts, and feeds, and fulfils us—this is our basal act of faith: by this faith, faith in the Name of God signed upon us, the Name energizing within us, the Name which is the vigour of God passing out from Him to seal us to Himself,—by the victorious efficacy of this faith alone, are we made whole, and stand upright upon our feet, and enter by the apostolic favour and presence into the temple, walking, and leaping, and praising God.

We start, then, from the side of God, and see what significance this has for the life here. It means that we live in this world, not as growing up out of it, not as its products, but as coming to it from outside, as those who are sent to it—sent, as He was sent, Who came down into it out of the Father's Presence, and felt His round of daily life here, so far as it was shut up within that short space of thirty years, to be but as an interlude in the Spiritual Existence which He had eternally on high: "I came forth from the Father, and come into the world: again I leave the world, and go unto the Father." We, who inherit the apostolic sending, have, therefore, to look out upon this world around us, not as if it were quite natural for us to be here, but as if our prime purpose in being here at all lay in the need to serve the purpose of God's love for man, which has made Him keep us out of that abiding place of His Presence, which is our only true Home, out of that bosom of God, where He is Who is our only Life, and where we long naturally to be with Him. "We are here as strangers and pilgrims," or rather as ambassadors of Christ, sent into a far country; messengers come from a distance, knocking at the vineyard door to ask for the fruits that are due to our Master. Our whole contact with the world, our points of attachment to it, are made such by coming within the compass of our mission to it. We love it; but we love it for the love that the Father has for it. There is our

The Spiritual Eye.   153

motive. We handle it there where God's determining and authoritative Will allows us to place our fingers. We move about in it only where the everlasting arms deliberately bear us. Not, indeed, that we fear at all the touch of earth—God forbid! but that it has become perilous to the fallen spirit of man, and can only become secure to him once more when he has been taken out of this fallen flesh of his, and has been bathed anew in the light and being of the Father of all Life, and been given back to the world, inspired by the reconciling breath, instinct with the transfused, and penetrative, and transforming energy of God, capable of being a channel through which the grace of God's love flows out to redeem the dead husk of the withered earth into the fresh, blossoming splendour of the new kingdom of heaven. Through man's fall the world lost its hold on the sustaining life outside it, on which it depended: through man, that life from without returns to recover its lost domain. Through us the Spirit is sent; sent forth, not out of us, but sent from far away; sent from that far heart of God to which the Son returned, when we, whom He left in the world, saw Him no more. The Spirit of truth and consolation is sent; and so it is that He comes suddenly from without, sweeping down as the wind upon us, we know not whence; and in the might of that great mission, we, even we poor worms of earth, feel ourselves changed, uplifted, borne along, as by a rushing mighty flame; the light of another world is quivering above our heads; the inarticulate tongue of a strange, a heavenly country is alive within our lips; the whole steady fabric of this substantial world is shaken and broken up at the incoming of this new power. Men of this world look at us, and stare, and wonder, for we are to them as drunkards, and they outside seem to us, who stand within the compass of this strong influence, as phantoms in a dream, as ghostly shapes in a vision—things that have no substance, but will melt and vanish away. For, indeed, our young men now see visions, and our old men dream dreams; only, the dream, the vision, is now the reality, and it is our old every-day life which has become the baseless fabric of a vision; a bad dream ready to pass away at the coming of the morning, when the sun, the centre of all that old substantiality, shall turn into darkness, and the moon, that steady witness in heaven, "into blood, before the great and notable day of the Lord come." Yes, my brethren, "we are drunk with new wine." We have tasted the fruit of the grape, as Christ gives it new in the kingdom of heaven. Which of us has not known this now and then? At the moment of any great spiritual crisis,—often at some time of prayer, often at the coming of Christ in the breaking of bread, often in the intensity of a searching sorrow, above all, as we stand round the open grave of any one dear to us as life itself,—the whole aspect of the ordinary earth is suddenly reversed to us; the spirit-world breaks open to us; that land into which our dear one has passed is felt to be the reality which we always profess it to be. It embraces, it touches us; its presence is poured about and around us; we breathe its air; our whole being, stirred and uplifted by the supporting grace of God, rises to greet the incoming love; every fibre of the soul is stirring with the exaltation of that Divine delight which washes round it like a vast tide, swelling up from some eternal sea of light, and life, and glory, whose waves are under us to carry, whose breeze is in our face to quicken. We know at last the vigour and sweetness of the love of Christ which passeth knowledge; and then, if we lift our eyes to look on the sky, and the trees, and the strangers standing about to watch our funeral, lo! they have become strange and alien to us; the forms, the faces, they seem to us hollow, ghostly, unreal, the mere husks and shells of the Divine force which is alive in us and them, quivering through us and them, threading its way in and out of our souls. We have to put out our hands to recover the reality of the world of sense: we have to touch our own limbs to make sure whether they are ours: we are surprised to find the tears welling out of our eyes, as if we had lost a friend, instead of our having found our and his true and only life. This exalted joy we are now and then privileged to feel; and when we do, then let us, I beseech you, us, who are Priests of God, cling fast to the memory of such a moment; cling and cleave to it, treasure it, cherish it, that it may be the fountain light of all our day, the master light of all our seeing, the upholding strength of all our years, the consecration of all our efforts. For it is in such moments as these that we pass into the attitude of spiritual dependence upon God: we drain the new wine of our spiritual priesthood, and the work of our holy office is nothing but this, to spread out the insight, the inspiration of such brief glimpses of God over an ever-increasing circuit of this earth we see about us: we have got to labour incessantly, that this whole vast and teeming world of ours may feel itself hung, as we then hung, in the suspended and floating atmosphere of spirit, in the breath of God, even as a word float in the larger, fuller meaning of Him Whose breath creates it. We have got to increase and emphasize the faith which overcometh the world; and what is faith, but the living declaration, the abiding sense, that by the spiritual eye alone is the earth seen as it indeed is: not, let me repeat, that the earth is in itself evil or unreal,—rather that the earth in itself is neither good or evil, real or unreal; in that it is nothing of itself, but utterly dependent upon the life of the Creative and Sustaining Spirit, and, therefore, that it is evil and unreal to abstract it from God, and to view it by and in itself; that any such attempt falsifies our insight, disturbs our moral balance, shuts out the presence of God, hardens, benumbs, corrupts our spiritual faculties; that you cannot, therefore, begin by isolating the world from God, to make sure of it first, for, by so beginning, you are tangled in a network of illusion, are ruining your capacity to see God, are only building up round yourself a hard and naked prison-house, which closes round you, till all looks cold and stiff, and impenetrable, a bare cell, in which your starved soul pines away, unfed and unwarmed, to its dreary death. No; our faith is that, since the world hangs still upon God, only, therefore, by beginning with God, by starting from the implanted and impregnated sense of this original reality, can we hope to pass onward to the gathering in of this wide and varied universe, into the fairness and the glory of God's almighty and all-pervading Love.

This, it seems to me, is one great meaning of our Christian antithesis, of faith and sight, of the kingdom of God, and the kingdom of the world; and let me just instance two immediate practical results for the ministers of the Church.

First, as to others. This faith of ours, starting, as it does, from the recognition of our spirit's essential dependence upon God, starting from the immediate contact of Creator with created spirit, finds itself at once in emphatic contrast with the way in which the carnal eye looks out upon nature and upon men. You remember how to the latter the vision of nature meant the disappearance of the self: you, who looked and saw, were a mere accident in the scene; the wider and larger the vision, the more *man* dropped out of the picture, as a forgotten, valueless incident; or, if you turned your view on to men, their whole individual importance vanished; they became mere mechanical elements in a social system, mere figures of a statistical class: you stood outside watching them, as you would watch ants at their building, guessing at this or that ingenious aim, admiring this or that patient enterprise, but still outside, shut out, indifferent to them, as they to you. To us who believe, how utterly all is changed! Every moment, every effort, of the sight which comes by faith, stirs our deepest self into wider, and intenser, and stronger life. Every insight into God's Being is an imperative summons of our own souls into more vigorous action; and, therefore, as we look out, with a seeing faith, upon nature, *we* are not lost or forgotten. No! the larger the vision, the knowledge, the more impetuously does the stormy fire of love rush with quickening energy from God to us, from us to God. We feel our very souls clinging closer to Him, as they drink in the light and life immortal from the Divine Presence, which they see, and know, and treasure, and worship in every hue of the heavens, in every grace of the flowers. And, above all, when we look on men, the outward, the fleshly, cannot stay or entangle our insight. We see straight through to the world within, correspondent to our own hold on God. Each man is, to us, no mere shell of some unknown self, whose character we can but grope after, and guess at, from the outside workings which our understanding detects and analyzes. Rather, it is this outside show which is to us incidental, and but half understood. It is the *inward self* which we know far better, know with a certainty, a closeness, a familiarity which cannot be gainsaid. It is with the inward soul that our soul holds high and sure communion. Can we doubt it? Why, we start with the immediate fact, that that man before us is not merely what our carnal mind sees him to be—a thing of outward shape and tangible stuff—but a living character, whose vivid existence is passed in a world we cannot ever see, or touch, or even dream of putting under a microscope; a world made up of his mother's love for him, his sister's tenderness, his wife's sympathy, his own hopes, fears, courage, sorrows, anger, passion, despair. That is the real world in which he lives and moves, in comparison with which

The Spiritual Eye.

the outward world is thin, and vague, and shadowy. And do we not *know* the inner world of this? Is it not just the very thing we can know best? Have we not complete and unfailing entry into the very heart of it? And if we enter it, as we may, every step we take towards fuller knowledge of it, increases the interest, the importance, the vividness of his individual personality: if we know him, as his mother or his wife knows him, he would stir with his personal presence the whole round and scope of our vision: and, my brethren, we have to know him, as his priest; to know him, as he floats, the centre of all this living movement of feeling, and thought, and love, and passion, in the unwavering, all-penetrating light of God's eternal eyes,—to know him better than wife, or mother, as one whose whole being is only known when seen to be hanging still upon the inbreathing and sustaining Spirit of God. To us, he is a holy thing; a living *soul*, knit in and in with our souls into the Being of God, a thing God loves, as verily as his mother loves him; for whom Jesus is anxious with all the anxiety of a brother; round whom, and through whom, is moving and stirring all that vast world of most real life, which is bound by the gold chain of the Holy Ghost about the heart of Him Who is Infinite, the Father of Spirits and the Lord of Souls.

Then, secondly, for ourselves! We, ministers of God, have got to strive to make our entry sure and easy into the spiritual life of others: we are ambassadors of its spiritual Chief: we are to emphasize before men the reality of this world they live in, and yet so terribly forget: and, if so, if we are to impress men with the reality of our embassy, we ourselves must be sure of our credentials; we must be ready to show them clearly and unhesitatingly, with unmistakable assurance of faith. The ease of our entry into men's souls must obviously depend on this clearness; and this clearness, dear brethren, can only be the outcome of our own intensity of living faith in our mission, faith in the reality of the spirit world with which we deal. This faith must be to us ministers, at least, no casual garment, kept hidden for Sundays and church, or hurried on suddenly at the call to a deathbed. It cannot be to us a shy, retiring secret, which we timidly venture to take a look at when we are quite alone. This will never make us the worthy messengers of a city set on a hill. By this we can never become as candles set on a candlestick. The ministry requires that we should be sure of our ground: we must have already examined it, and found it sure and steadfast: we must know well what we are at, whence we come, with what power, with what support: we must be continually testing our contact with the life of God; continually feeling after, and touching, and grasping hard and fast the everlasting hands which uphold and guide us and the world. Our witness, my brethren, before men depends for its power on the clearness and force of our own inward vision. Our ministrations of spiritual help will only be effectual means of grace, when they are no hasty and abrupt efforts to bring the spirit-world to bear upon human life, but are felt to flow easily and naturally out of the rich abundance of God's constant fulness of presence within us. The very Sacraments we administer will find a surer and readier way opened for them to men's hearts, if they are seen to be to us no awkward, exceptional strainings after an unfamiliar spirit-life, clashing almost violently with our daily experience. No, not this; but the sure expression, the steady outcome of a life lived in unbroken communion with Him Whose Sacraments we serve; with Him Who is to us as real and living as father or mother, or sister or brother; Whose love is dear and familiar as the sense of home; at Whose table we feed, with awe and humility, indeed, but yet without surprise, without constraint, with the quiet, natural freedom with which we delight in the tender presence of a beloved friend. And it is because of this need that our bishops are more and more anxious to summon us together before the day of ordination, to prepare for the holiness of our office, in that we are given a gift which is not to be hung on us, as an external charm, but is to become part and parcel of our whole lives; to suffuse its grace throughout every vein and nerve of our being; to take possesion of us, and dominate our every impulse and thought; to steep our very face with its felt presence, so that men may never let their eyes fall on us, without seeing at once Whose we are, without recognizing and realizing the vivid actualness of the spirit-world in which they and we all live, and may so ever and ever again, each time they catch sight of us, lift their heads from their toil in the world, to cry aloud in joy and affectionate remembrance, "Verily, the kingdom of God is come amongst us. Surely, we are called a holy people, the redeemed of

God, the City of the Lord, the Zion of the Holy One of Israel."

This, dearly beloved, is the call of our priesthood. God grant us grace so to live in its love and light, so to receive with care and patience this holy unction, that it may pass, in all its mystic power, into our heart of hearts, and thence spread abroad its loveliness over our whole lives, that men may be bound by our hands into that good and joyful union of Christ's Church; that union which sheds itself down through us, as the ointment upon the priests of the old covenant; that precious ointment upon the head, "that ran down unto the beard, even unto Aaron's beard, and went down to the skirts of his clothing;" that union which drops down from heaven, as dew of Hermon, upon all those who can know themselves to be as the Hill of Zion, no mere earthly height, bearing a temple made with hands, but a place where God Himself hath promised His blessing and life for evermore.

SERMON XI.

THE BREAKING OF DREAMS.

"Walk as children of light."—EPH. v. 8.

WE men, when first we begin to discover ourselves, find that we have been born into a world that is but half alive, but half awake; a world that sleeps and dreams. About us and around us, there works without pause, without stay, the infinite stir and movement of Nature. A thousand activities push, and thrust, and strive; a million sights flash in, and stand, and cease; and yet, lively and brilliant as all this motion seems, it is to us but as the brilliant and changeful life of a dream. How blind are its workings! how little, how slight, how momentary our hold upon them! How vague, how unsteady the purpose that runs through the endless sequence of changing visions.! Laws there are, underneath, we know, stiff, solid, mechanical, that govern the machinery of all this shifting transformation, but how little their law tells us of any inner secret! Still, it is a dream-world at which we find ourselves staring; a world which becomes, under the guidance of Science, more dream-like than ever; a world of things that strive and thrust unthinkingly, aimlessly, blindly; of movements that hold within them no purpose, and no clue; of agencies that start off into action, under some dull impulsion, and simply act on until checked by some sudden and blank obstacle. All meaning is lost: we gaze, and gaze, and still the feverish activity proceeds in the same wearisome round of ceaseless transition, without intelligible beginning, without fixity of purpose, without possibility of an end: we look on from outside it: we have no clear part in it: with or without our looking, still its wheels whirl, its passionless, unintelligent working goes on in dumbness, asking for no interpretation, seeking for no goal, like the weary and stupid recurrence of some horrible nightmare.

Nay! the poets have done better than this at times. Under their inspiration Nature becomes to us almost alive, almost awake. Something that we seem to know shines out upon us from its manifold scenes; its loveliness seems to greet us with a living welcome; its terrors shake our souls; its voices break out into articulate speech; they call, and we almost arise, and run, and follow after the flying cries, after the touch of these appeals. And yet how momentary is its speech! how elusive the shining of its face! We look round, and it is gone. We stop and listen, and lo! the cry has ceased. Not one clear undoubted word breaks the silence of those starry skies. There they watch and wait, those thousand eyes of the night; and we think for a moment, as they strike in upon us, in sudden hours of feeling, that they have tongues, and can tell what is hidden; and yet there is neither speech nor language! As we look, they fall back into their ancient secrecy: we can make nothing of them. The hills that stand together in solemn gatherings, while, all day, the shadows of the scudding clouds pass softly over them; the woods that lie bathed, hour after hour, in the flooding moonlight, through still summer evenings; these move us, and move us most deeply; and yet, can anything be more dreamy and untangible than the charm which they lay upon us! What is it! Where is it! Is it in them! Do they mean it! Can we fix it! or can we ask them what they would say! Can we put out our hand and touch! Nay, if we snatch at it, it is gone! If we define it, it eludes! It is but some strange breath that sighs through them for an instant into our spirits, and lo! it is over, and the hills are but dull earth again, and the woods are but blind trees, that stand, and grow, and decay! We listen to catch any sound, but it is as if we were watching the lips of a man talking in his sleep: the talk rises, and there it relapses: he seems to be muttering words, and then sinks back into broken noise: we strain our ears in vain. So with Nature: it seems ever on the point of waking, and yet it ever sleeps: and we, too, we sink back to slumber: we turn over on our bed after each faint knocking at the door, and that is all for most of us: we are not roused to full mastery of ourselves: we are not set moving to some decisive issue.

And if we turn to that dim animal life that bustles, and crawls, and leaps, and flies on every side of us, are we any more than before in presence of a world awake! Active and incessant as is the motion of animal life, it, too, surely moves as in a dream. It is pushed along by forces to which it is blind, under which it is passive: it is not the animal that is active, but the momentum that is lodged in the animal. It itself does not occupy and possess the forces that stir in it, but they occupy it: it obeys their direction: it is at the mercy of their propulsion. If they are strong, and full, it goes forward; if they fail, it, too, relaxes and saddens. It never, or most rarely and faintly, can put out exertions of its own, to control, or dominate, or govern the unvarying mastery of its unquestioned instincts. You can appeal to them through habit, but you cannot appeal to it itself, for it lives no life of its own: it lies passive and dormant, and over it pass and change the moving impressions, to which it offers no resistance, and of which it takes no stock: it is carried by them whither they will, and if you appeal to it for more, it can but look at you with eyes that distressfully wonder what it is you want. No new change ever comes, no shock rouses it to some novel and eventful start. It is shut up within dead and unshaken limits, which no outward call ever shatters, no inward effort can ever attempt to displace; and this is the life of a dream.

And we, too, we men, begin life as in a dream. A certain momentum has been thrown into us at our birth; a certain deposit of force occupies us; it carries us along with it. We move under it: we do not question it: we take but little part ourselves in the effort of the movement. The forces work, and we let ourselves go with them: we exert ourselves according to the measure of the compelling power: we push our way through home, through school, just as a plant that thrusts itself upward into the light: we resist oppression, as it resists: we clutch at the profitable occasions and opportunities, as it clutches: we work our way, but we are but half responsible for the way: it is more that the powers within respond to the powers without, that the good instincts, sharpened for us by long inheritance, answer to the touch and gentle pressure of outward appeals; or, again, that the evil passions sweep over us like a flood, if others undo or undermine the dams. Something we do ourselves; but it is but dimly, and, even then, it is under the force of outer demands —the demands of a mother's love, of a father's hopes, of a friend's admiration or reproach. Still, we trust chiefly for our position, for our success, to the impulsive strength of such powers as we found ourselves to possess; they are enough to secure us our place. We lie hidden and but half awake within them: they toil for us, they bear us along: we are not called upon to renew them, to set them going, to put them straight: they work fairly and well, they give us no trouble: we accept what they effect, we follow their lead, we are passive under the floating influences, that weave our life: we ask no questions, as they waft us from stage to stage, encircling us with some strange mystery of woven paces, and of waving hands.

Nor does Oxford, at first, altogether break the charm of this strange wafting, of this mysterious dream. It is true that the brain is more alive, the man more conscious of himself; but, I think, this may only hide from us how little the man is awake. The momentum that was thrown into the man at birth is still the chief propelling force. Such brain-power as he finds in himself, that, indeed, he puts out; and puts it out, how? Well, as a weapon chiefly of attack or defence: an endless game of battle is astir all about him,—a battle of wits, and into it he plunges: for everything that comes he is ready with a word, with a joke, with a criticism: he delights in the exhibition of this readiness: he is quick to all intimation, to all suggestion: he flashes out, as he can, when he can: he plays his part.

But all this is but the carrying on, in the intellectual region, of what the plant in the tangled, crowded hedgerow does in one way, and the beast in the crowded forest does in another. Still, the prompting energy that excites and sustains all this activity, wells out of the deep instinct of self-preservation. The thought, the inspiration, the rapid fancies, come swarming up, just as of old the feelings had swarmed, the man hardly knows whence and how. He is content that they should come, that the supply is inexhaustible: he does nothing to prepare: he exercises but little foresight or prudence: he husbands nothing: he anticipates nothing. It all happens: on each emergency, at every crisis, the quick retort, the sharp answer, the swift parry, the dashing question, drop from his lips: they turn up, they appear, they are there: they come without trouble, they go, and they are forgotten. The intelligence produces them instinctively, spontaneously, just as readily as eye-lids wink, or the hand leaps up to ward off a sudden peril. The man himself is borne along by his own inbred energies: he is their prey, their possession. When they flow strongly, he is pleased and buoyant: when they languish and fail, he is grieved, and despairs: but

The Breaking of Dreams. 169

HE is not in action; he does nothing; he is dependent on what happens; he leaves things to occur: if the fancies do not appear when he expects them, if the shock of circumstances is not enough motive force, he has no resource within himself. He does nothing to retrieve matters: he goes about moody and downhearted, until back the good stream flows, back the great tide flows in, and once more the strong currents lift him, and he lets himself go whither the happy wind and waves will beat him. Who does not know the endless delight of the young, in simply watching, noting, recording their own moods? They please themselves in being sad, in simply analyzing their own tempers: they take pride in their feelings; their mental changes seem to themselves full of inexhaustible, unutterable interest. Yes; because they are still so immersed in these moods, so dependent upon them. These moods are at once themselves, yet not themselves. They can observe and note them as they appear out of some strange abyss, whither no eye follows them; but they have no plummet yet to sound that deep abyss; they have no thought of changing, of varying, of correcting, of transcending these blind moods as they come. Nay, their very interest lies in the hidden mystery of their coming—that to-day the man is sad, he knows not why; that to-morrow he is glad, he can as little tell wherefore. So the changes of mind come, and so they go, good or bad, quick or slow, silly and serious, and the man himself is their victim: he attempts no control over them, he lies back still, and, more or less lazily, lets his eye wander along the moving flight of feelings; and all are equally strange, and wonderful, and uncanny, and unaccountable,—the evil as the good, the sorry as the joyful; he sees no reason for the one more than the other; he looks at all with equal interest. He is dreaming on still; his life is but a changing vision; he is not his own master.

Yes, as I look back and remember the old days, when I was what you are,[1] they seem to me, in contrast with later life, to wear all the semblance and the atmosphere of a dream. I was floated along day by day: I awoke to find the current flowing under me. It cost me but little effort; no hard shocks interrupted; up and down, in freedom and ease, the ready thoughts flew, and touched everything, and for a moment hung like fluttering birds, and then had flown elsewhere. Everything arranged itself; nothing violently obtruded; no loud call for strong action broke in. The very charm of the days lay in their easy flow. Everything seemed to be at our service, everything was possible; no harsh necessities forced upon us ungrateful limits, unpalatable truths. The mind ranged as it chose, the feelings found large room, the emotions knew but slight check or hitch; the very vastness that little griefs assumed was a testimony to the rarity of the larger and more real woes. We never looked much about. Out there, beyond the degree, lay some future, dimly felt; but we hardly cared to penetrate its dark precincts. Enough for us to notice and observe all the shifting scene, without any resolute desire to mend it, without any passionate craving to know how it would all end. It was the variety, the change of

[1] Preached to Undergraduates in St. Mary's, Oxford.

scene itself, which was continually engrossing, continually stimulative, continually sufficient. Why trouble to look beyond?

I do not say this was all: there were resolutions made, there were difficulties to master, there were moments of far-reaching intention; but these were not very pressing, not very salient, not very overpowering; and, in contrast with what I know since then of life, it is the passive joy of a vision that lies about those past hours! I feel as if I had then been wafted along by unseen powers, or if I had been walking in a dream, an unsubstantial fairy-place, haunted by a flying cry, that passed from hill to hill, an invisible thing, a voice, a mystery, after which I followed without any violent anxious distress, that it should still elude my chase, without any bitterness of angry disappointment, that it should remain a hope—a love still longed for, never seen.

"Walk as children of the light, and of the day." What is it to awake? What is it that shatters the dream? When does the break come? Let me ask a counter-question first; it may help. Why is it that, as we explore the records and writings now brought so wonderfully and delightfully nigh to us of ancient faiths, as we roam up and down their strange and varied stories, —why is it that, rich as is their splendour, and noble as is their range, yet to pass from them to the Jewish Testament is like passing from a world of dreams into a world of daylight? Those old faiths here get hold of the same matter and stuff as the Jew, but they fumble it about with such uncertain hands, with such a wavering will. Now, they seem to have gripped it, and a word leaps out that thrills, as the old Bible texts thrill; and then, again, on the very next line, is some odd, fantastic, unworthy imagination.

And yet they seem quite unconscious of the gulf that divides their best from their worst: it all seems to them alike; they have no sure canon to detect and divide the weak and the strong, the poor and the noble, elements of their belief. Their touch on high subjects is so unsteady as to seem almost unintentional: their greatest sayings read almost like guesses: they work at random, now high, now low: they do not go forward with any firm and unshaking advance; rather, they do not seem to move at all: they fall back as often as they go forward, there is so little getting on. And then how faint and feeble-hearted, in most cases, is their application to practice! They intermingle the moral and the immoral; no sharp lines stand out dividing. Their hold on life is slippery and vague.

But when we step into the Jewish Scriptures, we find ourselves in a new atmosphere. We are in company of another kind. These men are awake. Clear, sharp, strong, and sure run the great lines. They permit of no confusion, no fluctuating hesitation,— a single aim, a single purpose dominates the whole. Here good and evil stand out like black and white, like day and night. And, again, here is no standing still; a steady advance, undaunted and assured, is made from point to point. The intention clears itself from alien matter; it shows itself more firmly, more largely. For the sake of it, under the impulse of its heroes, the nation rises, and walks towards a goal that it distinguishes, towards a hope that grows fairer, a promise that waxes strong, under a covenant, a certified rule, a manifest guidance, a pillar of fire, a rock to which it clings. Here are no visionaries, no vague dreamers; here is no fumbling, no insecurity of footing, no doubtfulness of touch, no questioning guesses, pathetic through their very wistfulness. There men do not dream of other worlds; they deal with this earth's hope, in its solid groundwork, in its downright facts; they detect God; they see His handling; they demand His presence; they act by His law. Yes, these men are awake. The dream is broken; and when?

We can take our answer from St. Paul, from St. Stephen, from the Jew's own mouth. Looking back on the dim past, upon those masses of slumbering people, who filled the spaces of history, one moment there was when that Jewish people first broke their sleep among the sleeping nations; one man there was who first showed himself distinctly awake, amid a world of dreams; one man who first rose out of his bed, and looked, and saw, and understood, and made sure of his aim, and gathered up his powers, and broke with his past, and moved out on a new and open path.

Abraham, the father of the faithful, the friend of God! from him, and in him, they dated the hour when the eyes of the nation were opened, and they ate and drank, and saw God; the hour when they slumbered no more in the night, nor sat on still in darkness, nor wandered in the shades of death, nor sought after wizards that peep and mutter, nor cried any longer to lonely watchers, What of the night?—the hour when first, with sure and faithful ears, they heard the Word behind them saying, "This is the way, walk ye in it," when they turned unto the right hand, or when they turned unto the left.

Abraham, the first that broke the dream, and how? Three points there are I will shortly notice. First, the Promise. He had broken loose from the dreams that flit and crowd, the busy present dreams that unceasingly come and go, when once he looked through and away beyond to a far-off Divine event, towards which the whole creation moved, a purpose to be finally achieved, not now, but in the far years into which all this shifting scene of human history was slowly and painfully working. He would see it, but not now; he would behold it, but not nigh. There was something behind the dim and changing present. An intention, a promise, a blessing was at work, was moving, was ordaining. Day did not follow day without order, or advance. History was no endless round of unmeaning efforts, and dark, ruinous collapses. There would yet be an end. There would yet be a goal. It was pledged and sealed; in the Mount of God, at Horeb, at the end of the long journey; after all the blind striving and weary waiting, at last, at the Mount of God, it would be seen; it would be made clear. Towards that day, that far and hidden day, his whole heart moved out in resolute faith. He reaches out with prophetic soul. For the hope of it, he broke loose from the clinging present, from the bondage of daily incident. He rejoiced not in the loud clangour of the crowded moments as they passed, but he rejoiced to see that day of distant and dominant promise, and he saw it, and was glad.

And, secondly, the Call. Out from beyond the unresting shift and shock of circumstance, out of some deep eternity of peace, out of the steady and motionless silence, there fell upon him a sound, the sound of a compelling voice; there broke upon him the felt power of an imperial will,—a will strong, steadfast, supreme, that lifted him out of his dreams, and set him upon his feet, and bore him as upon wings, and drove him out of the slumbers of his hidden home; and he went forth he knew not whither, unmindful of the country from whence he came out, desiring a better country, looking for a city not made, a city that hath foundations, whose builder was God—that God of glory who had smote him with a cry, "Get out of thy country and thy kindred, and come unto the land which I shall show thee."

The Promise, the Call, and the Patience of Faith. By this, thirdly, he was delivered from his dream: that faith, unshaken, undying, free from all the rise and fall of passion, from all the gladness or the sorrow of each passing hour: a faith against which the present, with its mobile fancies and its disorderly impressions, fell powerless and beaten, as billows that foam away their broken strength upon a rock; a faith that staggered not when the winds stormed and rain fell; that, against hope, believed in hope; nor considered his own body now dead, neither yet the deadness of

Sarah's womb. Yea, "staggered not at the promise of God through unbelief, but was strong in faith, giving glory to God, that what He had promised He was able to perform." Patient faith! That faith which in His children never wholly failed, even when they were smitten with the plague of dragons or covered with the shadows of death: that faith which "subdued kingdoms, wrought righteousness, stopped the mouths of lions, quenched the violence of fire, through weakness was made strong:" that invincible faith, victorious in disaster, which, "though the fig-tree did not blossom, neither was fruit found on the vines, the labours of the olive failed, and the fields yielded no meat, though the flock were cut off from the fold, and there were no herds in the stall, yet, in dauntless loyalty, could still rejoice in the Lord, could glory in the God of its salvation."

My brethren, we may walk as the children of the light, as children of our father Abraham. Here is the waking of the spirit, of that spirit which alone bursts the hazy vision of the dreamful days. We wake as he woke. We are waking, when, first, through the shifting play of ever-moving forces, under which and in which we lie half passive, borne along as in a boat on some underlying flood, content to watch and notice all that comes—content with just that effort that ensures our own boat's safety, and keeps it in the full current—content to enjoy the sweet ease of motion when it is given, pining with powerless disappointment, when the eddies whirl us into dull back waters and blind corners, waiting, sick and impatient, until some happy chance discovers us, and wafts us once more into full and flowing waters—we wake, I say, when in upon us, thus dreamy and inert, there opens suddenly the hope of a larger promise than the run of days bring with it: a promise larger than ourselves, though involving ourselves: a promise, it may be, seen afar off; but yet a promise towards which we, and all our fellows, are moving, with set purpose, under the inspiration of some motive force that grows and dominates the whole mass of humanity: a promise of better things, of nobler aims, of purer hands, of more steadfast peace than we now can know: a promise in which, if not we, yet, at least, our children's children shall be blessed; in which blessing to come, we, from afar, even though we receive it not within this our little day, can afford to rejoice, content, ourselves, to be as pilgrims and strangers that walk through homeless ways towards a city that hath foundations, and will abide: a promise that shall, indeed, be no visionary ideal, but a solemn, sober fact on this our own earth, on that far day, to those born of our own blood, to men and women like ourselves; men and women like those who now grieve, and weep, and die, fast bound in misery and crime. Who of you does not begin to know this awakening? Who of you has not already felt the stir within his heart of that high destiny towards which we move, the prophetic touch of that hidden day when children shall no longer pine in hopeless, joyless, loveless homes, maimed and disfigured by pain and crime; when men shall no longer fall bruised, and crushed, under the fierce and grinding

M

pressure of a civilization, which is to them one long, dark, and perplexing riddle; when poor women shall no longer sink under the tyranny of men's reckless and horrible lusts? This is the promise—that such a day there might be; that sin is no necessity, nor misery the real law of our life. And the sense of this promise is to each of you a call, a call as real and living as that which drew Abraham out of Charran, and would not let him bide in Ur of the Chaldees. The spirit that is in you responds to that call: you know that the world may be bettered, that the world's anguish may be relieved; and bettered through you, relieved through you!

You, who once have felt the power of the promise, may never relapse into dreams, may never content yourselves again with old, easy acquiescence, with the light-hearted on-looking. Nay! it is you whom the loud call summons to be up and doing; to push through the hedge of tangling circumstance, and reach out, by prayer and action, to that far joy; to walk in the light of that hope, in the strength of that single purpose; to walk, and work, and strive, held and girt by the strong will of God, and carried whither you know not, only you know that it is towards the glory of that great day. Hazy no longer, vague no longer, you have gripped the purpose of your life: you may know now the sin of sloth, sloth so unsuspected, so unnoticed, in the days of your dreams: you begin to know the horror of moral evil, the devilish force of the adversary: you are restless and awake with a holy and earnest fury of zeal: you may know the sting and strain of the thought that drove our Lord to encounter the perils of hostile Jews. "Are there not twelve hours of the day? Work while it is day, lest the night come when no man can work."

Work! Work for men and for God! Work, and you are awake; and work not merely when the impulse warms you, and the hope carries you forward, and the heart moves freely; but work when the soul sickens, and the eye is heavy, and the limbs waste, and the blood runs slow and dull; when the momentum of youth slackens and fails, and the inspirations die away, and you see your clear path no more, and the shadows thicken, and the clouds darken, and the dark day of relief becomes even more and more impossible. The spirit that sinks under these trials is still passive, still but half aroused, still lost in dreams. Did you fancy, then, that it was *you* who would do the great deed; that it was *you* who could bring in the good day; that in your failure the whole promise fails? Yet Abraham, our father, staggered not through unbelief, when through faith he offered Isaac, in whom alone the promise could be fulfilled—Abraham, who, against hope, believed in hope, that he might become the father of many nations. Have faith! The spirit that is awake walks in faith, the faith of those of old who died in faith,—died without a sign of that great blessing, died stoned, sawn, slain, tormented, not having received the promises, but only seeing them very far off, and yet were persuaded of them, and yet embraced them, and yet never went back to that country from whence they came out, that country of dreams, but confessed themselves to be, not possessors of the inheritance for which they toiled and strove, but only pilgrims and strangers moving toward a city, which God, and He only, in His good time, will prepare for them. Walk in faith, for so alone does the Spirit keep its grip on the call that first broke its slumber. In the face of the awful wickedness that desolates and devours our cities, faith alone can hold fast the hope set before us.

And faith, the faith of Abraham, the faith which staggers not at the sight of its own dead, powerless flesh, nor at the deadness of Sarah's womb, this unstaggering faith in the goodwill and strong hand of an indomitable God, whither must it end? Whither must it at last lead us?

"Your father Abraham rejoiced to see that day; and he saw it, and was glad." So spake the Christ, the Child of Promise. Dearly beloved—you who, it may be, know not the full assurance of Christ, but only the first awakening of the Spirit; you who now feel only half dimly the compulsion of a great hope, have faith in that hope: have faith, enduring, patient faith; and then to you, as to the Jew, that hope, now so indistinct, so faint, will, God grant, grow clear, and full, and plain. Each failure of yours will but deepen your sense of God's needfulness; each despair of yours will but cry out for Him Who is seen coming from Edom with dyed garments from Bozrah, only then, when He has looked, and there was none to save, when He has marvelled, and there was none to uphold. You, too, will know the passion of prayer, that calls upon a God Who will rend the heavens, and come down: and as you learn more deeply, year by

The Breaking of Dreams. 181

year, the horrible corruption of that ghastly evil, which, wash as we will in Jordan, no tears seem ever to wipe out, no penitence to undo or put away, your hope will consummate itself in that faith which looked and saw a man stand at the end upon the earth, to whom it uttered its last triumphant cry: "Behold the Lamb of God, Which taketh away the sin of the world!"

SERMON XII.

SHEEP AND SHEPHERD.

"For judgment I am come into this world, that they which see not might see; and that they which see might be made blind."—St. John ix. 39.

THE chapter taken for this morning's lesson is one which is proverbially familiar; it calls up memories and pictures which have haunted the heart of the Church since her first sweet childhood in the Roman Catacombs, and which still touch, with ever-recurring grace, the soul of each fresh child that grows up under the power of Christian inspiration. Yet the chapter itself is full of confusing associations; its metaphors, its analogies, its suggestions, cross and recross each other with bewildering swiftness; the thread of its connection is hard to track with any steadiness or security.

We start with the allegory drawn out of the blind man's healing,—the keynote of its lesson is first started by the paradox of my text. It is caught up by the question of the Pharisees, "Are we blind also?" It is carried on by the still deeper paradox of our Lord's answer, "If ye were blind, ye should have no sin: but now ye say, We see; therefore your sin remaineth,"— and before we have had time to read this hard riddle, we are led off abruptly to new ground, to changed scenes. It is no longer the blind guides with whom we are dealing: we have thrown our eyes out from the Temple Courts, and over to Olivet, and we are looking at sheepfolds with their securing walls, and it is thieves and robbers who are now the symbols of evil leaders, climbing into the fold by violent and self-chosen ways. Our Lord is no longer the Healer of the blind; He is now the one Way of sure and acknowledged entrance. He is that which embodies all authority, all recognised privilege, all lawful rule; He is the Door, through which entry is assured by unhesitating right, without anxiety, or scruple, or suspicion. He is the Door, Whose posts are the posts of Righteousness, and over Whose threshold lies Peace,—Peace on the shepherd who knows himself at home, and in accepted paths; Peace on the porter who openeth with glad welcome to the well-known steps; Peace on the sheep who look up at the familiar coming, and move under the remembered voice, and pass out without fear behind the feet of him who goeth in and out freely through this Door of secure possession.

And as we ponder over this imagery, it changes under our very eyes: the picture of the pleasant peace of the sheepfold has brought forward the image of the Shepherd, who goes to and fro from fold to pasture, and, even as our gaze rests upon Him, He has become the chief figure in the parable, He gathers up into Himself the fulness of the scene. No longer the Healer of the blind—no longer the Door—our Lord is now the Shepherd Himself, the Good Shepherd that knows His sheep, and is known of them; and the Pharisees, the evil ones, are now no longer the blind guides, nor the robbers climbing over the wall; but they are changed into the hireling with the craven soul, whose very nature it is to leave the sheep when the wolf cometh; the hireling, who has no living bond with his cure, who has lent himself out for sordid purposes, who cannot therefore know the intense unity that knits a man to that which is his own, cannot realize that which is not, and who fleeth for this one and all-prevailing reason, "because he is a hireling."

And the believers who were once in the picture as the blind, who confess that they cannot see, they have now become the sheep, who hear the voice and know it; and still, at the last, the spirit of the whole manifold image is once more altered and heightened by that exalted refrain which places the secret of all this unity between the Shepherd and the sheep in that death under the jaws of the wolves, which He will undergo Who careth indeed for the sheep. The sheep know well the voice of Him Who will die to save them. "The Good Shepherd is He Who giveth His life for the sheep." "I am the Good Shepherd;" "I lay down My life for the sheep."

I cannot attempt this morning to tie together all these threads of thought, but I should like to try to suggest some main connections that underlie the general change of metaphor from the blindness to the sheepfold. Why are *we*, we for whom these things were written, why are we, first, the blind to whom our Lord came that they might see? and why should He then so quickly liken us to the sheep who hear His voice, who know the sound of that Shepherd Who is ready to die for them?

Let us begin with our Lord's first words. He starts

with the supreme fact of the Incarnation. He has "*come into the world*"—come to it, not risen out of it: He is an arrival from without: He comes to meet the world: He brings to it new powers, something that it had not before—new hopes and a novel purpose; and such an arrival from without, in offering itself freely to all who can recognise it, cannot but create a judgment, says our Lord,—a sifting of those who can see it from those who cannot. And who are those who will see it? Why, not those, surely, whose vision is bounded by the narrow compass of this world. The sight to be seen is one that comes from beyond the world; and a sight demands some sympathy, some unity, some kinship between itself and the eye which sees it. The sight, then, of our Lord's coming can only be seen by those who have already some receptive faculties by which light may be shed upon their souls from that far land from which He comes. They must be possessed of some kinship to that sunny world without and beyond the world, where God is the Sun, and the Lamb is the light thereof. Without such touch of sympathetic communion, the eye would remain blank to all the fair colour that shone in the dancing of that light of life, however close it might come, however richly it might pour its wealth of radiance over it.

Yet how can this communion be? How can we keep the eyesight of our souls ready for the Advent of this sight? Eyes live by use; unused, they shrink, and wither, and grow dark. How, then, can we use them upon a world so far, the world beyond our world, the world in which we are not?

True, indeed, that we cannot *now* look in upon that glorious land, or fill our eyes with its light, or feed our sight on its lovely colouring. Alas that it should be so! It need not have been; for, indeed, that land is very near; it is nearer to us than the very world that we think we live in; it is more verily the home in which our spirits would even now abide, than any earthly homes will ever be. It is these earthly homes that are far away, and strange to our real self. It is this sweet land of spiritual peace, that might be so close, so familiar, so akin. But sin has clouded our eyes, and dulled our seeing. Sin has eaten out our kinship to that eternity; sin has wasted us; sin has exiled us; sin has made it most alien, most strange, most unreal to us. Sin has driven us out from its joy, and has left us banished in a world that imprisons us in, with flaming swords at every gate, and hard-set barriers of sense. Our Lord does not deny this: it is because of this that He is come; but yet the imperative law holds good, no spiritual light for those who have no spiritual eyes! How can this law stand sure, and yet our Lord's coming be discerned by those who have no sight to perceive whence He is?

One way remains, and one way only. Man has blinded himself, it is true: he has ruined his spiritual senses; but still one thing, at least, is left him—he is not so ruined that he may not know his own blindness. He has lost the use and habit of seeing eternal things; but he is the same man still, possessed of the same possibilities, created for the same end as ever, endowed for the same Divine life. The faculties are there, however, unused and deformed. He has the eyes, though they cannot see; and, in recognising this his disaster, in recognising that he lives here in this world, with powers unworked, with functions that can never be fulfilled through sin, with senses that nowhere now can be enjoyed, he has already passed out beyond the borders of this earthly habitation, of this sin-clouded sky; he has proved his inner kinship with that other land, which yet he cannot see. His very sense of this life's blindness establishes his right to be a citizen of the Eternal Light, his openness to the Advent of Him Who bringeth the Day-spring from afar!

Yes! "I am come into this world, *for judgment*, that they who see not may see!" They can receive the new Gift; for to them, blind as they are, it is still allied; in them it can still find a point of contact, a door of entrance. But there is a blindness worse, far worse, than this; the blindness which does not know itself, the blindness which believes that it sees. The man who, looking round and about himself and the world he lives in, pronounces that he sees his way through it, that everything required is within his ken,—who finds no faculty fail him, who misses no expected capacity, who detects no blank spaces, no breaks of darkness, no collapse of power, no emptiness of fulfilment within or without,—the man who is conscious of no loss, of nothing wanting, who finds himself fitted with all the senses necessary, and needs none beyond, and feels at home with what is, and has no misgivings, no doubt about his own clear-sighted apprehension of things— what can be done for *him*? What good can be brought him from a land far off? What significance has an advent from elsewhere for him? What entrance can the Eternal Light find in him? What can avail to pour down upon him the splendours of the Heavenly Country? He has no faculties alive to receive them, and not only this, but he has no sense of alliance, of kindred communion with any world to which he is not alive. Not only are his spiritual faculties unused and dead, but he has no consciousness of possessing any dead and unused faculties. He is content, he is not on the alert for any new thing; yet he could not be so contented if there was any energy yet sleeping in the disused organ of life. No! it is died out utterly; it is gone: and not God's own Beauty can attract that which is dead. There is nothing for God to appeal to, nothing to recreate, nothing to enlighten, nothing to assist. This, then, is the judgment, that the Light comes, and that His very coming proves that some men have no eyes that can see Him; and this is the sin judged, not blindness that cries for the light,—blessed, most blessed is such blindness!—but blindness that declares itself to be unmaimed, unthwarted, undimmed; blindness that feels itself self-sufficient, and asks for no better, and relies confidently on its own powers, and believes itself to be seeing what it was meant to see. This is the fatal, the irrevocable evil: "If ye were blind, ye had had no sin: but now ye say, We see; therefore your sin remaineth."

And the sheep,—what of them? what has blindness to do with them?

Surely, now, it is plain. If there is anywhere in all

the living world a contrast with the confident, self-reliant, self-sufficing individualism of man's natural understanding, where should we find it so vividly realized as in the temper of a flock of sheep? We laugh at their stupidity: they are a proverb for weakness, for docile dependence, for silly herding together. Quite true: such laughter may be perfectly right, and genuine, and innocent. But our Lord, as His creating eye fell upon them, saw portrayed in them one quality, one principle, one gift, which endowed them with a peculiar crown of grace, and has made them, for all time and in all lands, the symbol of lively and tender community, of sweet and unruffled serenity, of ideal fulfilment, of perfected peace. We all feel the charm of the beautiful comparison, as it sounds through page after page of the sacred text: "He maketh Him households like a flock of sheep." "The Lord is my Shepherd: He maketh me to lie down in green pastures: He leadeth me beside the still waters." "We are the people of His pasture, the sheep of His hand. He shall lead His flock like a shepherd. He shall gather the lambs into His bosom. He shall gently lead those that are with young. As for His people, He led them forth like sheep. I will gather the remnant of My flock out of all countries. I will seek out My sheep, as a shepherd his flock, out of all places where they have been scattered in the cloudy and dark day. I will feed them in a good pasture, and upon the mountains of Israel shall their fold be; there shall they lie in a good fold, and in a fat pasture shall they feed upon the mountains of Israel. Yea, I will feed My flock, and I will cause them to lie down, saith the Lord God."

So the beautiful assurance lived on in the prophetic heart of Israel, their dream, their joy, their unfailing prayer, and still, as storms thickened, and ravage desolated, and ruin destroyed, the cry after their blessedness repeated again and again the old words that pictured all their peace: "Feed with Thy staff, O God, the flock of Thine inheritance that wander, scattered and alone, in the wood! Feed them once more on the slopes of Carmel! Let them feed, O my God, in Bashan and Gilead, as in the days of old!"

What is it that is thus attractive, thus lovely in a flock of sheep? It is just that wonderful capacity to rely on a world, on a life, *outside* their own. It is the bond between the sheep and the shepherd that has such grace in our eyes. The sheep may be weak, but, at least, they are not shut up within the narrowness of their own faculties, their own powers. By a Divine instinct, they detect in that, to them, far and strange human life, a marvellous efficacy to guide, to control, to aid, to bless. It appeals to them, it advances towards them, and they have the eyes to see it; they know not its secret; they have never penetrated its recesses, but something in them responds to it, something in them fastens upon it, and they answer to its appeal, they answer with absolute and unswerving steadiness, they completely throw all their trust upon it. They read its mind, they follow its footsteps, they catch sight by some hidden sympathy of its mysterious and awful will, they live in its royal and gracious supremacy. This is why they, of all animals, possess their lives in peacefulness, and are the type of minds at peace with God. We men are not to be unreasoning, inactive, tame, uninquiring, as they; but one good thing they have, which has won them the love, the instinctive poetic love, of all mankind; one good thing, which our Lord blessed as their glory, and has forbidden ever to be taken from them,— the power to find their strength, their life, in a world that is not their own, the power to walk freely and gladly in the might of the unseen presence, the power to keep their senses open to lights that fall from far worlds, to impulses sent they know not whence, to voices sounding from elsewhere.

My brothers, we have a harder task than the beasts that perish. We have to develop individually, we have each one of us to put out the strong energy of personal will, the force of an inquisitive reason. We are bound, hand and foot, to this task: it is not I who deny this; I insist upon it: I demand that no single one of us should refuse to take it in hand. I want to stir you this morning, if by God's grace I may, to realize the necessity laid upon every one of us, as he passes up out of youth into manhood, the tremendous and inevitable necessity, to put forth the highest powers that are in us to their fullest and noblest use. And it is just because this is so, just because no one of us may sit still and idly toy with life, just because no one of us can, with impunity, delay long to move upward and work onward, that I would bring before you the need of your recognising, as the ground of all aspiration, the reality of a world beyond and above your own, towards which you are to move, under the attractive and prevailing power of which you are to grow. You are not asked to be as sheep that follow blindly; your will, your reason, your conscience, all are to live, all are to be made strong; this is not what I deny, this is perfectly true; only they are to live a life of growth, of advance; and that means *they are not yet what they should be.* Not merely, that is, is continually new material to come under our faculties; but the faculties themselves are continually to develop, continually to advance to better stages, continually to improve in efficacy. They are not put into our hands full-formed and complete; rather they, together with our whole being, have yet to be made real, have yet to grow, are still imperfect, still misshapen, still are in their childhood. More than this, their very tendencies upwards are now twisted and enfeebled and stifled; they have yet to be re-made out of corruption; they have yet to be set free from burden and bondage; they have yet to renew their first childhood, and therefore it is fatal to limit our horizon to the capacities of our present faculties. It is fatal to take them, as they stand, as our true measure, and test, and gauge of life. It is fatal now, while yet we are incomplete, while yet we are corrupt, to suppose ourselves in full possession of our powers, to pronounce unhesitating judgments. It is deadly to say, "We see." Deadly, since to say it is in a moment to check our growth, to bar our advance, to turn the key on our spiritual life, to stop short, to lose all movement, to paralyse energy; from that moment the chill of death has struck us, we stiffen, we wither, we shrivel up; soon we shall have ceased to be.

Suffer me to urge this upon you[1] whose first physical growth is passing away, and upon whom manhood is

---

[1] Preached in Christ Church Cathedral, Oxford.

coming; because it is so slight, yet so terrible, a temptation for you, to stand still, to fail to make the effort forward to the higher level. In boyhood we may not think much or seriously about any further life, but then during all those younger days God has the matter more directly in His own hands. He does not ask *us* to do much: He Himself carries on our life. He fills us with overflowing, buoyant, springing energy. No fear in youth of our standing still, of our lacking movement; the impulse of our birth from God's hands is still upon us, its motion has not yet died away out of our souls. But with the end of boyhood ends too that first natural movement forwards. God stands off from us a little more, He leaves us more to ourselves; we ourselves are to do more towards carrying on the work, towards sustaining the growth. We may no longer, at our peril, trust to unconscious advance: consciousness, reflection, reason, these have all come forward now; these are now our tools, our engines, our mechanism, by which we are to fashion our destinies. With these, or with nothing, must we set to work. So it is that the temptation works. We stand still a moment, and look round, and find ourselves in possession of ourselves. We are in our own hands, it seems, to do what we will with ourselves. We have these faculties of reflection, we are fitted out with this apparatus, we are fully equipped, we can examine, we can consider, we can judge, we seem self-sufficient, we are content with our gifts, we feel a sense of power in recognising our mastery over our own lives, over ourselves. We consider ourselves complete; we think we shall always remain what we are at this moment, with the same tastes, the same likes and dislikes, the same wants, the same judgments. We set to work to scheme, to plan out our days, to map out our course. We throw our eyes round, and seem to sweep the whole field; we see all that there is to be seen, all that will ever be worth seeing. If there is anything beyond, elsewhere, why trouble ourselves about it? We are dealing with this present life, and with it we feel perfectly at home; it lies there before us, visible from end to end; we can go up and down its whole length and breadth, what more should we desire? We can pick and choose, we can settle what we like and what we dislike. If we like anything, that must mean it is intended for us to enjoy, to use, to possess. If we dislike anything, why should we trouble about it? It cannot be meant for us.

Ah! believe me, if once you fall into that temper, life is over for you! for life is growth, and you have ceased to grow! To judge as you are doing, to rely on such judgments, to feel yourself now in full possession of the canon of truth, or of moral right,—now, while you are incomplete, unfulfilled, at the start, and not at the end,—now, while you are still stunted and stifled by a thousand selfish desires, by a thousand unruly passions, disordered vanities, diseased imaginations, moody and envious discords—this is to condemn yourselves hopelessly to the unchanging prison-house of selfish lusts, lusts that will roam for ever round the naked wall that you yourself have built round your soul, seeking for some lost fulfilment that can never be found there, since it has fled far from your narrow cell, into sunny fields where flowers are ever renewing their delights, and rivers for ever flowing, and winds are free, and the vast world moves ever onward in motion, and beauty, and song. This is to condemn yourself not only to failure and death here, and now, in this human existence, but also to utter ignorance of the healing and the new life that Christ alone can bring you. His coming into the world must cease to have any meaning for you; you will be surprised, or proud, perhaps, to find His creed fading away from you, as a tale with little meaning. You will judge it to be untrue, for it will fail to commend itself to you; it will fail to make its proof clear. How should it not fail? How should it commend itself? What meaning can it have to you? It speaks of new things, new birth, new growth, new life, new heavens, and a new earth, such as eye hath not yet seen, nor ear heard, nor the heart of man conceived. No! it has nothing for you! You have no want of it, and therefore no key to its riddle. "If ye were blind," if ye knew yourselves heirs of far more than your eyes now range over, children of a heavenly country, to which all things move, but to which not even a St. Paul after a lifelong battle with self and sin may ever count himself to have attained—"If ye felt yourselves blind, ye had had no sin: but now ye say, We see; therefore your sin remaineth."

"My sheep hear My voice:" "I know Mine own, and My own know Me:" so our Lord confidently pronounces. We are His sheep. We must, if we would hear His voice, be as His sheep. We must know ourselves still, grown men as we are, to be dedicated heart and soul to another and a higher than ourselves, to be absolutely in His hands, absolutely bound over—impulse, will, reason, feeling, and all—to the service and good of One, Who has a vaster vision, an infinitely fuller capacity than ourselves. Do not let us be afraid; He will not dwarf us, He will let us use all our gifts, reason and will,—these we shall possess in full play, for they are His tools. But they will be used, not as if already perfected, but as if they had yet to grow to a far higher use, to a far nobler purpose. Our desires will not be crushed, but they will be accepted, not as a canon of right, but as prompting something greater than now they understand, as hints of a purer will, as glimpses into a better land, as flying lights from a clouded sun. Up to that higher guidance we shall ever be aspiring, ever hoping to be shown more clearly, to know more vividly, to seek more unfalteringly. Up to that higher service we shall be for ever moving, using what is, only as a step to what shall be, devoting all that we are now to the necessities that draw us onward to a purer life, to a less selfish end. All this will have become possible, if only we can yield ourselves to that self-surrender which makes a flock of sheep under their shepherd so lovely a picture of delicious comfort, of endless refreshment, of enduring peace.

Self-surrender! Reliance on forces stronger than ourselves. Self-sacrifice! Dedication to ends greater than our own happiness, or our own self-will. Here is the door of God's pasture. Here is the path that leadeth down to the still waters of eternal joy. By passing through this door we feed, we grow strong, we do not die. Let us but refuse to be content with ourselves, refuse to shut ourselves in within the circuit of what we now see, or know, or plan, or want, or desire. Let us but be ever on the alert, ever watchful for fresh light, ever looking for new hopes, ever striving after a purer life, ever feeling after a larger and holier world, ever praying for a hand to uphold, for a power to renew, for an eye to govern and direct. Let us only be ever expectant of a door that will open, of footsteps that will soon draw nigh. Then, the Lord promises, there will be the sound of His coming; He will come, and the porter of our soul will gladly open, and we shall see our dear Master, our good Shepherd, and shall hear His voice. We shall understand Him; His creed will not be so dark to us; His words will no longer sound unmeaning or obscure, for we shall hold now in ourselves the key that unlocks the mystery of His coming. We shall know the law of self-surrender, and by that very same law He appeals to us, by that law He offers Himself to our hearts. ' He, too, has surrendered Himself to the necessities of the virgin's womb; He, too, has fulfilled the law of self-sacrifice, and *therefore* it is that we are at one with Him, that we understand and accept Him, in that He, the good Shepherd, is one who surrenders Himself, and lays down His life for His sheep. So, by the power of this sympathetic identity of life-principle, we shall feel His presence; our eyes will be opened, and we shall see Him; our ears will be loosed, and we shall hear His voice: He shall speak and call us all by name, and we shall hear, and know, and follow, and shall pass out behind His blessed feet, out from the narrow fold which had for so long shut in our expectancies, our aspirations, our desires, out into pastures, where grows the fresh green grass that springs up for evermore, by streams that flow on unendingly with the water of inexhaustible life. God of His mercy bring us all to that gracious and abiding home!

SERMON XIII.

LOVE, THE LAW OF LIFE.

"Thou shalt love the Lord thy God, and thy neighbour as thyself."
—St. Luke x. 27.

WHAT a strange and startling command, to be ordered to love! We can understand obedience in a thousand matters: we can allow and justify an order to do this, or to do that: we might even go so far as to concede the right to dictate what we should think and believe, so ignorant are we of the reality of things, so dependent on the condescension of wiser and holier men: but love! Love, surely, is the one thing we cannot but retain in our own possession: love, at least, we fancy, is our own: into its recesses, into its deep privacy, who is there that will dare to penetrate without our leave? Why, we ourselves hardly venture to intrude upon the hidden places of our own affections! they escape, and thwart, and baffle, and elude our own inward grasp: we ourselves cannot presume to control them, so quick, so subtle, so indeterminate is their movement: they choose their own path: they defy all expectation, all prudence, all convenience, all intelligibility. We may advise and warn them as we will: they do not listen: they start out when we least desire it: they hang back when we are urgent: they laugh at rule, and system, and arrangement. We like this man, we cannot tell why: we hate that one, we cannot help it. It is no use talking: no one, so we plead, is answerable for his likes and dislikes.

And, if self-dictation over the heart is impossible, as we suppose, who is the master that can pretend to command us to love him? What tyrant, in his most imperious moments, ever dreamed of such a demand? Let him ask anything but this, if he will; but here, at least, he reaches his limit: his thunders and threats may do the worst, they cannot touch us: our love, at any rate, is free and unassailable. Yet God assumes the entry even of this last refuge, this secret home: even hither He penetrates with His searching decrees: He lays down laws, He makes personal claims: "Thou shalt love Me." It is a rule of His dominion that He should be loved. Nor is it to be merely a vague goodwill that we are bound to give Him: nothing general, or loose, or impersonal, or impassionate will satisfy Him: it is vivid, impetuous, enthusiastic personal love that He orders us to feel for Him: nothing short of this will do at all: love without limit, love without reserve, love without a rival, love without an end, this is His rule, the law of His state: "Thou shalt love Me with all thy heart, with all thy mind, with all thy soul, and with all thy strength." Nor is this all: our affections have yet more demands made upon them: not only are they to be concentrated, in all their force, upon the Lord of this kingdom, but they are to be distributed far and wide, over the whole length and breadth of the dominion: this, too, is to be done by order: we are under command to love every brother-man equally with ourselves: this, too, it appears can be dictated to us.

And these two laws, directing our love to God and our brother, are no general pieces of advice: they are real penal laws, with sanctions and punishments attached: they are rigorous necessities, on the breach of which follows inevitable, irresistible doom. Unless we do so love, in some measure at least, we are shut out from the kingdom: we are cast into the darkness outside the palace and the feast. Only on the condition of our loving His Son will the Father enter in and abide with us: "He that loveth not" is to abide in death: Whosoever hateth his brother is convicted of murder; and no murderer hath everlasting life.

Love of God—love of our neighbour: these constitute the sole titles of admission, the sole claims on life: without these there is no entry. We may plead a hundred other obediences: "Lord, we have taught in Thy Name, and in Thy Name done many mighty works:" but no! no other obedience is of any avail whatever: through the barred, relentless gates sounds the intolerable doom, "I never knew you! depart from me, ye cursed!" One command, and one only, has been given, "Thou shalt love!" "On this one command hang all the law and the prophets:" there is no other: "This is My commandment, that ye love one another: if a man will love Me, My Father will love him: he that loveth Me not, keepeth not My words: these things I command you, that ye love one another."

One thing, then, certainly Christ, our King, presumes

to do: He presumes to have the entire command of our affections.

What can justify such a claim? Why are we to be compelled to love any one? Why is it not the act of an unendurable tyranny? How is it not a contradiction in terms, to command love for oneself by law?

Let us consider, first, who it is who demands love of us. It is our Maker: He Whose fingers fashioned the innermost fabric of our souls, Whose very breath it is that makes us instinct with free and enjoyable life. He made us, not by any binding necessity, nor yet for any play or pastime of His own, but solely because the very core of His innermost Being is Fatherhood: He is God, because He is the Eternal Father: the Fatherhood is His Godhead.

Now, perhaps, we see daylight. For, even here on earth, fatherhood is assumed to necessitate love: it is abnormal and monstrous when these twain are severed: so that, as a fact, we do not really think love to be so incapable of rule and law as at first we supposed: for we assume that it follows, as a rule, the necessities of natural relationship.

Why? Why should we make demand upon love, that it should show itself under the strict limits of the family? Why should it be bound to appear within the lines laid down for it by the conditions of flesh and blood?

Because the conditions which constitute the family are identical with the conditions that constitute *love*. The sense in the father's heart, that he has been enabled to let life flow out from himself, and to put life into another. so that he himself, is no longer alone, shut up within himself, content with himself, satisfied with self-existence, but has called another into being to share his life, and joy, and movement, and freedom: this sense of expansion, of glad-giving, of self-participation, of condescension, of open-handed enlargement, of generous self-surrender—all this which constitutes fatherhood, what else is it than love? How is true fatherhood separable from love? Love *is* that free gift of self to others, that delight in opening the treasures of life to others, that longing to let loose all the gladness locked up within the narrow bars of an isolated soul, so that it may no longer hug its lonely happiness to itself, but may see others enter into its joy, and walk in the light of its surrendered glory. Love is Fatherhood.

And, again, how can childhood be other than love?

The sense of sonship, that which we feel in being sons—what is it but the delighted recognition that all our substance is instinct with living attachments to a father who has begotten us: that from him we are alive, and to him, therefore, our life returns, on him it depends, to him it clings as to its beneficent maker, its saviour, its continual help; by him it is guarded and assured, for his joy it moves and is, at his voice it gladly stirs, under his call it leaps into action, for his sanction it faithfully waits, in his word it lays its undying trust, to the wings of his unfailing shelter it creeps for warmth and protection, in his eye it reads its sure and confident security, within the compass of his fostering care it knows itself shielded, encouraged, sustained; to his mould it instinctively conforms; to fulfil his hopes it is ready and eager to devote every passionate impulse of loyal-hearted service, and to save him from disappointment and shame it would die gladly a thousand deaths.

This is sonship: this is the natural movement of the child, and this—what is this, but love?

Fatherhood, then, is that love which passionately delights in seeing its own life's joy reproduced in another.

Sonship is that love which passionately delights in recognising that its life is due to another, belongs to another, is dedicated to another.

Love, then, is a natural necessity between human parent and child: and love, therefore, belongs, by the same necessity, to our Divine relationships.

For out upon us that mighty Fatherhood of God has poured forth its abounding treasure: into our souls His fulness has flowed: without the workings of that fatherly love of His we should not be here on earth at all: in within each single soul, deep below all its flying fancies, and its surface feelings, and its unsteady desires, at all moments, without pause or slackening, the pulses of that great passion of fatherliness stir, and feed, and quicken, and inspire every atom, every fibre, every movement of our living selves. Within each one of us, to-day, hour after hour, minute after minute, the action of that eternal self-surrender of God Almighty reproduces in us His own image, the forces set loose by that Divine affection unceasingly inflow, inrush, invigorate: whatever our heedlessness, our forgetfulness, our sin, that labour of God's may never falter; His affection may never repudiate or forsake its handiwork, its insistent task: if it ceased for one second, we should have crumbled and vanished into dust. No! our Father worketh hitherto: and still He works, still His compassion never tires; still He pours out His life to make our life, His joy to make our joy; still His creative fingers move about our souls, and fashion out of His Will our will, out of His earnest expectation our hope of blessedness: in His breath we breathe, in His power we move: underneath us, without fail, now and always, His everlasting arms uphold us: our very characters are only alive in the illuminating fire of His immediate and animating Spirit: nowhere—in nothing —can we sever ourselves wholly from His untiring activity, from His unbroken presence, from His unstinted affection; and it is, in the sanctioning authority, in the undeniable right, of this His irresistible Fatherhood, that He lays upon us the command which no living soul can escape or refuse: " *Thou shalt love* Me, the Lord thy God; thou shalt love Me with all thy heart, and all thy mind, and all thy soul, and all thy strength."

And we, too, on our side—for our part—we cannot for one instant rid our souls of that sonship by which they belong to the Most High: we cannot, try all we will, we cannot shut up all the doors and windows by which our spirits look out beyond the narrow house of their own delight: we cannot check the currents of life that move outward from within our hearts, back to that great ocean which is their everlasting home. We are sons: the sense of sonship is alive: it works within: it cannot rest in itself: it feels abroad for that larger life, from which it came: it strains outward toward that overshadowing kindliness, that sheltering benignity, which appeal to it from out of the silences of Nature, and speak to it of the patience and the tenderness of a father that begat it: for this it yearns: towards this the great floods bear it. Something there is, higher, holier, mightier than itself, in Whom is security, and power, in following Whom is life, in clinging to Whom is rest, in serving Whom is perfect joy, in Whose embrace is the peace that passeth all understanding.

All this, inbred into our very blood and bone by the actual necessities of our creation—all this is what we are by the very fact of being sons; and such sense of sonship is, of necessity, love: its clinging dependence on another is what we mean by love: we cannot feel our sonship and not love: we can only deny the need to love by denying the fact of our sonship. If we could cut out of our souls all the fibres that knit our very being up into the movement of God's strong and compelling energies; then, and then only, might we decline His demand upon our love: but, as long as we have His breath in our nostrils, His quickening fire in our nerves, we are· bound over, by overmastering necessity, to His invincible appeal: " Thou shalt love Me, the Lord thy God:" " My son, give Me thy heart."

" Thou shalt love the Lord thy God!"

God has undeniable right to this demand; but, alas! who are we that we should love God? What possible meaning has this love to us?

We go our own way; we follow our own tastes; we pick our way along the world; we have joys and sorrows, friends and foes, of our own; we make interests; we laugh and cry, we fail or we succeed: all this fills up our days, and occupies our minds; and where is there any room for the love of a far-away, invisible God? How unreal such love must sound to us, in comparison with the pleasure and profits of this solid and companionable earth!

Yes! it is a strange, hard, surprising request. It falls oddly on our ears; it sounds thin, and alien, and unfamiliar. Yet on it the issue of our lives hang! God has no other test, no other appeal. It is vain to plead that you have kept moral, or that you have believed, or even that you have done in His Name many mighty works!—" Though you bestow all your goods to feed the poor, or give your body to be burned, and have no love, you are nothing." " Thou shalt love." Thou shalt love God! Thou shalt love thy neighbour. These are the only two commands. " He that loveth not never knew God: for God is Love."

We are here on earth to find out what love means: and all true love begins in the love of God Who loved us. At whatever risk, at whatever cost, we must attain to this love. How, then, to put some meaning into it?

We have found out that love is the necessary and essential outcome of our true nature. If we were living our true life—the life of sonship to God—we could not help loving. Here, then, is our mode of controlling and managing this love. We must secure and foster the conditions of our sonship; and what does this signify?

It signifies this: that the entire movement of our lives must set outward, away from ourselves; for we are sons, and sons, as they draw their life from another, so, too, find their glory and delight in devoting their lives to another. The first act of sonship, then, is faith. Faith is the first motion of the soul away from itself, away from its own interest and self-seeking, back to God the Mighty Giver. Faith, then, is the germ of love. Once let the current of the will be set running towards God in faith, and the whole force of the passionate soul of man will be drawn into the stream, will pour itself along the channel opened, until it flows with the full, swelling flood of love. In faith, the eye of the soul looks away from itself: in love, the entire heart follows the direction of the eye. Faith must begin : there is no love without faith : the soul's motions remain locked, dammed, and barred, until faith gives them free opening.

Have we no faith, then, faith, the first sign of the sonship within us ? No faith ? Ah, surely among you,[1] from whom the buoyancy and the good heart of young days have not yet been withdrawn—you, whose freshness of spirit the world's sins have not entirely soiled away—among you, I may rely upon it that my words will stir and rouse some living sense of your sonship, as yet unlost, some high touch of faith, as yet not wholly vanished away! You, at least, have aspirations, impulses, intuitions, that startle and quicken: you have not yet clipped, and cut, and pruned your desires down to the narrow round of your own selfish interest, your own private good: you are yet indignant when others are wronged, when wickedness triumphs and tramples: you are yet uneasy, and discontented, and

[1] Preached in Christ Church Cathedral, Oxford.

Love, the Law of Life. 209

restless, if the round of the week brings you nothing but your own gratifications.

All this is the witness of your sonship; this is the movement of faith. The soul cannot satisfy itself with itself: it seeks some higher service: it is issuing out of itself in pursuit of some unseen, unselfish end: it feels that life to be unworthy which cares more for itself than for any other thing in the world.

Come, then, trust that outward movement! Throw yourself in with it, move with it, let yourself go. Let no cynical scoff check it, nor any disappointment defeat it. You are meant to be disappointed, until you let that movement discover its end in God. By increasing disappointment you will learn, not to distrust the impulse after unselfishness, but to trust it all the more entirely as your guide to what God, your Father, is. That impulse of self-surrender, of self-devotion, which is the product of your sonship, cannot rest until it finds its true home within the Fatherhood of God. It is because you are His son that you instinctively long to give yourself up to some higher service than those of your own desires.

This is faith; and let me say that it is because we believe this sacrificial impulse of faith to be no casual, accidental fancy, varying with each varying soul, but rather to be the very essence and life-blood of every single human being, implanted in him by the sheer character of his creation, so that not one may claim to be without it,—it is because of this that we desire so earnestly to make chapel, to make the service of God, a necessary and essential part of our life here, included naturally within the daily business of earth; just because earth is not earth without its earnest expectation of the glory that shall be hereafter; just because man is not man without his aspirations of faith; just because man has lost his manhood when he ceases to feel himself a son.

If man is created, if man is a son, then worship, which is the rational recognition of that sonship, is as much a part and parcel of his nature as breathing is.

Worship is the exercise of faith—of self-surrender. Worship sets our sonship in action; and such a self-imposed exercise, in some form or other, is a necessity of human nature: for we are left to manage and develop ourselves; and if we neglect to use any part, that part will give way and die: we are bound, therefore, if we would keep our sonship alive within us, to give it employment, to keep it in use: we are bound to pray and praise. We can no more neglect these, without damage and loss, than we can neglect to use our legs or our arms with impunity. Faith will perish out of our nature, if we do not take care of it.

And, again, if we come here to chapel, let it be clear why we are come.

We are come, because we have that within us which leads away from us to God; that within us which aspires after self-surrender, after the high and devoted service and obedience of sons.

How pitiful, how hopelessly wrong-headed, then, if, when we are here, we bring in with us our wretched self-conceits, our absurd vanities, our affectations, our self-regard, our idleness, our listless indifference, our sleepy self-content, our lolling pride, our silly and self-satisfied complacency! We are here on purpose to forget ourselves; on purpose to break through our vanities; on purpose to wrestle with our own encumbering idleness; on purpose to have something in our lives which strives, and strains, and struggles, and aspires.

There is so much in life to drag our thoughts down to ourselves; there is so much, above all, in Oxford life, to make us self-conscious—conceited—self-interested. At least, here, where we profess to place ourselves under God's immediate Eye, let us attempt to lose ourselves. Let us strive together, one and all, to learn the humiliation of our sin, to look up to the glory which belongeth to God only, to throw ourselves at the feet of Him Whose love could find no way to the righteous or to the self-contented, to listen to the sweet, low voice that calls us out of ourselves, out of our own vanities, out of our own ease, out of our own lustful imaginations, up to the higher obedience, up to the humility of sonship, up to the service of faith: that, so nourishing and cherishing all the instincts that faith sets working within us, our faith may slowly perfect itself into that love of God which loves Him with all its mind, and all its heart, and all its soul, and all its strength.

SERMON XIV.

THE BLESSING OF GOD ALMIGHTY, THE FATHER, THE SON, AND THE HOLY GHOST.

"I looked, and behold, a door was opened in heaven."—REV. iv. 1.

WHITSUNTIDE came,[1] the flush of new life; the Spirit fell, a new beginning; man looked up, and found a new thing in his midst: and the especial form of the novelty lay in the increase of communion, of intercourse, of communication. Men had been isolated; now they understood each other, they spoke with "other tongues." They need no longer remain shut up, each to himself, narrowed, cribbed, confined; but something larger, freer, more open, broke out into man's utterance. No more "barbarians," staring, stumbling, stammering; but, as star answers to star, as, in that speaking silence, without speech or language, their voices are heard and understood, and a sound goes out into all lands; so with man, eye answered to eye, and tongue moved in sympathy with tongue; heart and hand and voice, all stirred, and responded, and aided, and gave accord. Everything had its meaning, everything became intelligible; man had at last got the mastery over language, just because he had got the mastery over the human

[1] Preached on Trinity Sunday.

The Blessing of God Almighty. 213

soul. Words became, indeed, acts of the soul, they throbbed with instinctive life, they were alive with spirit.

As at any great crisis, so pre-eminently here; under the sway of this supernatural energy, men, amid all varieties of character, found their point of union: they broke through all that sundered, they all heard and understood "in their own dialects" the wonderful works of God.

But not only have men found words, found a new language in which to understand *each other;* not only, when before his brethren, does the Spirit give him utterance; but also, as he lifts his eyes, as he stands before the Great King, as he feels the vast pressure of the Holy Presence, his tongue moves with new power, his lips frame new and strange sounds, communications pass and repass, communion is open and free; a fresh utterance breaks out, a larger intercourse, God and man become more intelligible the one to the other; He and we understand each other better, a new name is spoken, a new speech springs up; that which before was dark and concealed and unutterable, now shows itself and finds itself a voice.

Age after age man had striven to find a word by which to name God. Each fresh manifestation had brought with it a fresh intelligence, and called out a fresh name, yet still there was restlessness, still incompleteness, until the great wind blew, and the whole house shook, and the fire leaped down, and sat, and, filled with joy and splendour as with new wine, men caught sight of that final vision, in which all is sealed and perfected; and as their eyes gazed, and hung, and watched, their lips moved, and framed the fresh sound—the new name.

God is one God indeed, but within that holy flame Three Beings walk and live; Three Who are Lords, yet one Lord; one God, yet all Three are God, three Almighty, yet one Almighty. There they live, and move, and act, and love. We know them. None is greater or less than the other; the whole Three are co-eternal together, and co-equal; one Person of the Father, another of the Son, another of the Holy Ghost. Such as the Father is, such is the Son, and such is the Holy Ghost.

Yes, we had puzzled, and doubted, and wondered for so long how one God could be both this and that; how one God could be both entirely self-contained, self-contented, yet also a Creator of worlds, a Father of man, a Friend of Abraham. Now we know, now we see; God is One, yet God is other than One: God is Three. God is God alone, yet God has never been lonely. God is One, yet God is Love; He has never been unloving, never without full exercise of love; for there were Three eternal, Three uncreate, Who from before all time had the full intimacy of intercourse one with another, and fulfilled in devotion the one to the other the highest and holiest necessities of love. Yes! we are compelled, by the force of the Christian verity, to acknowledge every Person of the Three by Himself to be both God and Lord; and yet so instant, so unbroken, so complete is their entire unity, that we cannot divide them asunder, or pronounce them to be three Gods or three Lords. Rather, the Catholic faith is this, this is the new speech, this is the new understanding: we worship one God in Trinity, and the Trinity in Unity, neither confounding the Person, nor dividing the Substance. He that looks for sure salvation will think thus of the Trinity.

So the Christian body has pronounced, so we ourselves repeat; yet with what unready lips! what questioning hearts! How can we make it real? How can we give it meaning? Perhaps one way is, not to attempt imagining the self-existence of the Three in One, but to make distinct and clear their separate and peculiar relation to ourselves, their separate and peculiar action upon our souls. We know God by what He does to us; how does the Trinity make clearer the mode in which God applies Himself to the moulding of each separate soul? How does it show Him to you and me?

Surely we can distinguish at least this: God acts upon us first through His Fatherhood. We find ourselves existing, ringed round by an enclosing world of things— trees, sky, rivers, sea, family, home, nature; all close, compact, solid. Yet through it all man's spirit runs, sees it all, watches, comes to the end; and away, far away, beyond it all, his unceasing questions carry him. His head, his thought, cannot shut themselves in; he knows himself hid in a corner. How? Whence? Why? Whither? Right through the sky his thought pierces, seeking a higher Heaven; right below the roots of the earth his reason digs, discovering a lower depth, a profounder Hades. Away from all that has been, or is, or shall be; away, back behind it all, he strains and strains his eyes; the "I am that I am," the One eternal above all change, the One before all began to be, this he would see before he dies. So his thought works, and his heart echoes the voice of his reason. It, too, cannot feel itself at home; it seeks, and finds not; it knocks, and nothing opens; its weakness, its dissatisfaction, its hunger and thirst, and, as sin deepens, its horror of misery, its yearning after purity, all force it away, all drive it out of its home into desert places.

We long for the light, we crave for food; we are desolate, and know no peace, and win no satisfying love; we send out loud cries into the night. The Love, that our souls know, and cannot find; the Peace, that our souls seem to remember, yet never to attain; the Righteousness, that fashioned us, yet left us so wicked and unholy; where are they? How may we recover the lost joy? Not here is our home; not here our rest. Some other land there is with other mansions. To its dear shores and home-sweet hills we stretch unavailing hands, and send out the wails of our lament.

So it is, after this old fashion, that our Father draws us, that we are impelled to discover Him, Who, though He draws us near, yet hides Himself from us; though He calls, yet remains covered up in silence; though He loves, yet is sought in vain, and flies as we rise up to open the lattice and look out. So we learn the Fatherhood; and then begins the new Revelation.

Not only did God once make us, not only is God to be found in that dim vastness which lies behind all our present days, but God also enters into our life as it is; He acts in it, and through it; in Him it lives, moves, has its being; He is here, here with us, close by us; here in all we see, or think, or feel, or know. And this can be; God can be so intimately present in a created world, just because within the Godhead is One Who is Himself a result of the Father's action, Himself a Son, and so is in full sympathy with that yearning of the Son for the knowledge and blessing of the Father. He Himself knows that longing of dependent love, He can share in it with us, He can enter into fellowship with our hunger and thirst, He can stand by our side in our search; He knows what it is to seek after a peace that lies beyond, for He is a Son, yet none the less is He God. God, then, can be found, the voice of God can be heard, not only in some far land to which we move but which we never see, but here, in a world that seeks as a son seeks. This living, breathing earth in which we abide may hide the Father, but it does not hide, it reveals, the Son. His Sonship fills it from end to end; it is He, God Himself, Who speaks to us from out of all its changing scenes; His voice, the voice of God the Son, moved men from the first, as it spoke from out of all their joys and sorrows, spoke in the fire and the wind, and the earthquake, and in the still small voice.

And more than this; in the power of that Sonship God undertook to gather into Himself all that now is, all that makes man, all that stirs in human souls, all that aspires, all that suffers, all that wastes, all that weeps, all that is forlorn and wanders astray. God the Son will become one with us here and now; He will empty Himself that He may enter into our longings, He will know what it is to miss, to seek, to lose, to hunger, to deplore; He will do this, yet never for one instant diminish that which is His divinity, for that divinity is the divinity of a Son; His Sonship is His Godhead; He loses, therefore, nothing of His Godhead in experiencing all that it may mean to be a Son of God, even in the sense that we are sons.

He, the Son of God, then, becomes what we are; God is with us in our flesh, He can bear to taste what God the Father might never taste; He can become what the Father, as Father, is debarred from being. He has that in His essential Godhead which need not be ashamed to call us brethren; as Son in a higher sense than we, He yet can embrace within His higher Sonship that lower sonship which is ours. He is made our Brother, our Brother-Man. All that is brotherly in nature—far more, all that is brotherly in man; all that reaches out hands to greet and welcome us, all sympathy that grows up, all encouragement that flows, all help that springs to meet our need; all tenderness, all gentleness, all kindliness, all comfort, that soothe our misery; all pity, all compassion, all closeness of heart, all friendship, all love; all that comes to sweeten, to relieve, to support, to fortify; all courage to share, all unselfishness, all self-sacrifice—all this large brotherliness of man to man is the work, the secret work of the Son; all this is His prompting, His ministry, Who, now finally for our sakes, since the children partook of flesh and blood, Himself partook of the same; He, the true Brother, Himself, in His own Person, no longer content with the feeble service which those whom He inspired attempted to fulfil, came down, and stood by our side, and shared all our ills, bore all our sicknesses, was bruised, was chastised; among us He came in our saddest need, and drank of our bitterest cup, and was baptized with our sorest baptism, that He might bring nigh to us all help, all comfort.

He came, laying His hand upon our head in sickness, His fingers upon our eyes, sighing out His soul upon us, breathing His peace into us, touching, taking us by the hand as we sink, entering into our homes, lifting us up in fever, teaching, chiding, enfolding, upholding, enlarging, inviting, encouraging, drawing, calming, controlling, commanding. He drew near with His sacred, soothing words, "Be thou clean;" "Depart from him;" "Son, arise, and walk;" "Come unto Me, I will give you rest;" "Come unto Me, ye shall find rest;" "Learn of Me;" "Take My yoke;" carrying us in His arms, as little children; renewing us with the power of His love; summoning us into His holy service, "Follow Me;" "I have called you friends;" "My sheep, whom I know and love." He calls us all by name.

Yes, there is nothing He will not share, nothing He will not comfort, He will give His very life for the sheep; He will die, that we may receive of Him and bring forth fruit; He will divide to us, by death, His very flesh and blood, that we may eat, and not die. This He will give for the life of the world, He, Jesus, our Brother, made like unto us in all things; a High Priest, touched with the feeling of our infirmities, in all points tempted like as we are; a merciful and faithful High Priest, made perfect through sufferings, through strong crying and tears; Who, in that He hath suffered being tempted, is able to succour them that are tempted; Jesus, the strong consolation to all of us who have fled for refuge to lay hold upon the hope set before us; Jesus, the Captain of our salvation, able to save to the uttermost them that come to God through Him.

God draws us from above, then, as a Father, to bless; God stands by our side, as a Brother, to deliver: but, even yet, we fail our salvation, even yet the manifestation is not complete, even yet our redemption languisheth.

God's countenance looks down, the Father cometh forth to forgive; God, the Son, takes our hand, places Himself by us, His arm round us, to lead us, to cheer us, to cover our shame. Yet—who will not confess it?—our knees tremble, our heart is sick, our back is bowed, we fall a dead weight on the ground, we cannot move, cannot make the effort to rise and walk; the Son, our Brother, pleads, intercedes, He beseeches, invites; but we ourselves groan within ourselves, how can we dare to draw near? who are we, that the Son should shield us? We remain, utterly unworthy of all that has been done for us, powerless to do our part. Without is help, but within is weakness, deplorable, disastrous; within is the root of all our bitterness; within, in our secret self, wells up the foul and poisonous water; within, even yet, hideous things flap their wings—envy, malice, and all uncharitableness; within is excess, and rioting, and drunkenness; within is the tumult of passion, the gnawing disease of lust, the irritable distress of selfish pride; within is no peace, no sense of what holiness means, no desire to be like God, to keep our spirit and flesh unsoiled, unspotted, to love blessing, to love truth, to hate all that maketh and doeth a lie; within, out of the heart, proceed, still, evil thoughts, adulteries, fornications, murders, theft, covetousness, wickedness, deceit, lasciviousness, blasphemy, pride, foolishness; all these evil things come from within, and defile the man. We are defiled with a horrible defilement; we are dragged down by a clinging mass of corruption; and we are powerless, impotent. Christ, our dear Brother, may implore God, may kneel and beseech, may die to redeem, may offer His whole soul in blood to wash us clean. Still the unclean spot remains, still the impotence condemns, still concupiscence works, still death consumes; everything that we do is soiled, disfigured, profane.

And lo! the Godhead has still a disclosure to make, the redemptive energy is still unexhausted, it holds in itself a new spring of life.

The Comforter, the Spirit of Truth, the Holy Ghost, He it is Who, in the glory of the Blessed Three, completes the inner circle of entire communion, which binds Father to Son and Son to Father; He is the heart of all inward union; He it is in the energy of Whom the Father and the Son seal their perfect Fellowship of Love; He "proceedeth" from out of the heart of both, moving from one to the other, certifying their delighted intercourse of free and unhindered love.

He, then, is the inward spring of all joy, and peace, and blessing, and He, therefore, is the one to do on earth what for ever and ever He has done in heaven;

He will work within us, in the power of the same office with which He works within the Father and the Son. The Holy Ghost stands not outside, He enters in, He buries Himself in, within our deepest depths He implants Himself; He fashions for Himself a home, a dwelling, out of the substance of our souls; He, the Dove, the Holy Bird of God, will build Himself a nest within our spirit-home, out of the fibres of our very innermost self; He overshadows, He imbreeds, He inserts a germ of His own unswerving holiness, He makes Himself ours, He makes us His, from within our soul He sends up His cries and intercession to God; He mixes His voice with ours, He groans within our groans, He prays within our prayers, He calls from within our dumbness, He hears from within our deafness, He blesses from within our silence, He sees from within our blindness.

We are devoured by weakness, and passion, and sin, but deep within that which is our very self a new self is forming, a new man is growing, a new presence is conceived; the Spirit has descended upon us, and entered in, and a holy thing is born of Him within us; a new being, reborn, regenerate, with a new name that no one knows, born of water and the Spirit, within the husk of our old evil self; a thing, a being, that God looks upon, and calls by our name, and treats as us: for the sake of which new self, which one day may grow and be fully born out of the womb of the flesh into the light of life, He forgives us all that we, in our old lustful, passionate self, still work of harm and wickedness. That new self is the Spirit's own handiwork, He is the creating energy which moves once more over the deep waters of our spiritual chaos, and remakes a new world of grace. God the Holy Ghost works from within, not from without; not only the Father invites to the palace and the feast, not only does the Son secure our entry, but the Spirit remakes, reclothes, He makes Himself us. From within once proceeded adulteries; but now, He that proceedeth from Father and Son proceedeth, too, from within us. He proceedeth forth, in all His lovely works of holy grace, the works of the Spirit, the fruit of His activity, in love, and joy, and peace, and long-suffering, and gentleness, and goodness, and faith, and meekness, and temperance.

So it is that the Trinity shows itself to us. Surely it becomes real, this threefold Godhead, when we can distinguish so clearly its threefold action. In three separate ways God shows Himself to us, three ways which we can recognise distinctly the one from the other, so distinct, so separate, that, in a sense, they are contradictory the one to the other. I mean, each came in us to do that which the other, by its very nature, could not do. The Father could not become at the same time a Brother; we could not regard the same identical Person as at once both the one who begat us from above, and the one who shares with us in our nature at our side. It was to be that which the Father could not be, that the Son, our helpmate, became incarnate of our flesh and blood. And our Brother, again, cannot be wholly ourself. He is another; that is His very character: one Who takes our place, stands for us, fights for us, on Whom we rely, in Whose life we live. But we have yet a life of our own; a life sinful, corrupt, ungainly. We may fly from ourself to Him, but our self remains, an unsightly blot, until another than He enters in, and impresses the seal of His very nature upon our nature, and impregnates us with His prevailing efficacy, and purges out all corruption by the fire of His inward purification, and fashions us from within entirely anew into the semblance of His unspotted purity.

They are distinct, then; so distinct that we can sever each from each, and feel distinct gratitude to each severally as we recognise their separate action. Yet, in all, they are wholly and perfectly one God, none of them inferior or less than another.

Consider this Unity. It is not that we abandon the attempt to find the infinite Father, when we turn our eyes upon the incarnate human Son; but in turning to the Son we find the Father. The way to know the Father is to know the Son. "Come unto Me;" but in coming to Him we arrive at another, we find ourselves within the embrace of the Father. It is not a weakness, a failure, an inferior approach. We are indeed to believe on the Son, but in the very act of believing on Him we believe not on Him, but on Him that sent Him, so entirely and wholly One are they. "Have I been so long with you, and yet hast thou not known Me, Philip? he that hath seen Me hath seen the Father;" "I and the Father are One."

Nor, again, is it Christ, our Brother, Whom we lose sight or hold of as we pass under the action of the Holy

The Blessing of God Almighty. 225

Ghost. No, He teaches of Christ; in His coming Christ Himself comes; in His abiding Christ Himself abides. Christ Himself, in Him, takes possession; our very self becomes Christ's. It is not we that live, but " Christ that liveth in us." We, by falling under the activities of the Holy Ghost, become members of Christ, part and parcel of His heavenly Body. So entirely and perfectly one are the Son and the Spirit, that " He," saith Christ, " shall in all His doing glorify Me; for He shall receive of Mine, and show it unto you; He shall testify of Me."

Is this not wonderful? Is this not refreshing? God's action towards us is so many-sided, yet so unconfused.

Here, for instance, in this Eucharist, we can so easily, and so helpfully acknowledge the full plenitude of the Trinity: God the Father, the mighty Giver; God the Son, the perfect Gift; God the Holy Ghost, the clean and pure Receiver. Each one His office; each one His part and place; each one we bless, and glory, and thank; at no part do they fail us, the whole action is complete, on every side of us is support assured. We move forward to His high altar, surrounded, encompassed on every side by the whole fulness and abundance of the Godhead. It is the Highest, the Holy, the Eternal, Who spreads His table; it is the blessed, the everlasting Intercessor, Whose flesh and blood we eat and drink; it is the Holy Comforter Who spreads out hands from within us, to receive from the hands of the Father the Body of the Son.

And all Three are One. That which is given is holy as God Himself, the Giver; it is not less holy than He; the Gift is as utterly and entirely Divine as the Father

P

Himself Who gives it; the Receiver is no less holy and pure than the Gift or the Giver. Nothing is lost of the preciousness of the Gift, nothing is spoilt or sullied; whole and entire, the Spirit of God receives that holy thing which the Father gives and presents.

Yes! the whole united authority of the Blessed Trinity assures and secures to us our salvation by the Body and the Blood, and therefore it is that, in spite of all our miserable and hideous defilements, we, even we, poor, blind, maimed, impotent sinners, can venture without fear to lift up to-day our thin voices, and, with angel and archangel and all the company of heaven, to laud and magnify the glorious name, evermore praising God and saying, "Holy, holy, holy, Lord God of hosts, heaven and earth are full of Thy glory. Glory be to Thee, O Lord most High."

SERMON XV.

THE MEEKNESS OF GOD.

"The Son of Man came not to be ministered unto, but to minister and to give His life a ransom for many."—St. Matt. xx. 28.

HERE is a text that speaks home, at once, and with ease. It runs on our levels; it speaks in a language understood of all.

Every one knows the arrogance and the insolence of the kings of the Gentiles, who exercise lordship over their fellows. Every one in our Lord's day knew the pomp and the pride of those provincial governors of Rome, who broke in upon the rich East from out of the Imperial City, to despoil, and to devour, to suck out treasure, to recoup ruined fortunes by a few brief years of gainful and shameless corruption, and then vanished back to Rome loaded with ill-gotten wealth, leaving their place open to another spendthrift lord, as impatient as the last, to make full use of his splendid opportunity. They knew well the selfish greed of Gentile lordship: and we, too, in our generation, know too well the baneful presence of those who deem the world made for their advantage; who live to seize every occasion of profit; who use high position only that they may discover new modes of pleasure, new refuges from care, new apologies for idleness. These we know, kings of the earth, exercising selfish lordship, seeking gain: and those others we know, kings of the intellectual world, vain and self-seeking, who, in converse with their fellows, would take all, and give nothing; who see in life nothing but an opportunity for cleverly shining, and are irritated and fretful with the pettiness of the tyrant, if ever they miss the moments of display, or have no servile crowd to listen and applaud; men who spend their days hungering for new occasions of self-gratulatory success. We know what selfish men are, their repellent and ungenial company, the chill shadow that they cast on all that is sunny, and natural, and warm. Yes, "the kings of the earth exercise lordship:" they have their own interests to serve, and press, and assert: they are bent on aims which are not ours: they pit themselves against us, they challenge our right to all that they see in our hands, they are on the watch to put us to profit, to raise their black-mail, to weaken and to impoverish all whom they deal with: they bring us no help, they are felt as a peril: we are anxious while they pass by: we breathe more freely when they are gone: such is the blighting effluence, the deadly mist, that hangs about selfishness.

And it is in delightful and enticing contrast to this that we turn to greet, with heart and soul, the sweet coming of Him, the human-hearted, the tender Master of all loving-kindness, and all patience, and all goodness, and all long-suffering,—the Son of Man, Who enters in upon our earth in the might of a Lordship all His own, the Lordship of Him Who has everything to give, and gives it all: Who brings infinite power of

The Meekness of God. 229

helping, and sees no one whom He will not help: Who, having all things, keeps back nothing: Who has nothing to gain, and yet risks His all for us: Who cannot rest content, so long as He is not outpouring succour: Who came simply, and with this one purpose, "that He might minister:" with this aim He started: without this aim He would never have come. He brings help, not by accident, as it were, not incidentally, not with careless ease, not of mere blind good-nature, not in arbitrary fashions, not by after-thought, not under sudden pressure, not by fits and starts, not thoughtlessly, not by some flitting impulse of generosity, not in casual, free-handed good-humour: nay, He came, strong with deliberate intention, the intention to help. This motive alone, this and no other, drove Him out of His Father's home, into our troubled ways: by this one purpose was His soul prompted, and possessed: the very root of all His desires, the very ground of all His movement, the very end of all His action, was just this, that He might give. The Son of Man came to minister. He had seen an opportunity of giving, of helping; and so He came.

And of giving what?

Of giving Himself! His service was to be utterly unstinted. He would go the whole length with it. He saw that we should demand from Him all that He had; that we should use up His very life; that our needs and necessities would press upon Him so sorely, so urgently, that He would spend Himself, and be spent, in this hard service; that we should never let Him stop, or stay, or rest, while we saw a chance of draining His succouring stores. He foresaw no light and easy giving, no grateful and pleasant ministry, but that it would cost Him His very life. And yet He came: even *that* He would lay down for our profit: even that He would surrender at our demands; and just because the work of the faithful service would, indeed, involve this surrender of life, which is the final and utter proof of all loyal and unselfish devotion, He had found it a joy and gladness to enter a world that would ask so much of Him. In this hope, He came. "The Son of Man came not to be ministered unto, but to minister:" yes, and so to minister, so to serve, that He would "give His life a ransom for many."

He came, then, as the good Giver, as the Shepherd Who giveth His life for His sheep.

And it is this, His character, which draws us under the sway of His gracious Lordship. We cannot resist the sweet force of this irresistible appeal, "Come unto Me, for I am One that giveth all that I am to thee!" This is the allurement of Christ, by which His sheep are drawn after His feet: how can they resist the call of One Who serves them so loyally? Every sound of His voice has in it the ring of that true-hearted devotion, which would lay down life itself to save them from harm. All men who have alive in their souls any touch of nobility, of tenderness, of humility, understand the winning grace of One Who pleads simply to be allowed to give for their use all that He has, and all that He is. "I, if I be lifted up upon the Cross, will draw all men unto Me!"

And yet it is just this winning charm of which we miss often the true force. For do we not associate it

The Meekness of God.

entirely with what we call the humanity of the Lord? It is the human Christ Whom we picture so pleading, so meek, so unselfish, so good. It is the *Man* Whom we think of, toiling in our service,—the Man of Sorrows Whom we remember, with tender, loving hands that heal and help; with eyes that flow with tears of love, with a heart broken by our mistrust, and a brow bleeding under our scorn.

This is Christ, the Man, to our minds: and only when we come to deeds of power, only when He speaks of judgment and authority—of His Kingly Throne, of His Imperial wrath, of the glory with the Father before the worlds were,—only then do we speak of His Divinity. Our language seems to suppose, too often, surely, that the Lord's life can be bisected, and the acts of His humanity be decisively severed from the acts of His Divinity, as if He sometimes were wholly man, and, at another, set loose His Divine energy, in separate and solitary action.

So we draw our narrow and crude divisions: but this, of course, is not the Catholic creed.

That creed asserts that there is but One Person, Christ Jesus, both God and Man: One, Who in all His most human actions is still, none the less, the Eternal Word of God, Who alone is the Worker, and alone the Speaker. It is He, the Word, the Image of the Father, Who expresses Himself through that human flesh; and expresses Himself, not at rare moments of flashing glory merely, or in sudden efforts of peculiar prerogative, but at all moments, the moments of weakness as well as the moments of strength; the moments of meekness as well as the moments of kingly assertion. The whole life of the fleshly body is made His: He has poured into it Himself: He has made its features, and its limbs, its muscles, and nerves, and blood, to become His garments, His vessels, His instrument, the very organ by which He acts: He has taken to Himself its very nature and substance, which He indwells, and possesses, and animates, and fills.

And, if so, then it is in the action, and character, and movement of His Humanity, that we are to recognise, and interpret, and understand His Divine Person. Powers, and energies, and motions of the Divinity, indeed, there are, which cannot limit themselves by fleshly barriers, and hold themselves distinct from bodily circumscription. We are not confounding that which is divided: His Divine nature remains whole, and undiminished, and distinct; but there is no division of Person. That which acts in and through the flesh is the One Person, Jesus Christ, the Word, Who is ever with God, and Who is God; and all the motions in the flesh are, therefore, the motions of a God: His hands, His feet, His face are all the expression of an eternal Personality: that which we behold in the countenance of the Man Jesus, is the face of the Word, Who is in the bosom of the Father.

Is this unreal theology? Is this the useless abstraction of fanciful, Athanasian dogmatic?

Nay, surely! it is the very life and soul of the Christian faith. For, if it be true, then that charm which allures us to the gracious and tender-hearted Healer of sickness, is no temporary character assumed at the birth, no mere incident of the sojourn in the Virgin's womb; no lower and subordinate element in our conception of the Lord, no partial condescension to the weakness of our faith. That winning grace has in it the potency of God Himself. It is the manifestation of the Word, the revelation of what God is in Himself. The body, the flesh,—these make plain and clear what has been from of old, from eternity. They make effectual to us, attractive to us, apprehensible by us, the ancient and everlasting God. If Jesus, the Man, is tender and meek, then God, the Word, is meek and tender: God, the Word, is sympathetic, and gentle, and humble, and forgiving, and loyal, and loving, and true. It is God, the Word, Who cannot restrain Himself, for love of us; and comes, with overwhelming compassion, to seek and save the lost: God, the eternal Word, Who longs to win the heart of publican and sinner. He has not now begun to be all this: such as this He has been from all eternity; such as this He cannot but be. He shows us, not another, but Himself,—God Himself, Who loves, and weeps for Lazarus; Who looks upon the rich young man, and loves him; Who has pity for the forlorn and childless widow; Who takes up children in His arms, and blesses them; Who prays for His murderers, and tenderly remembers His mother, and forgives the dying thief: God, the Word, Whose Soul is exceeding sorrowful, even unto death; Who took bread, and blessed, and gave thanks, and so loved His own to the uttermost. It is, verily, no accident of His bodily life, all this! No character adopted, to be put on and put off; no mere growth of thirty narrow years! It is God Himself Who is incarnate, God Himself, the Son, Whom St. John touched, and tasted, and handled: it is He, in His everlasting characteristics, Who is made manifest in the flesh. The Son of Man is the Son of God; and, therefore, we know and thank God for it, that it is the blessed nature of the Son Himself, in His eternal substance, which found its true and congenial delight in coming, not to be served, but to serve, and " to give His life a ransom for many."

Nor is this all.

For he who hath seen Christ, hath seen the Father,—the Father, in Whose Name He worked, Whose word He spake. That last and uttermost pledge of unfaltering love, the death on the Cross, was no plan, no thought of His own. It was the Father that prompted it, the Father, without Whom He could do nothing: it was the Father Who moved Him to the task: this commandment He had received of the Father, to lay down His life for the sheep. That tender, gracious, devoted, patient, forgiving gentleness, that warm, overflowing sympathy, that invincible passion of sacrificial love, that sweet human-hearted compassion, that lovely persuasiveness, which flows down to us from the Cross of Jesus,—all this, then, is not only a revelation of the motives, and spirit, and affection of God the Son, but more than this, all of it is an outcome, an expression, of the character (if we may be allowed the word) of God the Father. His heart it is which the Passion of Christ makes manifest, His heart which it is given us to understand in the infinite piety, and beauty, and grace, and comfort, and goodness, and meekness of Jesus.

The Meekness of God. 235

These are all the signs, the sacraments, the interpretation, the outflow, of His Father's presence; for He and the Father are one. The winning tenderness, the wonderful humility, which look at us out of the eyes of the dear Lord, are the clearest and closest knowledge we ever here shall attain of what we mean when we name the Father, of what we shall behold when we see God.

Do we remember sufficiently that it is the Father Whom the Gospel story makes near, makes visible? that, in drawing near to Christ, under the strong pressure of the unstinting love, we are being drawn near to God, the Everlasting Father, made present and intelligible in His Son?

God the Father offers us a picture of that, His eternal substance, hid in excess of omnipotent light: and we press forward to look: and lo! we behold One Who is meek, and lowly, and gentle, riding upon an ass, washing the feet of His friends, serving, and not served, loving Mary, and Martha, and Lazarus, the Friend of publicans and sinners. That is the image of God the Father, the express character of His Almighty Person.

Are we startled? Startled to think thus of the God of the Jews, of Sinai, of Sabaoth?

Yet why should we be surprised?

What was it that the old covenant told of God but this, that He was one "Who led His people like sheep,—that He carried them as the eagle its young—yea, as an eagle stirreth upon her nest, fluttereth over her young, spreadeth abroad her wings, taketh them, beareth them upon her wings, so the Lord did lead them"? What can be more tender, what more pitiful? What other was the name by which Moses knew Him, Moses hidden in the cleft of the high and lonely rock, covered by the hollow of God's hand, as the Lord descended in a cloud, and stood with him, and proclaimed the name of the Lord, when the Lord passed by before him, and proclaimed, "The Lord, the Lord God, merciful and gracious, long-suffering in goodness and truth, keeping mercy for thousands, forgiving iniquity, and transgression, and sin?" So Moses knew Him: and by what other name did Isaiah know Him,—Isaiah, who knew Him by all manner of tender and gracious names—the Vinedresser, the Husbandman, the Shepherd, the Bridegroom, the Husband,—the God of pleading compassion, more faithful, more forgiving than a mother: "Yea, she may forget her sucking child, yet will I not forget thee!"

And the Psalmist,—did he know of any other God than the God Who is made manifest in Christ, when he sang of the Lord his God, "Who helpeth them to right that suffer wrong, Who feedeth the hungry; the Lord Who looseth men out of prison, the Lord Who giveth sight to the blind, the Lord Who careth for the righteous, Who careth for the stranger, and defendeth the cause of the fatherless and the widow, the Lord Who healeth those that are broken in heart, and giveth medicine to heal their sickness?"

True, there is thunder round Sinai; wrath, and terror, and judgment upon the lips of Prophet and Psalmist. But is there no dread anger, no terrible lightning, in Him Who, meek and gentle and lowly as He was, yet had words like leaping flames, of awful condemnation: " Woe unto hypocrites, generation of vipers;" in Him Who, against the faithless and wicked servant, will give scathing judgment: " Cut him asunder; cast him into outer darkness; there where the worm dieth not, and the fire is not quenched."

The holiness of the meekest of men has its searching fire: for God would not be all-holy if He were not terrible in His devouring fury against sin; and in being holy, He is, of necessity, meek, and long-suffering, and merciful. God the Father, then, for all His terror, is gracious and pitiful: He, the God of Sinai, is indeed the very God Who is made manifest in Him, Whom He sent and anointed to heal the broken-hearted, to preach deliverance to the captives, to refresh the weary and heavy-laden, to feed all hungry souls.

Are we still surprised? Do we yet find it difficult to associate so closely the picture of Christ, the lowly and the meek, with our conception of God, the Eternal Father?

What, then, is it that we primarily believe of God the Father which is inconsistent with the appearance in the flesh of God the Son, Who is in the form of God?

Surely His Name is, first, "the Father:" He, Who gives life, gives out of Himself His own Life: He, Whose actual Godhead lies in His free spontaneity of giving, in His gift of Himself to the Son: for His Fatherhood is His Godhead: His Divinity is not shut up to itself: it exhibits itself in the very act, wherewith it gives life: His very substance consists in the desire, the eternal readiness, to surrender His entire Being to another. From everlasting to everlasting, He is the Father Whose whole joy is to glorify the Son.

The Father, and also the Creator, One, Who, without any self-interest, without any personal need, without any external motive, without inducement, without necessity: solely out of the abundant largess of His own exceeding love: solely that He might see others live in His Life, and in His Light see light: solely out of the unbounded munificence of His everlasting compassion, set Himself to the six days' labour, poured out life upon life, power upon power, grace upon grace; each new work richer and fairer than the old: and all for this one end,—that those thousand times ten thousand worlds, hung in the vast spaces of heaven, might burn, and quiver, and roll in the gladness of the outgiven life, as thronging and multitudinous insects rise, and circle, and dance, with murmuring joy, in the splendour of summer suns.

God the Father, God the Creator, and God the Redeemer: the Redeemer, Who, after all the abundance of His first gift of creation, had still new gifts in store for those who failed, and fell. They fell; but, still, He works on, with the Son, outpouring fresh springs of healing. Still, on prophet and people, He spends the treasures of the Spirit, with all its manifold gifts: still, as sins increase, increases the abundance of the good giving, until, at last, pressed and driven by our insults, by our scorn, by our ingratitude, He gave His all; gave, like the poor widow, even all that He had: gave us that which is Himself, One with Him, of His substance, of His nature, laid eternally at His heart, in undivided union with Himself. Yea, "God so loved the world, that He gave His only-begotten Son:" gave Him, His supreme and uttermost gift, Life of His Life, Light of His Light: Him He gave when He had no more to give; gave Him when we had despised and outraged all other gifts, and would disgrace, and defame, and spurn, and spit upon this His holiest and dearest Gift also. Him, nevertheless, His only Son, His Beloved, Heart of His Heart, Spirit of His Spirit, Son of His Love: Him, still, at all risk, at any cost, He gave! So mightily, so unflinchingly, has God, the good Giver, loved this naughty world! Surely here is meekness, meekness even in the Most High! Surely here is humility, and lovingkindness, and pity, and long-suffering, and tenderness, and gentleness, and sympathy, and goodness, and mercy, and love, and inexhaustible compassion. Surely here is One Whose delight is not to be ministered unto, but to minister: here, in God the Father, Who gave His Son for us, we recognise all that melts us to tears of thankfulness in the sweet and pleading graciousness of Jesus,—Jesus, the human-hearted, the Man of Sorrows, Who gave His Life a ransom for many!

SERMON XVI.

THE POWERS THAT BE.

"There is no power but of God: the powers that be are ordained of God."—ROM. xiii. 1.

THE historic life of man moves under the impulse and control of God. So the first Church believed, as it read in its familiar Scripture how the long order of the Jewish revelation had interwoven itself into the actual history and process by which the race of Israel had moved forward, through its political changes, from the free domination of the Lawgiver, through the loose and sudden chieftaincies of the judges, to the full sovereignty of the kings.

Each movement in social organization was a movement in spiritual apprehension: it was God that showed Himself in each political expedient: it was the law of His manifestation, that it should shape and mould itself by the needs, and forms, and varieties of Jewish society. His revelations moved in intimate sympathy with the shift and change of history.

And this intimacy was not narrowed, so the Jews had learned, to the mere limits of the privileged people. As the shock of disaster shattered their homes, and scattered their sad exiles into all far lands, the eyes of their large-hearted seers were opened to the wider ranges, to the vaster horizons. As they stood under the solemn shadows of the immense Babylonian palaces, and gazed from out of their lonely sorrows upon those silent masses of Assyrian statuary, big inspirations stirred in them of far-reaching hopes, and grander destinies. Not that the holy nation was lost or forgotten: it still centred upon itself the eye and heart of the Most High; but round it and about it these enormous nations moved and shifted under the breath of that same God. At His Will they gathered; under His wrath they sundered and passed: it was He Who, by His mighty arm, uplifted them into supremacy: it was He Who drew them by strong pressure from the east and from the south: it was He Who drove them out of the hills of the north: it was He Who poured them out of the river-watered plains.

For each He had an office; for each He had appointed a beginning and an end. One by one they rose in orderly succession, those stupendous kingdoms of the East. Babylonian and Persian, Egyptian and Greek, God had required their armies: He had lain His hand upon their captains: Assyria was His hammer, Cyrus was His shepherd, Egypt was His garden, Tyre was His jewel: everywhere He was felt: everywhere the Divine destiny directed and controlled: and far from the especial revelation of Himself, which he concentrated upon the Jews, being severed sharply and decisively from these large social growths, it interlaced itself most closely and intricately with their motions: it mixed its story with theirs: it is round it they turn. The shuttle of God passes in and out, weaving into its web a thousand threads of natural human life. All history is put to the uses of God's holier manifestation: He works under the pressure laid upon Him by the wants and necessities of social and political progress.

Nor was this association of the spiritual and natural confined to the Jews. The faith of the Incarnation enlarged and crowned this anticipation of the prophets. Christ, indeed, came down from heaven: He was not of the world; He came from above, not from beneath: but He came to find what the Father had already given, what the Father had already drawn to Him. Nothing could come near to Him but that which had already in it the force and impulsion of God. The revelation, then, of Christ entered a world already informed by a premonitory impulse, already responsive to the touch of Divinity. The sheep were His, and He entered only to find and gather them: His voice would be to them no strange, unfamiliar thing, but the sound of a friend, known, beloved, expected, sympathetic: the world to which He came was a world already His, already made by Him: it was true of the whole as it was true of the part, that He came unto His own; and, if so, His entire manifestation would proceed in intimate union with the process and movements of the natural order of life; it would answer to them; it would be congenial to them it would meet them; it would find them to its hand; it would mingle itself with their aspirations and welcome their aims. Everywhere that Spirit of Revelation would recognise itself: it would greet its own handiwork; it would encounter its own countenance; it would come unto its own; it would raise this faint and stifled humanity to life, as Elisha raised the dead boy at Sarepta, by laying face to face, and hand on hand, and feet to feet, by close and binding correspondence.

And it was so. We have been hearing lately in London,[1] from lips that speak our accents without our inspiration, how largely Christ admitted, within the shaping of its Divine system, the influence of that imperial dominion which had laid its vast arms about the world from the Thames to the Euphrates. We, indeed, may insist, with unshaken force, that the power so to put Rome to use could hardly proceed from Rome herself, as our puzzled critic is inclined to suggest; while, yet, we admit with ready glee that the Church found in Roman organization, in Roman skill, in Roman order, in Roman obedience, that which had for her an overflowing suggestiveness, and won from her a free and delighted adaptation.

"The powers that be are ordained of God." So cries St. Paul: this great empire is His voice, His call to us, His symbol: in it He invites us, He welcomes us, He holds out hands of greeting. It is the response from without to our mission from above; the mercy and peace that look down from heaven encounter a righteousness that springeth up from earth : they meet together and embrace. So it was, as we know well, that the vision of the vast Christian kingdom, whose citizens should break down all partitions between Greek or barbarian, bond or free, male or female, draws its imagery and wins its intelligibility from that wide fabric of Roman law which spread its marvellous

[1] M. Renan's Hibbert Lectures.

dominion from the prison-house of Paul on the Palatine, over the wide forests of Germany and Gaul, over the shores of the Mediterranean twinkling with towns, over the sweeps of African land, and the wealth and wonder of Syria. The Church never ceased to praise and admire, even where it slew her, the imperial justice of Rome: her apologists, even when pleading before it for their lives, turn to it as to a friend: they appeal to it from the blind fury of the mob, with the proud assurance that it cannot, if it be true to itself, be against them. They are as convinced as St. Paul himself that the law was bound only to be a terror to evildoers, and a praise to them that do well: they recognise, with all their hearts, the nobility of the Roman ideal of a law that stood over all personal distinction, all local enmities: and when it fell to the Church to organize her own dominion and ministrations, she used, wherever she could, the model of that civil order which Rome had perfected, and followed Rome's lines for her diocesan divisions, for her parishes and her provinces, for the summoning of her assemblies, and the fashion of her appeals. Rome was to her a perpetual suggestion of the form and direction which her Divine work should assume; and the Church of Revelation was in no sense afraid to use and follow the fashions of human civilization.

"The powers that be are ordained of God." Round and about us those same powers are moving; they are breaking up, and reshaping the old world order to new issues: and if we were asked what was most peculiar and predominant in their working at this hour, we should answer, I think, the tendency to fashion vast cities. The powers that belong to immense masses, the powers that lie in concentrated efforts, the powers that create and move into being these huge combinations of human skill and human interest, with all their infinite multiplicity, their intricate variety, their untold complexity, their splendid range of massive achievements, their silent transformations, their noisy turmoil of business, their struggle, and pressure, and competition, their rises and falls, so swift, and yet so slow, so sure, yet so unforeseen, so regular, yet so arbitrary, so steady, yet so blind; their push, and press, and insistent strife, their endless steps, and degrees, and grades, circle within circle, their changes and chances, their wealth and poverty, their shocks and convulsions, their ebbs and flows, their heavings and subsidences, their network of influences, their growth of involved habits, their intricate co-operations,—yes, and their restless anxieties, their constant strain, their quickened brains, their unknown agonies, their unlooked-for cruelties, their enormous disasters, their boundless pains: these, these are the powers that are shaping human history under our eyes; these are the powers that hold the future in their grasp; these are the powers that govern our immediate destiny; these are the powers put into action by that Divine impulsion which underlies all social movements; these are "the powers that be."

And these, therefore, I would beseech you to believe, are "the powers ordained of God." Here, in London, we stand at the very centre of this new working, at the very point where the pressure of the incoming energies is most strongly felt. Never before has society attempted so complete or so gigantic a combination; never before have men succeeded in so extending their efforts; and all the ingenuity of human invention is spent in rendering this union of manifold interests more intimate and more intense. Here, then, in London, more than anywhere, do we see the suggestions of God: here, more than anywhere, we understand the task that is before us. Christianity may not pick and choose its own field of work, nor dream of some favourite and congenial society, where its creed would find itself more easily at home. It is bound to undertake the task God sets before it; it is bound to follow His invitation, to encounter His challenge. God in each successive fashion of civilization challenges His Church: He challenges it to measure its strength with His, to wrestle with Him as Jacob wrestled, until the dawn broke over the hills of Mahanaim.

Come! He cries, here is My new offer; here is the new stuff from out of which you must shape for Me garments of beauty; here are the new stones out of which you must build My Holy Temple; here is the new food which you must gather in to be transformed into the Body of My dear Son.

The Church fails herself, if she fails to be adequate to the needs of this invitation: she is faithless to her hope, if she falls below the standard of mankind's historic progress, if she has no answer to his problems, no interpretation to give to his movements. These great cities into which the life of humanity is throwing all its endeavours, and which have in them the seed of the days to come, must be as welcome to the Church as was ever that ancient Roman empire: she has to learn to apply herself to them, as she applied herself of old to Rome: she has to see in them the finger of God preparing her the way: she has to listen for their tones and assimilate their experiences. The Church of the Fathers would have been doomed, if she had fallen short of the largeness, the width, the dignity, the universality of Roman imperialism: if the citizenship she offered had been a narrower and pettier thing than that lordly freedom to which St. Paul was proud to lay claim, even under the shadows of the Temple. She triumphed because she was brave and strong enough to give a yet nobler response to those wide and splendid cravings after equal justice and a common-hearted brotherhood, which Rome set moving, but failed to content. And we have, then, a like task, which we shall fail at our peril! It is our task to be equal to those thousand influences that vast cities foster and increase: it is our task to prove that the Church has it in her to deal with these new powers, to measure herself with their aspirations, to be large and full, and strong, and masterful, and immense as they. If they exhibit the enormous scale which combination makes possible, she, too, will show that she knows how to combine; she, too, will prove her power of concentrating efforts, of doing things in the mass: it will never do for her to be puny and small in the face of a vastness like that of London: it will not do to be content with securing the safety of our own little corner of the world, in the face of an immense system of co-operation.

How, then, is such vastness attainable? How is London possible? London is possible, because thousands upon thousands of men and women work that others may reap the fruit, work for results which they themselves never see. London is possible, because men trust one another, because men rely on those they never see or hear of, or overlook: it is possible, because, for instance, every man can work all day in confident security that the huge machinery which provides him with his food will most certainly accomplish its daily necessary task, even though he know nothing of the laborious process. And the evangelization of London will be possible when Christians exhibit an equal largeness of confidence in one another, and enter into co-operation with something of this width of view, this ungrudging freedom. Again, London is what it is, because no man lives for himself, because no district in it narrows its interest down to its own limits. London lives as a whole: it is no mere conglomeration of parishes: it is powerful just because its influences, its organization, work in the mass, work in the spirit, and on the scale, of an immense community, with a common interest, and a common welfare: and by the side of this great life our Christianity is only too apt to look such a poor, and mean, and small thing, with its local and partial efforts, its isolated endeavours, its lonely and disunited struggles, its selfish and timid narrowness, its feeble and intermittent exertions.

This is our shame! and what you are asked to do to-day [1] is to overstep the boundaries which too often

[1] Preached on behalf of the Bishop of London's Fund.

confine our charities and our care: you are asked to attempt the larger task, the worthier endeavour: you are asked to recognise the scope and range which is demanded of our Christianity, if it is to be adequate to the work it has proposed to undertake: you are asked to deal with London, not in scraps and fragments, but as a whole, as a living thing, as a single, vast, and inspiring fact, in the welfare of which you are profoundly concerned, and for the good and evil of which every one of you is in a measure responsible. You know its enormous outgrowth: you know its unceasing increase. Not only have we been insufficient in the past, but the present is daily enlarging the difficulties already so gigantic: all round you, to the north and to the west, entire towns are at this very hour springing up as fast as the armies of masons can lay brick to brick, and all of them will be quickly filled by thousands, whose lives will be spent in close contact with yours, working for your needs, called thither by your wants, knit up by countless threads into the life that you live, into the commonwealth that you share. Let me implore you to remember that this swarming and multitudinous city is no horrible evil, which you are to relieve with your charity; it is no huge disease, whose worst bitterness you are begged to assuage. This city, in its strong and wonderful immensity, is as high and superb an ideal as that imperial system of old Rome. Such a city is the fullest and noblest expression of that supreme effort of mankind which we call civilization: it is the triumph of combination, the crown of friendly and orderly intercourse between man and man. Only by the subtlest skill, only by untiring labour, only by most tender, and manifold, and delicate mechanism, can its hourly existence be sustained. Into such a city are gathered the stored forces which create history: these multitudes are drawn into its net by the movement of the deepest human energies. Such a city is the achievement of large spiritual impulse : it is pre-eminent among the " powers that be : " " it is ordained of God."

Here, then, is our task; here, and nowhere else. This is our trial hour. Can we, or can we not, Christianize this fresh fashion of human life, for God and for his Son?

History will not ask whether, in nooks or corners of London, a few faithful met together to praise and worship God. It will ask, was the Church faithful to the big work to which she was summoned? As of old she encountered and won imperial Rome, and banded Vandalism, so now, did she once again rise to the new task? Did she run the course set before her? Did she seal to God the powers of the great cities? Did she enlarge herself to the measure of the new organization? Did she learn and use the secret of combination? Did she discipline herself to the handling of vast masses? Had she the courage for this? Had she the largeness of heart? Had she the confidence in herself? Had she the generous trust in others which alone could make it possible? Had she the inspiration of faith? Had she the splendour of love?

Or did she quail? Did she shrink up, creep, and fear? Was she poor, and thin, and niggardly, in her attempts? Was she weak and insufficient? Did she abandon the huge hordes of crowded men to that ruin which she knew would be inevitable, unless Christ became their Master, unless Christian faith bonded them into that communion which alone hallows and endures? These are the questions to which we, in our generation, are asked to give answer.

It may not surely be that this National Church of ours will be content to ignore or falsify her claims to run level with the national life: she has responsibilities which it is criminal to decline, and these responsibilities compel her to make sure that her labours be no narrower in their scope than those of the entire nation. What England does, the Church of England must not be afraid to do; and England is now massing her works and population, as she never massed them before. The Church, then, must forward her energies with no stinting hand, with no captious or suspicious heart, if she is not to fail England at the critical hour.

Nor is it England only that she will fail: it is God,—God the Father, Who summoned her to undertake: He it is Who moves (unseen, yet felt) this whole heaving world of men: His breath impels and shifts these massing multitudes: He shapes their destiny: He prepares their paths; and yet they know Him not! They cannot know Him, until the Son, the Beloved, the only Righteous, stands before them in human flesh, in living Presence, to show them plainly of the Father.

The Father, in His silent, unseen working, desires with strong longing to know His own, and to be known of them: and He cannot make Himself plain to them, except through the face of Christ Jesus, His Son. For that hour of Revelation all His vast creation travaileth and groaneth. And we—we hold it back: we let or hinder it: it is in our hands to bid the Revelation open: it is in our hands to suffer the Father to meet and embrace His children: it lies with us to allow the Word to come unto His own, to find and gather in all that the Father has patiently and laboriously drawn towards Him.

It is the Father Who cries to us out of the Eternal Silence in which He ever labours and hopes. He has laid His hands upon the multitude, shaping them for His Son: He has prepared the way. How? He has taught them the large hopes of brotherhood: He has instructed them to combine,—to hold by one another, to trust one another; and lo! He waits that we may interpret to them the secret of all fraternity, of all combination,— the secret of Jesus, in whom they may all become members one of another; of one Body, of one Spirit, of one Hope, one Lord: He has quickened their instincts, their sympathies, their aspirations, that, out of the sharpness of disappointment, out of the bitter and keen anxieties, out of the restless fears of impatience, they may be ready to know and receive the everlasting consolation of His dear Son; that they may understand the power of the Passion, the victory of His Cross, the peace of His Resurrection.

They groan in pain, toiling for no end, suffering without hope; shaken and tossed by the shocks and storms of a troublesome, tumultuous world; thrown up and down, from wealth to poverty, by laws which they cannot master, by accidents beyond their control, amid riches they may not share, though they know not why, in sight of endless plenty, which they may not touch; held in, and hedged, and confined by necessities which they never made, and in which they see no purpose nor benefit. Their children starve, yet they may not steal: diseases rack them, and miseries depress, yet none comes to succour, no man helps. How may they ever gain peace, and comfort, and belief, unless we will suffer the dear Lord of all consolation, the Man of Sorrows, the Prince of Life, to draw near to them, and touch, and heal?

Oh that we may not, by blind indifference, by careless sloth, hold Him back! Oh that we may help to let Him in, amid their streets, at their doors, to their beds of suffering and death: that He, through us, may see at last of the travail of His soul, and be glad.

SERMON XVII.

THE SWORD OF ST. MICHAEL.

"There was war in heaven: Michael and his angels fought against the Dragon."—Rev. xii. 7.

THE very exhaustiveness of the Gospel of Christ constitutes its chief peril. Its reach and scope are so large, that the lines of connection, which hold it fast into consistent unity, lose themselves, vanish, outspan our sight. We cannot follow them home, and are thus thrown back upon the one refuge for the baffled brain, —the use of paradox. Paradox is the expedient by which our thought expresses its sense, its intuition, its anticipation, of an underlying unity which it cannot thoroughly master or unravel. It detects the action of a single principle throughout a mass of dissimilar incidents. It sees too little to be able to exhibit the singleness of the principle amid all its variable and intricate transformations; but it sees enough to be sure, by some touch of living instinct, of the profound and dominant unity which all this intricacy makes manifest. And in order to give force and insistance to a truth which it cannot adequately express, it summons in the imagination to its aid,—it seizes on the two most extreme and contradictory of all the manifestations,—and, by the very act of placing them in startling neighbourhood the one to the other, it emphasizes their real, yet hidden, similarity.

Thus it is that the Christian faith revels in paradox. It delights in binding together in one statements apparently intense in their mutual opposition. The further it pushed its intellectual conquests, the more vivid and extreme became its sense of the power that lies in the recognition of paradox,—the more secure its confidence in the reconciliation of contradictions. Its deepest heart throbbed in response to the reverberant counter-song of the Creed of Athanasius: "Three who are Lord, yet but one Lord; three who are God, yet one God; three Almighty, yet one Almighty;" its whole soul rose to the great repudiation of Pelagius, as it cried, with the strong voice of St. Paul, "I live: yet not I, but Christ liveth in me;" for, indeed, in the pronouncement of these far-reaching oppositions, it felt itself in possession of that infinite truth which holdeth all in one, and stretcheth from end to end, and is never broken. It knew its power, and its triumphant glee could not conceal its victory, as it broke out in creed, or collect, or hymn: The Word of the Lord is a double-edged sword: it turneth this way and that.

But this double character has its natural danger. At the slightest weakening of the high tension which paradox expresses, we slide into the easier and lazier course of contenting ourselves with one or other of the opposing sides of our truth. This has been familiar enough in the history of heresy: perhaps it is hardly so familiar in the moral domain.

Yet that paradoxical character of the Christian creed, which has left its mark so forcibly upon its theology, is no less remarkable in its moral aspirations and development. There, too, Christ revealed, as embraced within the compass of a single principle, actions and effects of intensely opposite tendency: "Blessed are the hungry; they shall be filled." "Blessed are the meek; they shall inherit the earth." "He that loseth his life shall save it." "He that saveth his life shall lose it." So ran the startling message, and as men stood bewildered with vague awe at words so double-sided, they found themselves uplifted to the level of their solution by the impulse of a compelling faith in Him in Whom paradox attains its climax of astounding surprise, yet attains it without extravagance, without strain, without effort, without violence, in the perfect peace of assured fulfilment—in the ease and the quiet of a natural, an irresistible reconciliation. For, indeed, where was there to be found one trace of discordant contradiction in Him, Who was at once absolute Lord and absolute Servant of all; of Him Who lived that He might die, and died that He might live; of Him Who claimed the entire control and possession of our whole will, and heart, and soul, on the ground that He, and no one else, was meek, and lowly, and submissive; of Him Who obtained and demanded all glory, because He sought not His own glory; and could do all things that the Father doeth, because He could of His own self do nothing; of Him Who showed Himself Son of God by the perfection wherewith He proved Himself to be Son of Man?

There are two opposing sides, then, to the moral

character instilled by the graces of Christ, just as much as there is a double-sided opposition in the intellectual expression of the Godhead, revealed in Christ; and morally as well as intellectually, therefore, we have to guard against any one-sided development—against any jealous exaltation of a single factor of the opposition. Such partiality would be a moral heresy, however true its actual aim, however pure its aspiration; just as any attempt to ignore the counter-side of a theological position becomes intellectual heresy, however exact and genuine the actual statement itself may be. It is heretical not because it is wrong, but because it is partial, because it is deficient. Let us try to recall the double and Divine aspects of the Christian's spiritual manifestation, that so we may know more surely whether we stand at all in peril of such moral partiality, such moral heresy.

The Christian character, then, may be compared, on the one hand, to the leaven which leaveneth the whole lump; to the mustard-seed, which groweth no man knoweth how, until, from being the smallest, it increaseth to be the largest of herbs, and the birds can lodge in the branches thereof. Here is a familiar and most beautiful ideal! This secret, mysterious, unseen growth, by which, below all outward surfaces, beneath all form, and show, and fashion, in the hidden place, in the quiet chambers of the soul,—there, where no eye penetrates, no sound disturbs, no tumult disarrays, no vanity deceives,—there, where the roots and fibres of the spirit run back into the deep silence of God's awful presence, and drain from His dark founts their unnoticed supplies, and feed on His secret food, which He delivers, by hands invisible and unfelt, out of His own incomprehensible fulness,—there, where there is hushed and breathless stillness upon angel and archangel, as with open eyes they gaze on the Hiding of God's power, on that process of condescending love in the might of which God lowers Himself to secrecy and concealment, and is content to creep into our hearts through dark passages and overlooked ways, to creep as a thief in the night, under the cloud of shame and contempt, into the houses of our souls, whose doors we have barred and bolted against free and open entry, to creep as a thief, digging through the wall at an hour when no man knoweth, in mean disguise, with noiseless tread, unsuspected, unannounced, unforeseen,—there, at the dim base of our innermost being, where God waits in unspeaking patience to instil His grace, drop by drop, slowly and lengthily, into our graceless and unready minds;—this marvellous growth, by which God succeeds in pervading and penetrating our life by continual, unceasing effort, day by day and hour by hour, until at last He has won complete acceptance, and has moulded the whole man in us anew to His liking, and can move forward into fuller use, into nobler attainment; and can show out His Divine glory; and can make His presence felt and revealed; and can gather in new stuff to the work; and can spread, and enlarge, and increase, and break out on every side, so that the man becomes a living expression of God, a lump leavened through and through by the lively ferment of the infused Divinity; and men, his fellows, are startled to find themselves in the sudden neighbourhood of a Holy Thing; and all gifts, and joys, and pleasures discover themselves to be lodged within this outgrowth of God, as bright birds that live, and throb, and sing within the mustard-seed branches;—this marvellous and lovely growth, the blessed fruit of Christ's wonderful Incarnation, may well fill our hearts with amazement, and delight, and endless thanksgiving. Who, indeed, can ever tire of watching and telling all the beauty of the character formed on this ideal? Such a character, slowly built up, slowly perfected, inexplicable in its working, yet so obvious, so intelligible, so unmistakable in its action, captivates us by the very invisibility, the very mystery of its peculiar charm. We are in the company, let us say, of men or women, like ourselves,—such as move amid human circumstance, busy in our worldly business, amid the toils and sordid cares that eat away our souls,—of our household, or of our company. No lofty task, no immense and ennobling responsibility is laid upon them, but only the trivial round of daily things—the fretting littleness of unnoticeable anxieties. No halo glitters above their heads; no large and moving tragedies hedge them round with splendid sorrows. Nothing marks them out; nothing signifies their coming or their going. They make no prominent claims; they shrink from public gaze; they have, it may be, no position, no remarkable gifts, no ambitious expectations. Yet, as we look, as we watch, as we live with them, what breath is it of sweet, and strange, and unknown odours that steals from their souls to ours! What unearthly power is it that moves in their movements, and fills every look, every motion, with help, and wonder, and attraction, and comfort, and delight! What soft and holy grace is it that plays about their presence, and calms us when they are near, and draws us closer and closer to their confidence, to their intimacy, and quells rebellious imaginations, and speaks of peace, and of purity, and of every lovely thing! How helpful are their hands! how inexhaustible the deep sympathies in their eyes and in their hearts! How tender, and gracious, and lowly, and unselfish is all their activity! How full and rich the sound of their voices! How gladsome and cheering their entry! how dismal their going! And if sorrow strikes us, how surely our hearts turn to them! how confidingly we give ourselves up to their undoubted delicacy of touch! How prevailing, how persuasive, is their goodness! How blessed is their publishment of peace! Whence is it that they draw their strength? From what land of far delight do they bring good news of great joy to a world without them so comfortless, so unsatisfied, so dismaying! O blessed, thrice blessed, this secret working of Him Who hid His glory in a virgin's womb; of Him Who strove not, neither cried in the streets, and yet brought out judgment unto victory! "Is not this the carpenter's Son? the Son of Joseph and Mary? Whence, then, hath He this wisdom?" The Brother of James, and John, and Simon, and Judas? And His sisters—we know them—are they not still with us? Yet, verily, He is come down from Heaven. "He is the Bread of Heaven, the Living Bread, of which if any man eat, he shall not die, but have everlasting life!"

Here, then, is one side of the Christ-bearing character. It grows within the womb of flesh. It hides, it works in secret, in the night, when men sleep; slowly, invisibly, by degrees, it enlarges, it leavens the lump. But here begins the moral paradox. This very same character has another aspect,—takes an entirely different form. There are counter-pictures given us to that of the leaven. There is a world of imagery taken from light, from fire, from salt, from the sword, from the wedding, from things that flash, and glitter, and smite, and sting; and here, to-day, while still we stand within the light of Michaelmas, I cannot but single out that one supreme expression of this counter-ideal, which we yesterday commemorated. If we want to express the warrior-aspect of our spiritual life, we know no nobler, no more inspiring image than that of St. Michael, captain of the great hosts of the God of Sabaoth.

St. Michael! Prince of the Most High! Ah! our life, meek, gentle, hidden, as it may rightly be, has something in it of another fashion. It is not all secret, all mild, all subdued and submissive. This it is; but with this it has something more,—something utterly different. It has in it a touch of fire, a scent of flame. It has in it the tingling of loud trumpets, the ring of keen and quivering swords. The breath of St. Michael is astir within its heart, and his glory kindles upon its head. St. Michael! how strangely changed is our ideal from that on which we dwelt under the image of the leaven, or the mustard-seed! St. Michael, Prince and Captain! he it is now who leads and shapes our moral history. After him, we follow. In his name we stand enrolled. St. Michael! how he flashes as he moves! how swift the lightning of his flight! how terrible the shining of his eyes, and his sword, that leapeth as a living flame! Like the wind, he springs down from on high! he hurls his glory from the heights of heaven! He follows hard after him who fell as a star. He shoots along the sky; he smites like a thunderbolt; he pierces, he slays with every motion of his glittering spear! Who does not know him, hung as Raphael saw him, above the foe, whom, with one stroke of his passing wings—with one flying look of awful scorn—with one touch of his pointed steel, he has smitten into writhing and powerless ruin? Or who, indeed, can forbear to remember him whom Perugino painted with a deeper mind—him who stands, young, ruddy, strong, triumphant, girt with shining armour, belted and greaved, yet swift, ready, and at ease; with free, uncovered face, and the wind moving in his hair, as he waits with his hand upon sword and shield, in the pause between task and task, poised at rest in the evening stillness, before another day dawn, and his labours begin anew? How invincible the beauty of his mouth! how large and enduring the patience in his eyes! how quick, how generous, how radiant, how untiring his glorious service! He has done much; he has fought and won; but not yet is he weary. He looks round, after all his long labour, to see if there be not yet some deliverance that he might work before the night come. Call upon him, even now, and he will answer. Summon him, and he will save.

Such is St. Michael, Captain and Deliverer, swift,

sudden, irresistible; and in the light of his indarted splendour—in the glory of his coming—*evil* reveals the full horror of its naked and disgusting deformity. It no longer drapes itself in fair veils, nor pours round itself a concealing vapour of soft and melting delight. It is no longer that mixed, indefinite thing, of changing shape and shifting hues, which is so intricately intermingled with all that is good, and pure, and holy, that we know not where to lay our finger on it, or where to denounce it, or what to purge and uproot, and burn and destroy. No; it is driven, by that swift insight of the warrior angel, out of all shape and disguise. It knows the touch of that penetrating steel: it tumbles down into hideous confusion under the mastery of his eye. It creeps, and crawls, and writhes at his feet in its bare reality, a vile, brutal, base, and hateful thing,—a thing at which our gorge rises,—grotesque as Dante saw it, sickening, ugly, repulsive.

The Christian, then, is not only a penitent,—not only a sufferer,—not only a poor, and meek, and gentle slave of Christ: all this he is—all this, by the very law of his forgiveness—by the first principle of his deliverance out of sin into life—he must be. In all this, he begins. It is the root from which his whole being draws its succour of grace. It is the ground of all blessing: "Blessed are the poor in heart." It is the very secret of his call to Christ: "Come unto Me, all ye that labour and are heavy laden;" "Learn of Me, for I am meek and lowly of heart." Here are the foundations: here is the spring and source of all life. But the perfected Christian cannot rightly stop there:

he is to be a soldier as well as a sufferer. He carries a sword as well as a cross. He moves, indeed, with tears and shame; but he moves also with glee, with courage, with defiance. Not that the one character is inconsistent with the other: nor is the one to be pitted against the other. Neither of them discredits or repels the other: rather is it true that the one tends to produce the other. He who is perfected in meekness wins to himself the grace of force and courage. He who stoops discovers himself to be more than conqueror. He who bends himself to receive the humility and gentleness of the Spirit finds himself gifted with the sword of the Spirit. He who gives his back to the smiter is, by the powerful efficacy of that very act, girt round with the whole armour of God, with shield, and breastplate, and helm. Yes! in very weakness he is strong—strong by the high grace of Him Who reconciled both in one man; of Him Who, though He strove not, neither cried, yet had a voice of thunder, and a sword of flame, for Pharisee, and Sadducee, and Scribe; of Him Who, though He might be led as a lamb to the slaughter, and be dumb as a sheep under the shearer, yet uttered a cry of woe, and vengeance, and war, and judgment, not one whit less severe, not one whit less relentless, than the cry of the Baptist amid the rocks of Jordan: "Woe unto you, hypocrites! ye fools and blind! Woe unto you, ye serpents, ye generation of vipers! how can ye escape the damnation of hell?"

My brethren, beloved in the Lord! you [1] who have received, and you who hope to receive, the awful

[1] Preached to the members of the Clergy School, Leeds.

sanction of the priesthood, I want you to consider whether we of the Anglican ministry have been loyal to the full ideal of this double-sided character of Christ. One side, indeed, we probably have already, by prayer and aspiration, set before our souls, to be desired of God. The ideal of the leaven has never, in spite of all our terrible falls, failed to work and to gather in examples of its wondrous loveliness, in our English Church. Always there have been those whose ministry was found to possess that hidden force which works from within the secret chambers of the soul, and subtly penetrates on the right hand and on the left, in the dark night when no eye sees; that force which creeps like a tide, with noiseless motion, with unceasing advance, until men wake up astonished to find themselves encompassed by the wide waters of Divine and mysterious love. Meek, holy, pure, gentle, sacred souls, whose patience has had its reward, whose labour has hallowed the earth in God's Name, blessed are your lives, your services, your prayers! Blessed are ye, the salt of the Church! the light of all our day, the comfort of our eyes through dark hours, and dusty ways, and weary years of distress! So good, so true, so enticing has their high example been, that I need not stay to express what they have so richly taught. But we have still to ask ourselves the further question, we have yet to remember the counter-side of the Christian paradox: Have we, as a ministry—have we, as individual ministers—had enough of the spirit of St. Michael in our moral life? in our moral ideal? I want you to ask yourselves this question, each in the way he knows best. Have we, as a priesthood, in the history behind us, shone in upon the dark and cruel habitations of this world with the sudden glory of deliverance? Have we flashed in, with the splendour of the warrior angel, to succour the oppressed? to bid the captive go free? We have spoken of peace —well enough; but have we sold our coat to buy a sword? Have we avenged the heathen, and rebuked the people? Have we bound their kings in chains, or their nobles with links of iron? The praises of God have been in our mouths; but has there been a two-edged sword of the Spirit in our hands? Where has been the Helm of salvation? where the spear of St. Michael? We have toiled for the relief of the poor and the unhappy; but have we toiled for their release, for their deliverance, for their enfranchisement? We have comforted; but have we set free? Have we broken bonds in sunder? Have we thrown open the cruel gates of brass? We have pleaded; but have we denounced? We have listened in the secret chambers; but have we proclaimed upon the housetops? We have moved with the still secrecy of the wind; but have we leaped with the power of the flame? We have refreshed with cool waters; but have we run and kindled, as a fire? And yet, if not, why not? Has there been no need? Is there no need *now?* Ah, my friends, we know too well to our bitter shame what it is in the midst of which we stand!—we, who have seen and touched, however briefly, the wild life that rages up and down the crowded and reeking streets of our vast cities,—the cruelties, the brutalities that rend and tear; the wicked selfishness, the heartless indifference, that deaden, and corrupt, and blind; the sensuality that devours; the gambling that maddens; the pride that tramples; the ambition that slaughters; the violence that tyrannizes; the covetousness that feeds on blood; the loathsome diseases of the soul, that sicken, and debase, and kill. We know the sins, large, and gross, and vile, not of individuals, but of *classes*. We know the villanies which society perpetrates in the mass,—villanies at which any single member of society would shudder with horror, We know the enormous evils of mere heedlessness in wealth, of mere carelessness in luxury, of mere recklessness in commerce. We know how whole masses are driven under by the mere pressure of competition—driven down into that dark and tyrannous domain of ignorance or crime, of drink or lust. We know how herds of men and women are shoved and huddled along the hard roads of a dreary world, without hope, without light, without comfort, without grace, without God. We know how many souls lie shut up in dull and dumb despair, whom the sickness of doubt has troubled, and discoloured, and withered. All this we see with fearful eyes and failing hearts. We know it but too well. No need for St. Michael! Oh, when was the need more sore? when was the cry for help more loud and dreadful? The Church has her task clear and decisive before her —the task not only to work within the heart of all this trouble in the gracious activities of consolation; but more than this—in complete consistency with this inward work—to come down from above as a deliverer; to break in as the day-spring from on high. Men who lie, bound with chains, between soldiers, ought to feel her shine in their prison as an angel, as she smites them on the side, and raises them up, bidding them rise up quickly, so that the chains fall off from their hands. The Church has her high task of emancipation. But how has she fulfilled it? Do men, who lie in sore need, in oppression, in social degradation, look to the Church—look to us, her priests, to be to them as their St. Michael—to save and deliver? Do men, in the pride of selfish power—in the lust of reckless success—fear the Church or fear her priests? Do they hear her loud judgments—her swift denunciations? Do they feel her victorious spear, as Satan feels the onset of St. Michael? Does her sword smite? Are the vast sins of society seen, and detected, and condemned by the glory of her eyes? Are they devoured by the flame of her wrath?

My brethren, these are no idle questions. They search, they pierce; they may not be gainsaid. I know not whether, at this hour of England's life, there are to be found for us ministers of the Church questions more urgent or more imperative.

The history of the days behind us is not without shame. It is for us to retrieve, by God's grace, before it is too late, the things that have been lacking. A whole society is remaking itself. The life of an entire people is shifting and resetting its assumptions, its habits, its landmarks. We cannot stand outside: we may not shrink from touching the large issues of social order. It is our duty, as it is no one else's, to assert the widening of the range of righteousness—the advance of sweet and comfortable light; to denounce and condemn unsparingly the cynical idleness that despairs of bettering the world's order. We, who have before our eyes the vision of a new heaven and a new earth, may never pronounce the old sufficient—may never be contented with a partial equity—may never rest satisfied while one soul languishes in unworthy fetters, while one heart withers under beclouded and unseemly skies.

O my God—God of the spirits of all flesh—pour down upon us, together with the holiness of priests, the power and inspiration of prophets! Alas! we have lost our heart of grace! we have sinned away our life of hope! We have not dared to clamour for the entire removal out of the earth of evil, and misery, and wrong. We have not, with our whole souls, believed in the war by which Michael and his angels cast utterly out of heaven that old serpent, the Devil.

Oh remember not, we beseech Thee, our old sins! But send down Thy Holy Spirit to fill us more full with the Spirit of Him Whose eyes are as a flame of fire, and on His head are many crowns, and out of His mouth a sharp sword goeth—of Him Who in righteousness doth judge and make war, and Whose Name is faithful and true: the Word of God, King of kings and Lord of lords!

Enlighten our eyes, that we may see the sins that encompass our days. Inflame our courage, that we may without fear denounce what Thy light has made manifest. Draw us out of the easy paths of acquiescence—out of the chill shadows of distrust. Compel us to speak and act with a larger mind and a loftier purpose, that we may boldly rebuke vice and patiently suffer for Thy truth's sake, and so prepare a people for Thy coming, O dear Lord, Who tarriest long, but to Whom the Spirit and the Bride must for ever say, Come! and let him that thirsteth say, Come! Even so, come, Lord Jesus.

SERMON XVIII.

THE KINGDOM OF RIGHTEOUSNESS.

" Are your minds set upon righteousness, O ye congregation: and do ye judge the thing that is right, O ye sons of men."—Ps. lviii. 1.

WE have learned much, in our day, of all that world of spiritual interests, which lies, secreted, within and behind the veil of outward things.

Behind that busy turmoil of superficial life which meets the eye, behind its loud noises, and its fair show, behind its vulgar commonplaces, there move, and stir— (we know once more by a thousand vivid proofs, by voices within and without)—strong and momentous forces, powers, and passions, and desires. These are awake once more: we see men and women impelled, and swayed, and mastered by these invisible influences: we ourselves know, thanks to God, something of this spiritual stress.

It is a religious revival. We have become alive to unseen movements: we are sensitive to the touch of religious emotions: the deep pathos of human life affects us, as it never affected our fathers: its cravings, its intentions, its possibilities, its infinities, its mysteries, its despairs—all these have become familiar, and intelligible: and so fast as these are felt and understood, we have moved out of the land of sight into the land of faith. We know now the barrenness of the present, and the tangible: we have passed under the pressure of the Unseen, and the Eternal: and so there has sprung up out of the ground of passion, watered by tearful sorrows, the flower of Spiritual Faith,—Faith, which is the discovery of the inner powers of Spirit,—Faith, which is the act with which the Spirit, in the joy of that self-discovery, severs itself from all that is without, frees itself, detaches itself, and enters on its own life, holding its life within itself. In Faith, the Spirit comes to itself; it holds revealed within itself, within that world which is its own, a new order of being, a new region of emotion, of which it enters into possession,—a region withdrawn from all the rough handling of the flesh, beyond the touch of worldly weapons,—a region unearthly, unseen, that fadeth not away, within which a great drama is everlastingly enacted; a drama, crowded with incident, rich with passionate hopes and fears, awful in its issues; a drama which no eye sees, nor ear hears, yet a drama, real, incessant, exciting, absorbing, the Drama of Spiritual Salvation.

This drama has once more in our generation been felt in all its thrilling intensity; and hence, there has been in our midst this wonderful revival of worship. Following with our hearts that momentous action, by which the world is lost and saved, we have known once more the strange motions of spirit, which to the outside eye seem so extravagant, so fanciful,—the rapture of praise, the absorption of prayer, the joys of contemplation, the outpour of song, the living flame of adoration, the prostration of penitence. This we have known; and, with it, came the inevitable sense of communion, of a common effort, and a common interest, of united participation in a single action, the redemption of all in the one Lord. The spiritual life is no lonely, isolated thing, no solitary possession, but a citizenship in a spiritual country: we are admitted members of an immense company, of a new race, of a single body: and our worship, therefore, which should give spiritual expression to the new conditions into which we had entered, must be united, must be the action of the entire body.

So it was, through the needs of common worship, that we rediscovered and revived the reality of the Catholic Church: and this Church, again, as the home of spiritual aspiration, and of the free spontaneity of faith, must have that detachment from earthly things, that freedom, that inner self-possession, which is the peculiar gift of faith. By faith, spirit shows its self-mastery, its self-completeness, its independence of local tie, or circumstance, or external accident: and the Holy Church, built without hands, the spiritual home that faith inhabits, must, so we have slowly learned, be also self-complete, self-mastered, with a life, and substance, and reality of its own, independent of circumstance, capable of free detachment from all temporal and earthly conditions.

We praise God for all we have gained.

But let me ask you whether we have not yet to make another step.

The spirit comes to itself in faith; but does it keep

to itself? Is it of the nature of spirit to remain detached and withdrawn, severed from earthly circumstance, self-possessed, and self-contented? Does it abandon to its own ways and works that outer world, from the bonds and cravings of which it has joyfully severed itself?

Nay! Spirit is always, by the very essence of its being, an activity, a movement, a quickening power. It cannot exist at all without issuing in act, in motion; wherever it is, it is felt abroad as a wind, strong and masterful, under the pressure of which we see the reeds shake, and the trees bend and bow, and the waters curl and roll: it is felt, sudden and alive, like a flame, under the touch of which things stir, and change, and melt, and kindle, and start, and quiver, and shine. Spirit is a power; and in coming to itself, it has discovered the secret of its power: in finding itself, it has gained an increase of force: in freeing itself from the rule and limit of outward things, it has won to itself new activities, new capacities, new domination. It is more alive than before; and it makes manifest its increase of life by the power which goes out from it; the power of the wind, and of the fire.

Spirit never lives shut up within its own secret pleasure-house, nursing its own musings. It is always a force: if it fails to find scope for action, it loses strength, it wanes. Spiritual emotion cannot sustain itself, unless it become more than an emotion; for spirit holds within it the power to will, its life lies in the free exercise of will; and a will must act, or die. And spirit, too, is love; and love must ever be seeking occasion to show itself, to pour out its gifts, to put itself to use, to carry help: kept to itself, then, unused and ineffective, the love, that is the heart of spirit, withers, and faints.

A revival of spiritual emotion, then, must of necessity involve a revival of spiritual activity. The spirit that is sought and won in the hidden chamber must make itself manifest on the housetops. The spiritual secret that is whispered in darkness must inevitably utter its cry in the broad daylight, must make itself heard in the crowded streets.

This is the law of its life; to win its power from the Father Which seeth in secret, but to exhibit that power in victorious sovereignty over this earth, that our eyes see, and our hands handle.

If spirit is present in our midst, then virtue must go out from it; the thrill of its presence cannot be restrained; it will make itself felt out and beyond the very skirts of its clothing in sudden motions, in marvellous efficacies, in electric touches, in healing breaths. This poor earth of ours, bound over in bondage to Satan, worn and weary with ancient evils and the burden of intolerable wrongs, has but to draw near to this new power, and lay its finger on the hem of the garment, and lo! the change has passed over it, the mystery of iniquity is loosed: it knows within itself that it has been made whole!

If it be true, then, that no revival of spiritual life can be real and enduring from which virtue does not go out, to better the world's estate, to unloose its sins, to banish its sadness; and if, as we discovered in the region of worship, spiritual life is, always, no isolated, individual matter, but a movement of many souls, a movement that knits men together, and spreads by sympathy, and gathers heart by gathering masses, and works and grows in companionship; and that the needs of perfect adoration are fulfilled only in the united movement of the Catholic Church, of the Body of Christ: if so, then must this *social* character belong, also and as much, to the correspondent activity of spirit, of which we now speak, this activity of the wind and of the fire, with which spirit issues out, in power to redeem and renew the earth. If the Church be necessary to the perfection of worship, then is it also necessary to the fulfilment of righteousness. If our spirits cannot mount upward with strength, and persistence, and courage, until they have been embraced and unfolded by the upward motion of a whole spiritual society, then neither can they move outward in acts of truth, and purity, and love, unless that same society be about them and around them, to sustain and encourage, to nourish, and enlarge, and enlighten.

My brethren, Christ our Lord, as He stood upon our earth, found Himself in face of no casual and isolated fragments of evil. What He saw and met was a vast, and ancient, and weighty dominion, huge with gathered stores of sin, strong with interlacing bonds, knit tight and fast by link upon link, by tie of blood, by touches of hideous sympathy, by dire kinship, and hateful affinity—welded and soldered by the strokes of heavy centuries into a single, solid, compact, and enduring mass—*the kingdom of evil*, moving in steady persistence under

The Kingdom of Righteousness. 277

captaincies, and principalities, and powers: and what He strove, even unto blood, to raise up over against it, was a massive movement of concentrated energies, all working together, with one heart and one spirit, one law, one hope, one baptism, pledged one and all to loyal companionship, bound up into the powerful unity of a single organic frame, a body of faithful men set upon fulfilling righteousness, a society for well-doing, a Holy Church, whose very breath, and life, and being should be instinct with goodness, and temperance, and kindness, and purity, and love—a kingdom of God, offering to sin a counter-force as united as its own, as multitudinous, as entire—a kingdom of God which should not struggle, and sink, and struggle again in rare and solitary efforts of moral heroism, at loose intervals, in disappointing disorder: nay! but a dominion that should stand, and not fail—should grow, and increase, and gather force—should withstand the shock of disaster, the battering of the hostile years, the fall of kings, the uncertain shiftings of the peoples—should slowly and painfully raise its fabric of holy living, line by line, and stone by stone,—a dominion with the strength of the everlasting hills, a kingdom that should have no end, against which the gates of hell, with all their ordered and marshalled hosts, should never prevail.

So He planned: and where but in this Divine plan do we find the secret of that victorious joy, that burned like fire within the heart of the early Church? What was the blessed change that then came over men? Was it that there had never been, before Christ, any heroic striving after righteousness, any superb hatred of wrong? Nay, there had been much, much most high and fair. But each effort had been as the unavailing battling of some breathless swimmer against the loud inrush of the buffeting waves. He may struggle, but he must sink at last, and he knows it! Alone and desperate, this and that noble soul strove to retain some white purity of heart, some sweet touch of gentle peace; but higher and higher the great floods rose, the floods of foul imaginations; fiercer beat and roared the storm of malice, and cruelty, and all uncharitableness. The entire set of the world was against him. It was rushing down into ruin: no strong hand or wary foot could stay the headlong fall. So such men had felt, and fainted, and fallen: and lo! now, not in pitiful loneliness, but in inspiring unity of hope, a whole brotherhood are about them, pledged to pure living, pledged to undo wrong; an entire society surrounds them, with the warmth, and glow, and fervour of a crowd, all swayed by the one high motive, all moving, hand in hand, towards one aim, all thrilled by one expectation, the enthusiasm for right.

The Greek philosopher, who set himself to hold his own soul in purity and peace at any cost, felt himself to be (so he tells us) as one who, in a wild tempest of sleet and hail, crouches behind a wall, content if he may but keep himself, at least, dry while the storm swept by. So it had been: but these Christians crouch no longer: out from behind their sheltering walls they come to find themselves, boldly and in broad day, dreaming of new possibilities altogether,—of whole multitudes knit into the endeavour after good, into the

Body of Christ; of a society in which holiness should be the law, and purity the possession; of a society which should begin to make manifest, even now among men, the blessed peace of that new heaven and new earth, wherein dwelleth righteousness.[1]

My brethren, is this so? What have we done with this splendid hope? We have learned something of the power of united worship: but what have we used of this power of united well-doing? The Church cannot, indeed, stand out from the Christianized civilization, in the vivid contrast with which, in those early days, it rose up from out of a dark Pagan society. But we still must most anxiously ask, how far does it gather into itself, and concentrate into a single effort, the movements that, in our day, make for righteousness, the movements that make against wrong?

How far does it make itself felt, as a body of constant well-doing and pure living, throwing itself, with the weight and momentum of a solid and single mass, into the cause of justice, and mercy, and uprightness?

How far does it devote its splendid heritage of tradition, and position, and wealth, to the loosening of iniquitous bonds, to the lifting of burdens, to the bettering of the crushed, and the outcast, and the forsaken?

And to bring the question nearer home to each separate soul, let us seriously ask ourselves, one and all:

Are we at all sure to find that, as we pass from out of the talk and company of the ordinary world into the society of Churchmen, we have changed at all, for the better, the moral atmosphere that we breathe?

[1] *Cf.* Church Gifts of Civilization, pp. 147-207.

Are we sensible, always, that we have stepped across a line, inside which there is a sweeter air, and cleaner ways, touches of a higher peace and of a fairer tenderness—touches that soothe our feverish hearts, and smoothe down our ruffled petulance, and cheer our troubled gloom, and scatter our beclouded tempers? Do we find a better, brighter life about us?

I would not have us forget, indeed, the examples of helpful and devoted work, that each of us can, praise be to God! easily recall; but how personal, how lonely, how separate, how fragmentary have they been! Each man has been left to struggle, as he may, almost as heavily over-matched as if he were back in some huge old-world civilization.

And those larger movements and agitations that have set themselves to remove injustice, or clear a new space free from base encumbrances, for goodness, and fair living—the very movements, which a National Church exists to inaugurate, and make possible—well! how perilously have we left them to others to achieve; others who, as often as not, owe no conscious loyalty to Him Who died to found, in His Blood, a kingdom of uprightness: died to loose the prisoners out of captivity, to give sight to the blind, and speech to the dumb, and life to the dead, to bring in the great and acceptable year.

As we speak with devout Church-men or women, does the higher man in us, that is stifled and choked by the dusty turmoil of the world,—does it wake up, as if by magic? does it bestir itself to nobler dreams? does it recall its best hours of enkindling aspiration?

The Kingdom of Righteousness. 281

Does it freshen, and brighten, as the sea under breeze and sun? Is it natural to us, in their presence, under their eyes, to speak of righteousness, to denounce the cruelty of evil-doings, to scheme for justice to the injured, and for comfort to the suffering? Is it easier, with them than with others, to pour out our compassion for the weary and heavy-laden? Easier to believe that the poor shall not always be forsaken, that the patient abiding of the meek shall not perish for ever? Easier to believe that man shall not always have the upper hand, that verily there is a God that judgeth the earth? Are we, when with them, as in a home of hallowed grace, secure of sympathy with all high appeals, all splendid endeavours,—the quick, eager sympathy, that is sure to flow out of the hearts of those who hunger and thirst after the kingdom of righteousness?

Ah! surely, these questions are searching, are humbling! How little security have we that those who have knelt praying together with us in the Church of God, will not, in deed and speech, outside the church door, take upon them the lower tone of cynical indifference to public wrong, will not give the pitiful shrug of easy disbelief; when possibilities of fairer days are opening upon the tired earth, will not drop from their lips the light scoff, the sharp sneer, at those who dream of a purer justice, of a larger freedom,—dream of undoing oppression, and of curbing sin!

And is it only of others that we have to sorrowfully complain? Alas! why, then, are we, each of us, so pitifully conscious of cramped enthusiasms, of half-hearted beliefs? How little of prophetic fury is there about us! How passive, how indifferent, how unstirred we remain, while huge sins walk abroad, and the earth is full of cruel habitation! What evils are there that shrink before our indignation? What wrongs are there that dread our loud outcry? What low and base ambitions are there that creep off abashed when we are near? What worldly man feels uncomfortable in our presence? Why is it, that no rebuke, no repugnance, goes out from our very being against iniquity? Why do sins flourish so close to us, without fear, and without scruple? Something is wrong. We pray, we know spiritual hopes and joys: we are far more alive than many men about us to religious emotions and religious inspirations. Why is it, then, that we are not equally conscious of a purer moral tone than they, of a more delicate sense of right, of a nobler, and more victorious wrath?

My brethren: such questions, however humiliating, are profitless, unless we can win some answer to them. I can but attempt one slight answer to-night.

Our individual weakness is, surely, due to our isolation. We do not hold our moral life as a debt due to the Church; we do not work righteousness as members of a corporation, of a body pledged to holy living. Alone, and fearing the terrific odds that are against us, no wonder that we faint, and quail.

But if there were about us a large and rushing movement towards God—the pressure of multitudes, the fervour of a crowd: if there stood about us a fair brotherhood, bound to this high chivalry, warring for the right,—ah!' *then* there would be nothing we could not hope to achieve!

Why, then, is there so little of such movement?

Because each struggler strives alone, unconscious of his responsibilities, of the call that is on him to bear his share in creating such a mighty moving of the waters.

Dear people, in working out salvation we are working for others: for we are members of a body—which suffers or gains as a whole, according as each member loses or sins.

All these our brothers, each in his lonely strife against sin and wrong, look for our support, look for encouragement from our companionship: and, when we fall, when we yield to the seductive influences of lust, or vanity, or sloth, or moral doubt, we not only outrage God's honour, not only defile the temple of the Holy One, but, also, we fail our brother in his need; we sin against the Body of Christ; we lower its tone, we degrade its office, we decrease its efficiency for good; we obstruct its life. Each sinner about or near us misses from us, who have so sadly betrayed our trust, the rebuke that might have stirred, and saved: each penitent struggles, through our sin, under a blinder weight, under a direr burden of evil: each saint who thirsted for sympathy in his agony, fights a harder battle, suffers from more grievous infirmities, because we have brought him no help, because our lives carry with them no power of inspiration, no fire of love.

We owe it to them, we owe it to all, that our minds should be set on righteousness.

Remember it! remember that it is for others, that we wrestle and pray! Remember it, when the dark hours hide us from all eyes! when loneliness at once weakens the will, and empowers the temptation! *Alone* we fight! Yes! but others will feel, and know, the issue of that conflict!

Others, toiling, striving, suffering as we, will catch from us in the day to come, some touch of tender, helpful comfort, if now, in the hour of trial, we hold fast to God and to holiness.

Others—if we loose our grasp on purity and goodness now—others will look to us from out of their sad bitterness of soul, from out of their broken endeavours —and will look in vain! No virtue will go out from us! No fountain of living water will spring up to refresh their hot lips! The hem of our garment will bring with it no blessing, no power to heal and save!

We fight not for ourselves alone. These are they— our brethren—the cloud wherewith we walk encompassed: it is for them that we wrestle through the long night: they count on the strength that we might bring them, if we so wrestle that we prevail. The morning that follows the night of our lonely trial would, if we be faithful, find us new men, with a new name of help, and of promise, and of comfort, in the memory of which others would endure bravely, and fight as we had fought.

Oh, turn to God in fear, lest, through hidden disloyalty, we have not a cup of cold water to give those who turn to us for succour in their sore need!

SERMON XIX.

THE PRUNING OF THE VINE.

"I am the true Vine, and My Father is the Husbandman: every branch in Me that beareth not fruit He taketh away, and every branch that beareth fruit, He purgeth it that it may bring forth more fruit."—
ST. JOHN xv. 1-2.

OUR Lord has many offices, and gives Himself many names. He is the supreme Lawgiver, the unique authority; and, as such, He names Himself the Door, the narrow, but one and universal Passage, by Whom all must enter who would come into the peace of secure allegiance to God.

He is the King; and, as such, He names Himself the Good Shepherd, Who shepherds His flock with undoubted devotion, and is followed hither and thither with unwavering loyalty by the happy sheep who are known of Him by name, to the pastures of delightful tranquillity, and by the ever-flowing waters of ceaseless content.

He is the Saviour, the Deliverer; and so names Himself the great Physician, Who will heal the broken-hearted, and bring health to them that are sick and at the point to die: yea, even though they were dead, yet shall they live, for verily, He is the Resurrection, and the Life, Whose voice the very dead shall hear, and they that hear shall live for evermore.

He is the Revealer, the Truth; and so names Himself the Light, in Whom men recognise the reality of all their works, and of all their high imaginings, and of all their longing aspirations, and to Whose blessed Light they press forward that their deeds may be made manifest that they have been wrought in God.

He is the Son of Man, Whom God has sealed to be His one and only Minister, His sole Servant; and so pronounces Himself to be to all humanity the very Bread of Life, the Flesh and the Blood, by sharing in Which mankind lays hold of eternal sustenance, and will be raised again, body and soul, complete and transfigured, at the Tremendous Day.

All this He is, and much more; and, under every figure, we seize some glimpse of our many-sided relationship to our Master and Lord, and we bless Him that gave, and we rejoice in what we receive.

But now, when the last hours of the Lord's life are hurrying to their close, and the tenderest, nearest familiarity of the last sweet converse between the Master and those whom He now deigns to call His friends, is attained:

Now, when all evil has been sifted, and purged, and cleansed, and he who received the sop has gone out into the night, and they who remain have been washed and sanctified every whit:

Now, when the Lord's heart pours out its most impassioned utterance, its most secret love, over the souls of those with whom He sits as He shall sit no more for ever, in the pure intimacy of human-kindness:

Now, at the close of that memorial hour, that unforgotten feast, into which our Lord pressed all the fulness and the wonder of the crowning memories which would hereafter fix and hold the prevailing and imperishable remembrance of Him among men until His coming again :

Now, as He stands amid His chosen, His beloved, His own, with, it may be, the very cup in His hands, which but now He had blessed, and uplifted, and enriched with the Promise of that atoning Blood which He was to carry for ever from henceforth into the Holiest of Holies, before the Eyes of the Most High :

Now, He Who is, to the Church of His love, the Lord of all her innermost life, has one figure more in which to embody that hidden, unceasing, continuous intimacy of union which would, for ever and ever, draw faster and closer to Himself the souls of those who had passed, by the power of His great Sacrifice, within the secret place of His love; within the circle of His Church's perfecting grace; within that upper chamber in which for ever the Lord Jesus comes, and moves, and shows Himself, and sits at meat, and passes in and out, and breathes perpetual blessing, and shows His hands and His side, and takes the cup, and gives thanks, and gives to them whom He has sanctified, and is known in the breaking of bread.

This is the familiar intimacy which He is now sealing by His last parting words, and out of the midst of which He speaks the parable of its mysterious laws, " I am the Vine, the very and only Vine, and My Father is the Husbandman. I am the Vine, and ye are the branches. Abide in Me, for without Me ye can do nothing."

"Abide in Me."

When our Lord is describing the first activity of Faith in Him, He has another metaphor, "Come unto Me." "He that cometh unto Me shall have everlasting life."

Faith begins, for man, in an act of approach. It is true such a coming can only be by virtue of God's prevenient action: all those who come are already given of God; it is the power of that gift which moves men to come; no man comes, unless God the Father draws him. Faith is a gift; it presupposes an activity on God's side: but man has still his part to play; he, too, is to be active; he, too, is a living motive-power; he has, by his own exertion, to make that act of approach which God's precedent gift of his soul to Christ has made possible. He has still to throw his own personal energy into the needful belief: he has to come, to draw near, to the life; and such coming is fulfilled when the soul has drawn so near that it can put out its hand and receive the very life that it desires; when it can feed on it, as it can on bread; when it can eat of the very Flesh, and drink of the very Blood of Him on Whom it believes. This act of eating is the crown and culmination of the act of approach. That activity of the man's free-will, which was begun in the energy by which he set himself in motion to come to the life, is continued in the energy by which he sets himself to eat and to drink of this most marvellous Food.

But the final act by which Faith attains the end of its approach, and is knit to that to which it was drawing near, and touches, and handles, and receives, and is made one with, that which, by its charm, draws the soul towards it from afar—this act, however vital, and crucial, and essential, does not close the history of faith; man cannot now fall back into idleness, or security, because his faith has at last touched its goal. That goal is the Living Personality of Christ, the Son of the Most High: it is an eternal Fount of endless and infinite Life. He who has so terminated his approach, finds himself encircled by a power of inexhaustible grace and strength, in the might of whose everlasting glory he may for ever and ever be quickened by undying fires, and renewed, and replenished, and reinvigorated by the ever-new and ever-increasing splendour of a life that can never fade, or diminish, or slacken, or fail. His faith, therefore, finds itself pledged to a new trial, to a new task: it has succeeded in coming; will it succeed in abiding? To abide; to cling and adhere; to sustain the contact; to keep the grasp firm and sure; to hold fast through all shocks of circumstance; to keep open all the passages, that the life-influences may pass in and out freely—this is now the work of the faith which has once entered into Christ. The man has passed within the action of his Lord's Personality: he has partaken of His substance: he has been included in His Body: this is his astounding privilege. But still he may not rest, may not be content, may not trust to this achievement. He must even yet put out all his force of faith in order to retain the position that he has won. He must be himself in full activity, if he is to *abide* in the Body. His faith must put to use all its ties and bonds of persistent devotion, if it is to hold

T

its place. The Twelve who listened on that parting night had indeed been made branches of the perfect Vine: they had been chosen, and taken, and grafted in; they were, even then, alive with Christ's life, instinct with His grace, held fast in His Heart, made clean, and sanctified through the Truth; and yet He has still to insist, with anxious and loving entreaty, "Abide in Me, as I in you." "Abide! Let nothing slacken; let no effort fail; let no energies run down. As the branch cannot bear fruit of itself except it abide in the vine; no more can ye, except ye abide in Me." "He that abideth in Me, he it is, and he only, who will bring forth fruit." And then the earnest beseeching to abide unfolds the two strong cords by which their souls will bind themselves to Him with the irrevocable strength of the Eternal God: (1) "Love," the unfailing force that knits two souls in one—this is the band that will never break. Let their love be living and vigorous, as the love that binds the Father to the Son, and then they will surely abide. "As the Father hath loved Me, so have I loved you: abide in this My love." And (2) love that binds, tends also to assimilate: it reproduces its own likeness: therefore, by loving Christ, they will be like Him; they will become fashioned into His resemblance—into the similitude of His love; they will obey His inspiration; they will keep His commandments: "If ye keep My commandments, ye shall abide in My love; yea, even as I have kept the Father's commandments, and abide in His love." "Ye are My friends, whom I love, and who love Me, if ye do whatsoever I command you."

And bound by these two cords of love and likeness into an abiding unity with Christ, they will retain a permanent and undiminishing gladness of soul: "These things have I spoken unto you, that My joy—the joy that belongs to the unshaken unity of the Father and the Son—may abide in you; and that this your joy may be full."

And, in the might of this abiding hold on Christ, they shall have power with God; their prayers shall prevail before Him. "For if ye abide in Me, and My words abide in you, ye shall ask what ye will, and it shall be done unto you."

And yet more: the permanence which belongs to their own fidelity to Him Who is their continual life, will pass out from them into the very work that they will do in its strength. Not only will he, who abideth, bring forth much fruit, but the fruit itself will abide, and not wither: for that choice of Christ, which, by love and righteousness, they hold fast with unswerving vigour, has "ordained them that they should go and bring forth fruit, and that their fruit should abide."

All this is theirs, if only they abide; if only their faith continues to cling; if only it fail not to preserve the life-giving unity. But for this they must not be idle: yea, for this the power of the Father must be called in, must be secured, so urgent is the need, so real the peril: and so Christ prays, in that last great prayer in the strength of which His true Church stands to this hour, "O Holy Father, keep"—not only bring, but keep—"through Thine own Name those whom Thou hast given Me, that they may be one, even as we are one,

While I was with them, I kept them in Thy Name:" "Those whom Thou gavest Me I have kept, and lost none, but the son of perdition. I pray Thee now, that, as I once kept, so Thou, Father, wouldst keep them from the evil of the world."

So anxiously did our Lord entreat His friends to hold fast to the union with Him to which they had attained: so earnestly did He call on the Father to continue His fostering care, to guard and shield the gift that He had given. "Keep them, Holy Father! keep them, that they may abide in Me!"

And two pictures are given us, that admit us still further to an insight into the Father's action upon those whom Christ has once chosen.

They are chosen, and ordained to abide, in order that they may bring forth fruit. This is the point to which, above all, the Father looks. "Herein is My Father glorified, that ye bear much fruit." The Father is the husbandman: His whole care, His whole hope, is to find fruit. This is the terror of the Father's face, that He, the Holy, looks for the holy; He, the Righteous, seeks for worshippers, those who are such as He is; He, the Life-Giver, looks for those who can give life! Nothing imperfect, nothing sterile can abide before Him. The whole energy of His eternal love spends itself in the tremendous effort to form, and retain, and enjoy the image of itself, the likeness of its own loveliness. This, and this only, can content it, can satisfy it, can satiate its conscious yearnings. For this He has given His Son: for this He has planted His vine, and digged His winepress, and built His watch-tower: for this

The Pruning of the Vine.

He laboureth hitherto, from the foundation of the world: He seeketh the fruit; the fruit of His long travail; the fruit of all His husbandry. Nothing short of this!

And, therefore, surely, it is that Christ insists so persistently on His "abide in Me." "Abide; for without abiding ye will bring forth no fruit." It is not enough to be merely grafted in; fruit must be found upon us, or else the Father will have spent His labour in vain. Abide, then, abide in the Vine, for there is much to be done—much that requires time, and patience, and waiting. Fruit is long in coming: it is slowly matured: it has many long hours to pass before it ripen. Abide, then; cling fast; hold yourself close; keep on the grasp of faith without fail, without slackening.

For there is no exception, no escape. The Father will one day look for His reward: He will seek for the one thing needful; and every branch, every single branch, that beareth not fruit, "He taketh away!" That is His rule, His constant, unvarying practice: "He taketh that barren branch away!" And what happens to such dry and broken fragments we know well, our very experience tells us, it is an inevitable fact, "Men gather them, and cast them into the fire, and they are burned."

Most terrible, most horrible! To have once been in the Vine; to have been ingrafted within Christ; to have had His life working through us; to have been knit up into the unity of His Immortal Humanity, quickened by His Spirit, fed with His Blood, upheld by the power of His living Body.

And, then, to have let the flow of grace slacken; to

have dropped our energies; to have suffered our faith to loosen its hold, to deaden, and sink, and fall back; to have allowed the slow torpor of sloth to creep over us, the feeble weakness of forgetfulness to sap our strength; to have seen hope, and spring, and joy, and aspiration die away out of our hearts, like sunlight out of an evening sky, until a coldness, a chilling whisper has crept round the dull chambers of the soul, and has told us that warmth had finally fled, that the day was over, that night had come; to have ceased to strive; to have folded our hands; to have closed our eyes; to have remembered no more the inspirations that once summoned us to action; to have been content with the lower level, with the weaker effort, until effort itself has become impossible, and each lower standard is deserted for one still poorer, and principles grow vague, and shifty, and indecisive: to see dimly what once we saw clear, and feel feebly what once stirred us like a trumpet, and hear no more the voice of God in the Garden, nor ever again rise from our bed to listen for the far sounds of Christ's chariot wheels, nor catch any more the cry through the night of the Spirit and the Bride who wait for the coming:—this is the incredible thing! Yet this is what *may* befall us! Yes; we all know it: we all have shuddered to find suddenly within us the beginning of what would have such an end! This is that against which our Lord warned and prayed on His last night. This is that fruitlessness of which He records the terrific close: "If a man abide not in Me, he is cast forth as a branch, and is withered; and men gather them, and cast them into the fire, and they are burned."

But it is not on a prospect such as this that I would fix your eyes this morning.[1] We are here in hope, and joy, and thankful praise; and, though it may not be without its good purpose to remember, for one brief moment, the terrors and the perils that underlie our Christian gladness, the scorpions and the adders, the young lions and the dragons, which we tread under our feet as we move along the pathway of glory and salvation, yet I would lead your thoughts quickly on from this to the nobler and more inspiring revelation that Christ makes to us of the Father's action on those who are abiding in His love, and doing Him good and acceptable service.

How strange, how startling is the mystery! Just as arrival at Christ our Goal was, after all, not the crowning accomplishment, the final close of faith's victory, but was only the beginning of a new, and increasing, and most anxious task to be plied by faith, of *abiding* in Him Whom it had found and enjoyed; so, too, the very pledge that we succeed in giving of that true abiding in Christ,—the good works, the fruit in which the Father is glorified,—these are no final result, no assured close, in which the great Husbandman of our souls can rest content. He takes great delight in them, it is true, but His delight is the delight of an Almighty love, and such love is infinite, is inexhaustible in its requirements. He rewards them, indeed, but His reward, His seal and crown of joy, is to raise the level of His demands. We have done something for Him: well and good, it shall be the happy privilege allotted to us, to be given

[1] Preached at the Festival of the Wantage Home.

the power to do much more. We have been faithful over a few things: well done, ye good and faithful servants! this, then, shall be your gain,—to be set over many things, to rule over cities.

Nor will this gain be easily won; this privilege will not be without its own anxiety, and trouble, and severity, and rigour, and patience, and pain. No, the Lord promises no light and easy move upward: for the life that has already been working in us, and has brought forth such good results, is nevertheless richer, and more exuberant than any fruit that we have suffered it as yet to produce in us; and hence comes our new task. We have not yet concentrated all our efficacy on God's sole service; we have not yet dedicated all our force and energy to the purposes of that fruit, for which alone the Husbandman trains, and tends, and succours us. That life, that is in us of Christ, as yet pours out its abundance into a thousand odd tendrils and superfluous leaves. Showy and splendid as these may look, they are yet but passing and perishing gifts, without an aim, without a work, ending in nothing, useless to others, unprofitable to that sweet purpose of love which ever seeks to pass out beyond itself, and to devote all its whole strength to the service of others, to the fruit that others will enjoy. These, then, are not the fruit that the Father asks for, the fruit that can be put to profit, the fruit that will abide: and, therefore, there is stern work yet to be done, there is nervous and hard discipline yet to be endured. We have not yet done with that law which bade us cut off the corrupted hand, and pluck out the eye that offends,

No, the reward that we have won by our high aims, by our holy success, is just this, that the Father deems us now worthy of His sharper handling, of His more imperative care. He looks upon us now with something of hope: He looks upon us, and His Heart frames grander possibilities, and a finer end: He has higher issues in mind: He schemes for us a nobler perfection than any we have yet attained, yea, than any we have dreamed of: and, therefore, He will draw His knife; He will shape us, and fashion us; He will clean off and cut away all that now uses up for its own delight the flowing sap, that might be dedicated, with a more single aim, to the purpose of fruit. Quick, sharp, and clear, the biting edge of the Father's tool passes in and out of our soul's desires, its pleasant fancies, its manifold imaginations,—the pretty leaves, the merry curling tendrils! there they all lie, so swiftly, on the ground, given over to the burning: and all about us are little gashes and naked boughs,—where we miss that which once delighted, and sigh for that which was once our pride.

"Every branch that beareth fruit, God purgeth it, that it may bring forth more fruit."

Dearly beloved, we are met together to-day to celebrate, with hearty thanksgiving to the good God Who giveth all, the precious and blessed work which has been done for Him and for the love of His dear Son, by that band of devoted Sisters, whose beautiful home is in this place.

Not for compliments, not for complacent self-praise, are we here; but for the true and invigorating profession, assembled together in the sight of God, of our grateful sense of His unspeakable mercies, Who has shielded so tenderly the days of this holy society. Blessed, most blessed, is the life of those who have been permitted to devote their whole hearts and souls to such a service of love, of tenderness, of helpfulness, of peace. Blessed is the thankful and overflowing sympathy of those who, outside and apart from any direct share in this sweet working, have come to-day to acknowledge the delicious relief, that again and again has lightened all their labour, and illuminated all their weariness, as they remembered, when their own work seemed clouded with failure, and ruined by opposition, and defiled by sin, the constant, and pure, and unfailing devotion that was passing out from this Wantage Home, in peaceful and gracious loveliness, with no check or stint, bringing comfort to dark places, and healing to bruised and broken lives. For this, and for His enduring mercies, we thank and praise and give glory to God with one heart and with one mouth to-day.

But it is our Christian boldness to be able to be severe even in our joy, to recall dangers even when triumphant. It is ours to keep our footing sure then when gladness is most overpowering. For, indeed, we Christians well know that all our triumphs, all our gladness, are not our looked-for reward—it is not for these that we strive. They are but helps, but encouragements, but refreshments, but omens,—pledges of far more to come, symbols of larger fulfilments, parables of that infinite glory of God up towards which we may never cease to move. Therefore it is that our moments of thanksgiving are moments in which we gather our forces for new efforts, and gird on our armour, and brace up nerve and sinew. For well we know that the love of God can never content itself, kind and tender as it is to our poor handiwork. Well we know that where it finds anything, there it delights to ask for more, that to him that hath done work, to him shall still more be given; that whenever it discovereth a branch that bringeth forth fruit, it purgeth it, that it may bring forth more fruit.

"He purgeth it." My brethren, if we think over all the vast Church life of which this Wantage Sisterhood is so encouraging a sample, do we not know what this purging may mean? do we not understand that this purging may be even now in action?

There is trouble behind and before us; there are searchings of hearts, and fears, and sufferings. We catch glimpses of principles which it will be painful and perilous to hold faithfully, yet most desperate to abandon. We see ahead many storms to brave, much hatred to encounter, many hearts to wound, many sympathies to afflict.

Is it hard, we think, having done so much, having worked so loyally, having won our way so gallantly, to be met still by the dismay and confusion, by the alarm and terror of war? Is there never to be rest, never to be satisfaction? Will there always be tumult and anxiety?

Yes! for this is God's promise; this is His care; this is His reward; this is our testimony! We cannot read St. John and be surprised. Why should the hardships make us doubt? For certainly, if we are on the right way, if we are doing good work, there will be this increase of trouble and endurance: for this is the way of the great Husbandman; this is His mode of showing favours; this is His mode of blessing; this is His witness to the branch that bringeth forth fruit for His glory: "He purgeth it, that it may bring forth more."

And we,—are we not ripe for this purging? We are puzzled, perhaps, to see how this pain and doubt, that surround us, attach themselves to so much that belongs very closely to our highest and best spring of life. The attack seems to fall sharpest on much that, for itself, we should not care for, but which is so intimately bound up with our flow of holy enthusiasm, so interwoven with the whole movement of grace, that we cannot but feel as if it were hard to be severe on that which certainly springs out of the same spirit as that which we know to be our life and law.

It is our devotion,—it is our fervour, we say,—this very fervour which we all allow to be Divinely prompted, which impels us to do this or that which offends. Surely it is harsh to be too critical about what has so good and true an origin! Surely to attack the results is to attack the principle! Surely we may be allowed a charitable latitude,—a measure of kindly indulgence!

So we wonder and, perhaps, fret, and grow impatient; and yet, what does the Father's purging imply? These leaves, these tendrils, that His knife chips away, are they not, too, works of the same Divine sap as that which holds the branches fast in Christ, and which draws out of them fruit? Are not they, too, witnesses to the exuberance of rich and flowing life? Are they not delightful and lovely belongings of the Vine, true products of its abundant energy?

Yes! they prove life; they prove capacity; they are a sign and pledge of overflowing hope. But the Father still asks—are they fruit? Are they not absorbing force that might go to the making of fruit? Are they not for temporary delight, for passing gratification? They are pleasant to ourselves, but do they benefit others? Can they be dedicated to an abiding service? If not, even though they be lovely, even though they belong to the true root, and drink of the true sap, yet cut them down, chip them short, save their sap for purer and less selfish uses.

Far from expecting indulgence for a larger self-gratification, as we advance in God's work it is this very gratification that He sets Himself to curtail in those who serve Him best. This is His pruning. Those who know less of God can be allowed this plenitude of leaves, their present feelings of contentment, their sense of gratified satisfaction, their easy-going self-pleasing. But the more we show signs of aspiration, then the higher rises the rigour of self-sacrifice; the less are we allowed for self; the less can it be permitted us to stray outside the strict and rigid lines of a complete dedication.

You have offered Me something of yourself—says our God—try, then, to offer Me the whole; let Me cut off *all* that, however good, and fair, and pleasant, yet diminishes the completeness of your self-surrender.

This is the force of Christ's question: Will ye

abide in My love? Your faith has been bold enough to come; has it then the strength and the courage to abide while I work? abide while I purge and perfect it?

It is this question which we of to-day have now to face. We are of those who trust that it has been given them, by no merit of theirs, to sit within the upper chamber, among Christ's friends: we have been suffered to take our part in the great mission of the world's evangelization: we have been knit into the Vine; we share in its wondrous growth.

That growth has been, in England, a rapid and unchecked triumph for forty marvellous years; and God forbid that any one should bar its advance now, or should attempt to cry to it—Enough, so far and no further shalt thou go!

There is much yet before us; we are not yet near the turning-point; it is not the main onward flow that is to be nipped and stopped—thanks be to God!

But there is still about us—who will deny it?—so much of that audacity, that overflow of spirits, that free and heedless abandonment, that exuberant looseness, which are easily forgiven to the first flush of excitement, but which cannot be suffered to outlive that early time. They have a certain charm—the charm of frankness, of ease, of confidence, of spontaneity: they may even have done good work for a moment. But, nevertheless, God, Who looks for abiding fruit, for permanent proof, cannot for long away with them. For quickly, if we cling to this temper, quickly these almost innocent habits turn into vanities, into self-pleasing fancies, into wilfulness, into hardness, into offence, into extravagance, into insolence. They were hardly sinful when they first came; rather they were the signs of brimming power, the overflow of noble enthusiasm; but the sin is to refuse to let them go. Charming, graceful, captivating as this exuberance of youthful feeling may be, God's knife is out, and woe to us now of this generation, if we will not suffer Him to cut away what He will!

The sterner demand is once more to be made upon us; the more solemn and momentous days have arrived; the severer discipline is being applied; we must put away our childish things: "We have brought forth fruit!" yea, we are a living branch; and therefore God is preparing to purge us, that we "may bring forth more fruit."

One word on our own inner lives. There, too, how surely, how sagely, this law penetrates. God, in His Fatherly tenderness, allows us, in our early days of spiritual living, so much emotional attraction, so much of childish conceit, so much of self-confidence, so much of ready outflow! He smiles over our little wayward imaginations, our tiny insolence, our gaieties, our careless freedoms. These are but the testimonies of His abundant Presence within us, and He can lightly forgive them.

But, since they are signs of His present power, that power may be put to better use; and, soon, the higher light breaks in upon our souls, and we see the more rigid principle, and we become aware of the selfishness, of the wilfulness, of the pride, that were but half concealed in our religious excitement, in our spiritual delights, in our godly service.

Then it is that we shall know ourselves beneath the searching eyes of Jesus in the secrecy of His familiar intimacy with His friends.

Then it is that He will beseech us—" Abide in Me ! Do not fear ! it is *because* you have abode, and have brought forth some fruit, that God's weapon is now sharpening itself for you; to purge you of all these gay tendrils and overflowing leaves—to purge you that you may bring forth more fruit: Summon up your faith, then, to abide in Me—to abide, even though you pass so swiftly from that happy upper chamber to the bitter agony of the garden, and the shame, the misery, the blow and darkness of the Cross."

Is it depressing, to have spoken thus to you this morning ? Surely not,—surely, it is the keenest of all joys, to feel ourselves under the direct handling of God; the most bracing of all triumphs, to know that all our present victories are to be left behind, that we may pass on to still finer achievements, to still purer glories.

Welcome, thrice welcome, in God's Name, the pangs and perils, the wounds and the scourges that may await us, if these come to cleanse our souls, and purge our selfishness, and perfect our sanctification, and complete our self-sacrifice.

SERMON XX.

THE SLEEP, AND THE WAKING.

"Then shall the Kingdom of Heaven be likened unto ten virgins, which took their lamps, and went forth to meet the Bridegroom."—
ST. MATT. xxv. I.

THE Service is already full of Christmas;[1] but let me, before Advent is utterly passed away, recall your thoughts yet once more to that great prophecy of the last things in St. Matthew, towards the close of which our Lord suddenly introduces the parable of the Ten Virgins.

"Then!" We look up, astray and bewildered, into our Lord's face, as He sits there on the Mount of Olives, the Mount of His redeeming agony now so nigh, and gazes out across the narrow valley over to the walls of the ancient city, to the glories and loveliness of God's Holy Temple; and, even as He gazes and speaks, the walls dissolve, and the towers, and all the cloud-capped palaces; the very stones, great and wonderful, seem to move under His words; the whole mountain of Zion begins to shake and displace its solid frame under the power of His unearthly faith; and with Jerusalem, the kingdoms of the world, too, and all their storied histories, shift like unsteady clouds down the long and changing centuries, under the motion of His breath;

[1] Preached on Christmas Eve.

and still He speaks, and still new visions come, and shape themselves, and go. And we, we who, like those faithful four, Peter and James, and John and Andrew, have been stirred by some dark utterance of His on the ruin of the temples which our hands have built, and have pressed into our Lord's Presence to know more of what He meant, and have caught Him alone, and have asked our questions, "When shall these things be? and what shall be the sign?"—we, I say, find ourselves caught up into an answer which overfloods our senses with its fulness and compass; an answer which seems to play with time and space, as with creatures of its own handiwork; an answer which seems to be speaking of a thousand things at once, of Jerusalem, and of the Church, and of the world, and of our single souls, and of life, and of resurrection, and of death, and of judgment. Into this vast answer, epochs are swept up indistinguishably; whole masses of mankind and of life pass from transition to transition: in vain we attempt to lay hands on them, and hold them fast; in vain to fix and compel a clear and single response: even as we lay our finger on the place, and on the date, the vision has moved, has widened, has escaped. We cannot keep our footing: we are ourselves not outside the vision, but are included within its scope: we and all are lifted and swept along with its rhythmic changes, with its endless movement: the laws of time and of transition are the same within the circle of our little being as they are in the larger schemes of humanity's evolution: what is spoken of the one is spoken of the other. "Then," says our Lord, "then shall the kingdom be likened." "When, Lord?" we ask, and a hundred voices seem to give us an answer,

Then, when the end of the world draws near; then, when the Son of Man is close to His coming; then, when the Advent dawn is breaking in the skies of time. And yet, again, that Advent is always nigh in the process of history, nations, and races; that coming is always approaching; that end is always ending: and, therefore, then, whenever Jerusalem falls; then, when nations go down to dark ruins; then, when the people are shaken, and the boundaries are removed; then, when new lights are in the heavens, and cries of redemption are sounding, amid the falling of stars and the darkenings and shudderings of sun and moon. And yet, again, no generation shall pass away until that Advent is fulfilled, until that end is begun; and, therefore, once more, then, when year by year and hour by hour souls break up, and earth melts away, and strength ebbs from hearts that feel the blood run slower, from souls that are sick with the sure touch of decay; then, when the eyes grow dimmer, and the darkness and the desolation of death gathers in upon man and woman, upon young and old; then, when the old is ready to vanish, and the awful Presence of the Unknown New is felt to be suddenly drawn close, and many are calling to the hills to fall upon them, and to the mountains to cover them; then, when this or that generation of the faithful lies waiting on its deathbed, in trembling hope, for the inbreaking of God's tremendous Majesty; then, and then, and then "shall the Kingdom of Heaven be likened unto ten virgins, who took their lamps, and went forth to meet the Bridegroom."

This is the force, therefore, of that mysterious "Then," and this, therefore, the lesson; that whenever things of earth fall into fragments under the feet of men, whenever death is in the air above us, and dissolution is at work within, whenever there comes the day when "the keepers of the house shall tremble, and the strong men shall bow themselves, and the doors shall be shut in the streets, and the sound of the grinding is low, and the grasshopper shall be a burden, and desire shall fail, and man goeth to his long home, and the mourners go about the streets," whether it be the deathday of a generation or of the whole earth,—*then*, in that day of gloom, and disquiet, and horrible sadness, the Kingdom of Heaven shall not sit down with the trembling people in the dust, the Kingdom of Christ shall not be brought low with all those daughters of music, the Kingdom of God shall not be afraid, nor look in blank grief out of its darkened windows. No! it is then, when all is failing, that it shows itself to be possessed with the splendour of an immense hope, with the joy of a fulfilled expectancy. Till then, till that hour of terrible crisis, this hope, this expectancy, may have lain hid and smothered. Men may have looked upon the Kingdom of Heaven, and seen no such likeness to ten virgins in it,—the shape, the attitude of expectancy had not yet come over it: it seemed to belong to the everyday life of earth, to be indistinguishable from the turmoil of the kingdoms of this world. But now that the kingdoms fade and the earth darkens, now, at last, the sign of power is upon the Church; now, at last, the secret of her life breaks out. Over all else there is falling the ashy pallor of despair; but with her a new life quickens: she lifts up her head: she listens for the call, for the shining of the glory: she gathers up her limbs, and rises with joy and grace and beauty:

she arrays herself in splendour, and over her is shed the delight of virgin youthfulness : she is seen, through the clash and ruin of worlds, going forth, amid the light of her lamps, to the triumph of a festal procession, to the merry gladness of a wedding. "Then shall the Kingdom of Heaven be likened unto ten virgins, who took their lamps, and went forth to meet the Bridegroom."

Would that we could sometimes have it given us to see this likeness of a great expectancy come over our Church! Would that she herself could throw herself, in Advent days, into the attitude of those who look away from earth for One Who cometh from afar ! Our Lord, you see, speaks of the whole Kingdom of Heaven being like to ten virgins. Not this or that saint in it, but the whole kingdom, in its entire mass, is to be as those who pass out from our homes on earth to a marriage meeting. One single passion is, as it were, to thrill through the whole bulk of the Church. She would seem no longer the mixed, and complex, and intricate thing that she is apt to seem, without clear outlines or distinguishable purpose; rather, the whole body of the faithful would disentangle itself from the crowd of cares and busy confusions of the day, and with one impulse, decisive, strong, supreme, with one undivided will, would rise and pass out to meet the coming Lord. The whole kingdom would be as ten virgins going forth with their lamps.

And, observe, it is not the invisible Church of the Faithful, not merely the Church of the Saints, the Mystic Bride of the Bridegroom's election, that is so to appear; but *all* the virgins that bear her company, be they wise or foolish, all the mixed Church militant, with its good and its bad alike—it is this Church, as it is on earth, which is so to be possessed with this spiritual outlook for Christ, that it will show its strange, its superhuman purpose in its every shape and attitude. The very gesture, the gait, the aspect of the Church, are to be instinct with the impulse heavenward, are to be set away from earth. Not that she is not to serve Christ here: the parable of the talents is given to teach her the character of her earthly service: it is no idle day of contemplation that is here allotted to her: she is to work well and heartily; but, still, when the daylight dies, and when man, the man who is the creature of nature, the lord of earth, going forth to his work and to his labour until the evening, is creeping home tired and weary, worn and wasted with long labour, to the night of death, the night of terror and dismay, the night wherein all the beasts of the forest do move, lions roaring after their prey; *then* the Church ought to clearly show itself to him, as something not dying down to its end like him, but as something whose joy is only beginning when its day of earthly work is done, as inspired by a spirit that looks away to a new heaven and a new earth. Men of the world would look up, if our Christian lives were all tuned to the music of Christ,—the natural man would look up from the dull embers of his fire where he sits, sad and forlorn with age and weariness, in the dark house of the flesh: he would hear a sudden noise in the streets, a rustling of garments, a gleam of lamps, a passing to and fro in the night: he would look out of his lattice-window, and, lo! the Church of Christ goes by in the darkness, sweeping along, amid song, and gladness, and light, to some joy that earth knows not, to some triumph that the day of man has never seen. A new youth has come upon her, just when age and decay ought to drag her down: she sweeps along, white, fresh, glistening, like a band of virgins, like a troop of shining stars. For her, "the winter is already past, the rain is over and gone, the time of the singing is come: she sleeps, but her heart waketh: by night she seeketh Him Whom her soul loveth, for already the voice of the Beloved knocketh at the door of her soul, crying, Open to Me, My sister. Rise up, My love, My fair one, and come away."

Let me bring before you one or two points which this character of expectancy, which our Lord so vividly ascribes to the Church on earth, may help to clear up.

We are all often puzzled how to use the high ideal language about the Church, or about Christian souls, which is so frequent in the Epistles of St. John and St. Paul. For, after all, how very vague and fluctuating are the lines that can be drawn between the Church and the world, between the baptized and the unbaptized, between the religious and the irreligious soul! We pass up and down the world, and see and hear men of all sorts live, and move, and talk, and all look very much alike, and all say very much the same things,—a little better, or a little worse, it may be, but still all appear to be of the same stamp and calibre, turned out at the same manufactory. And if we turn to history, the Church seems to push its way along by much the same process as earthly societies: it has its clever ministers, its good occasions, its mistakes, its hopes, its fears, its ambitions, its intrigues: it works by the everyday influences: it learns by experience: it profits by circumstances: it lives for the needs of the day: we can trace out, according to the degree of our knowledge, why it succeeded here, why it failed there. And, then, still closer we can go. How much effort we ourselves seem to make to live the life of holiness! How many hours we spend in prayer! How often do we go on, week after week, year after year, receiving the Body and Blood of our Lord Jesus Christ! How much watchfulness, and care, and anxiety we spend upon our spiritual welfare: and yet there is so little result! We get on such a very little way: we are so very little, if at all, better than people who take no trouble whatever: they keep their tempers as well as we do: they are kind, often so much kinder than we are: to others they are quite as pleasant and helpful, if not more: they do their duty, as it appears, quite as faithfully: they are upright, honest, sober, hardworking,— would we were always as true, as devoted, as self-sacrificing, as they! and yet they do not pray or worship; they do not use the Sacraments; they do not think about God; they do not seem to strive after a higher life, as we do. It seems so strange, as if all our efforts came to nothing, as if our religious life did nothing for us, as if we were wasting our strength on what brought in no adequate result. Where does all the force we spend go to? What has happened with it all? Why is there no more difference?

This is a most real, a most serious, sometimes a most startling question, to all who have striven along the way of holiness; and, I think, this parable of the virgins is full of help towards an answer. It tells us that it is this

The Sleep, and the Waking. 313

very *expectancy* which explains our difficulty. The Christian life, the Christian Church, these do not reveal their strong and vivid distinctiveness here on earth, just because their day is yet to come. We may live, and eat, and talk, and work, and play, and laugh, and love on earth among our fellows; we may do all this in the full spirit and truth of our faith, under its influential sanction: we ought to do this with a freedom, and a power that, without our faith, would be impossible. Christian gentleness ought to inherit the earth. This is all true. But, still, not here is our abiding city, not of the world are we: our home, our reality, our true society are elsewhere; our conversation, our fabric of life, are in heaven. There, with God, and with all the companies of heaven; there, with angels and archangels; there, with prophet, and apostle, and martyr; there, with the household of God, the fellowship of the saints, the assembly of the firstborn; there, with all our beloved dead in Christ—there it is that we humbly hope to live, and move; there we should be indeed at home, in the haven where we would be; there, if it may be, we would eat, and drink, and see God, and sup with Jesus: and, if so, then we can never show our real strength, our inner dignity, while we are yet outside the New Jerusalem, while we are yet on the pilgrimage to the golden gates. Here, on earth, is not our rest, our satisfaction: here, on earth, therefore, we cannot put forth all our powers, or know the full significance of our spiritual graces: the meaning of our innermost life is still unrevealed; it is shut off from its true sphere of work. Our life is still hid with Christ in God. Here, in the world, and by means of the world, we prepare and shape our souls for heaven; we fashion our spirits to the likeness of God: but here we do not see God as He is; we do not meet Him in cool evenings amid the trees of the garden. Still, as yet, for us on earth, He is a God Who hideth Himself, a God Who seeth in secret; and, therefore, still our souls do not meet their fulfilment, do not find their satisfaction, do not prove themselves to be what they are. Only when the light of heaven breaks in, only when God shows Himself in the tremendous majesty of His awful splendour,—only then shall we know the interpretation of our long preparation; only then, will the Spirit's hidden and mysterious faculties, long matured in the secret womb of the flesh, start into life at the summons of that for which they have been made ready, and in which they are alive; only then shall it be seen which soul can endure the Presence of God, and which has no answering capacity to greet that appearing. Then, in that fearful moment of decision, when God advances to welcome the souls that are His, it will most surely be determined, with the vigour of an undeniable fact, which of us are good, and which are evil. Plain, sharp, relentless, the line of division will run along between man and man, between mother and child, between husband and wife, between friend and friend; and to those on the one side, the light of God's shining will come as a friendly thing, enfolding them in the joy of a welcome long known, long waited for, a welcome to meet which all the full force of the soul breaks out in confident exultation; and to those on the other, that very same glorious shining will seem as a flaming fire, which scorches, shrivels, devours, blinding the eyes which are focussed

The Sleep, and the Waking.

only to the darkness of earth, burning up, with the horror of open shame, the flesh whose foul hiding-places it makes manifest with its merciless glare. Yes, we Christians live for another day than this our day of earthly life : we live in view of a crisis to come. For a crisis it must be, that day of the Lord's appearance, in that it first will bring in the new conditions, our true home ; and, therefore, it first will show who is ready for the new, who can accept the life of the hereafter. The coming is the coming of the Bridegroom, the coming of Him to Whom our whole souls go out, the coming of immense and eternal joy. But it cannot, for all that, help being a coming to judge between good and evil, between light and darkness, between sheep and goats. For He Who comes, cometh to count up His jewels ; and, therefore, then, at least, it may no longer be kept hidden which are flawed and which are soiled.

Let us remember our parable. Our ten virgins had waited for the tarrying Bridegroom, with one purpose, one impulse, one beauty. All were as one body, all were clothed in the same garments, all bore the lamp of expectancy. There was no outward sign to show which was wise and which was foolish ; for as yet they only waited ; they only prepared for a coming hour. So soldiers, who prepare for a great battle-day, give no obvious sign as yet, in the everyday drill, which of them will be brave, and which be cowardly, in the day of blood, and fire, and vapour of smoke. All wheel, and march, and skirmish with equal precision, with the same skill and sureness. Perhaps, indeed, the officer, who watches closely day by day, may have a suspicion that this man will prove himself a better man than that; but to the general onlooker the outward effect exhibits no distinctions. Only, when the great day of trial comes, with its fiery demand to do or die, only then, will the fatal decision be made clear between the man who stands loyal to death and the man who turns pale and flees.

So it is with the virgins, who picture the Church in its time of preparation. And this outward sameness lasts on throughout the whole interval of delay. They all, wise and foolish alike, slumbered and slept, while the Bridegroom tarried. Until the day of the Lord comes, the Church is still in the night, still slumbering and sleeping. Our life on earth is a slumber: it is not our real life: we are not putting forth our life in it: our spiritual secret is asleep, is waiting to reveal its strength; it is not acting yet in all its power; it only makes itself felt in dim, dreamy movements, prophetic of a larger and richer awakening. So here, while the spirit slumbers, all are the same, all equally sleep, whether possessed of spiritual grace or not. The sleep of the good may be more quiet, more confident, more restful than the sleep of the unready, the bad. But still, to all and for all, it is sleep: the spirit sleeps. And so, too, to all equally, the slumber of earthly life closes in the long, dull sleep of death. All, good and bad alike, lay themselves down indistinguishably in the bed of the tomb. The gloom of an awful silence covers them all; the heavy earth hides all; the blind grass grows over and covers them; it asks not whether they be wise or whether they be foolish. No line of fire divides and saves. Impenetrable, speechless darkness engulfs them all into its secret places: "One thing befalleth them; as the one dieth, so dieth the other. All go unto one place. All are of the dust, and all turn to dust again." "We see that wise men also die and perish together, as well as the ignorant and foolish, and leave their riches for another." They all slumber and sleep,—true and false, wise and foolish, pure and impure, holy and unholy. Why not? Death is but the tag of *this* life; and as in this life they are more or less indistinguishable the one from the other, so in their physical death, too, they are not divided. It is not for any day of earth that we trim our lamps; and, therefore, not on this side of death shall we see the truth of our lives made manifest in full relief. The day beyond death, the day that tramples on death, the day of resurrection, the day of immortality,—that is the day for which we live; that, and that only, is the day for which we make ready; and therefore it is that then, and then only, shall be seen the fruit of all our long toiling: then, and then only, shall we know the secret of our efforts: then, at last, after many days, shall we find the bread that long ago we cast upon the waters.

This, then, is our lesson. We live here, not expecting to see why, until the day of the Lord comes. The holiness at which we labour is not to have its full life here. We must spend effort after effort upon it, though we see so little difference in our daily lives in comparison with the effort spent. For the question is not, do I now stand off openly from evil, as light from darkness, as life from death?—there, in this dull gloom of night, such a marked separation is impossible—but, am I such as could rise to welcome our Lord, the Holy, the Pure, the Righteous? When He breaks in in all His glory, have I secret strength stored up for a critical hour hereafter?

And the parable makes this question more searching, by addressing its warning to all those who are already embraced by the Christian life. It bids them beware, lest the life into which they are born becomes itself the peril. All the virgins have lamps lighted; all of them are on the way to greet the Bridegroom; all have been set in tune to the great Hope. They are all, wise and foolish, stepping heavenward. And so, we who are Christian-born, we of the latter days, we, too, be we wise or be we foolish, start with our lamps already lit. The heavenly oil of God's grace has already filled the lamp of our souls: the flame of the Holy Ghost has lighted upon us: we are not mere children of nature, even from the first: already, before we choose, we are made children of the Most High; we grow up in a Christian atmosphere; we inherit a Christian breeding. The gifts of forgiving love are taken in with the air we breathe. The natural passions are already soothed and trained under the discipline of the Cross, without any effort of our own. Anger, envy, lust, witchcraft,—these are somewhat cast out of our souls, by the long action of Christian influence through many centuries, through a hundred generations. The Christian home, the Christian society —these, the work of the unwearied Spirit has sanctified and sweetened. In a word, we find ourselves living *by nature*, as it were, for Christ, for heaven, for the hereafter: we find ourselves, of necessity, drawn along in the glee of the bridal procession. And this is what may deceive: we are in the right way, indeed, but it is by no effort, no will, of our own; and, therefore, this by itself will not suffice us to carry us safe home. No; this is the foolishness of the foolish five, that they trust to the lamp already lighted; and yet the oil already in the lamp cannot hold out through the long slumber and sleep. Here lies the sole difference between the wise and the foolish: the wise had private additional store of oil hid away in their own little vessels, so that the lamp lighted for them may be trimmed and refilled by their own peculiar oil. The common inheritance of grace brought down to us by a Catholic Church,—this is the beginning of salvation. But this cannot carry us through, unless deep in our own secret heart of hearts we have stored up the hidden oil of expectant love,—the expectant love that looks with a personal and peculiar tenderness to the days of the coming; the love of the inner heart for Him Who, after long delay, after long slumbering and sleeping, after long watching in life, and long silence in death, is still waited for with intense devotion, with living personal earnestness; the thoughtful, anxious, careful love, that does not rest in its own vague impulses and shallow fancies, but makes itself ready with given grace of God, so that, when the day comes, there may be not merely the blind, impotent, human impulse, crying, "Lord, Lord, open to us;" but more than this, the oil prepared of God; the grace which the flame of the spirit recognises as its fuel, and with which it is glad to replenish itself; the oil which each single soul must have laid up, with secret forethought, in the recesses of its own being for that day.

Be wise, then, in time,—now, on the day of the first coming, when He comes to light our lamps for us Who is Himself the Bridegroom of the Second Advent. Oh! be prudent, be quick, be wise: for, indeed, heavy is the slumber that must so quickly creep over us,—soon, so terribly soon, cometh the irrevocable sleep! We are in the night still; but yet we may not be idle; now, or never, in the dark hours of waiting, the heart must be made ready. For that day, when it cometh, as come it will, can then no longer suffer one moment's delay. Then, at that hour, if we be not already prepared to go in, we may never enter. No loud cry will avail, no tardy preparation: the day is past: "Too late! too late! ye cannot enter now!"

One thing, one certain hope, remains: the time is short; but yet, while there is yet time, let us urge, let us beseech each other, to make sure that we lay up once again, and with more devoted faith, more passionate earnestness, more steady love than before, each in his own soul-vessel, the one oil of gladness, the one gift of grace, that very Flesh and Blood of Him Whose pierced Body every eye shall see hereafter. Let us lay it up, not looking for the glory of fruition here, not looking for fruit, for ease, for comfort, but storing it up, in silence, and patience, and love, for that great day when the trumpet shall sound through the night, and a great cry is heard under the stars, "Behold, the Bridegroom cometh! Go ye out to meet Him,"—and we shall rise from our slumber, and shall, with joy and gladness, trim our lamps once more with the oil of our old earth-gathered devotion, and press in within the gates to the marriage feast, before it be too late, and the door be shut.

A Catalogue of Works

IN

THEOLOGICAL LITERATURE

PUBLISHED BY

MESSRS. LONGMANS, GREEN, & CO.

39 PATERNOSTER ROW, LONDON, E.C.,

Abbey and Overton.—THE ENGLISH CHURCH IN THE EIGHTEENTH CENTURY. By CHARLES J. ABBEY, M.A., Rector of Checkendon, Reading, and JOHN H. OVERTON, M.A., Rector of Epworth ; Rural Dean of Isle of Axholme. *Crown 8vo. 7s. 6d.*

Adams.—SACRED ALLEGORIES. The Shadow of the Cross—The Distant Hills—The Old Man's Home—The King's Messengers. By the Rev. WILLIAM ADAMS, M.A. *Crown 8vo. 3s. 6d.*

The Four Allegories may be had separately, with Illustrations. 16mo. 1s. each. *Also the Miniature Edition. Four Vols.* 32mo. 1s. each.

Aids to the Inner Life.

Edited by the Rev. W. H. HUTCHINGS, M.A., Rector of Kirkby Misperton, Yorkshire. *Five Vols.* 32mo, *cloth limp, 6d. each; or cloth extra, 1s. each.*

With red borders, 2s. each. Sold separately.

OF THE IMITATION OF CHRIST. By THOMAS À KEMPIS.

THE CHRISTIAN YEAR.

THE DEVOUT LIFE. By ST. FRANCIS DE SALES.

THE HIDDEN LIFE OF THE SOUL.

THE SPIRITUAL COMBAT. By LAURENCE SCUPOLI.

Allen.—THE CHURCH CATECHISM : its History and Contents. A Manual for Teachers and Students. By the Rev. A. J. C. ALLEN, M.A., formerly Principal of the Chester Diocesan Training College. *Crown 8vo. 3s. 6d.*

Barry.—LIGHT OF SCIENCE ON THE FAITH. Being the Bampton Lectures for 1892. By the Right Rev. ALFRED BARRY, D.D., Canon of Windsor, formerly Bishop of Sydney, Metropolitan of New South Wales, and Primate of Australia. *8vo.*

Bathe.—Works by the Rev. ANTHONY BATHE, M.A.

A LENT WITH JESUS. A Plain Guide for Churchmen. Containing Readings for Lent and Easter Week, and on the Holy Eucharist. 32mo, 1s.; or in paper cover, 6d.

AN ADVENT WITH JESUS. 32mo, 1s.; or in paper cover, 6d.

WHAT I SHOULD BELIEVE. A Simple Manual of Self-Instruction for Church People. Crown 8vo. 3s. 6d.

Bickersteth.—YESTERDAY, TO-DAY, AND FOR EVER: a Poem in Twelve Books. By EDWARD HENRY BICKERSTETH, D.D., Bishop of Exeter. One Shilling Edition, 18mo. With red borders, 16mo, 2s. 6d.

The Crown 8vo Edition (5s.) may still be had.

Blunt.—Works by the Rev. JOHN HENRY BLUNT, D.D.

THE ANNOTATED BOOK OF COMMON PRAYER: Being an Historical, Ritual, and Theological Commentary on the Devotional System of the Church of England. 4to. 21s.

THE COMPENDIOUS EDITION OF THE ANNOTATED BOOK OF COMMON PRAYER: Forming a concise Commentary on the Devotional System of the Church of England. Crown 8vo. 10s. 6d.

DICTIONARY OF DOCTRINAL AND HISTORICAL THEOLOGY. By various Writers. Imperial 8vo. 21s.

DICTIONARY OF SECTS, HERESIES, ECCLESIASTICAL PARTIES AND SCHOOLS OF RELIGIOUS THOUGHT. By various Writers. Imperial 8vo. 21s.

THE BOOK OF CHURCH LAW. Being an Exposition of the Legal Rights and Duties of the Parochial Clergy and the Laity of the Church of England. Revised by Sir WALTER G. F. PHILLIMORE, Bart., D.C.L. Crown 8vo. 7s. 6d.

A COMPANION TO THE BIBLE: Being a Plain Commentary on Scripture History, to the end of the Apostolic Age. Two vols. small 8vo. Sold separately.

THE OLD TESTAMENT. 3s. 6d.   THE NEW TESTAMENT. 3s. 6d.

HOUSEHOLD THEOLOGY: a Handbook of Religious Information respecting the Holy Bible, the Prayer Book, the Church, etc. etc. Paper cover, 16mo. 1s. Also the Larger Edition, 3s. 6d.

Body.—Works by the Rev. GEORGE BODY, D.D., Canon of Durham.

THE SCHOOL OF CALVARY; or, Laws of Christian Life revealed from the Cross. Small 8vo. 3s. 6d.

THE LIFE OF JUSTIFICATION. 16mo. 2s. 6d.

THE LIFE OF TEMPTATION. 16mo. 2s. 6d.

Bonney.—CHRISTIAN DOCTRINES AND MODERN THOUGHT: being the Boyle Lectures for 1891. By the Rev. T. G. BONNEY, D.Sc., Hon. Canon of Manchester. Crown 8vo. 5s.

IN THEOLOGICAL LITERATURE. 3

Boultbee.—A COMMENTARY ON THE THIRTY-NINE ARTICLES OF THE CHURCH OF ENGLAND. By the Rev. T. P. BOULTBEE, formerly Principal of the London College of Divinity, St. John's Hall, Highbury. *Crown 8vo.* 6s.

Bright.—Works by WILLIAM BRIGHT, D.D., Canon of Christ Church Oxford.
MORALITY IN DOCTRINE. Sermons. *Crown 8vo.*
LESSONS FROM THE LIVES OF THREE GREAT FATHERS: St. Athanasius, St. Chrysostom, and St. Augustine. *Crown 8vo.* 6s.
THE INCARNATION AS A MOTIVE POWER. *Crown 8vo.* 6s.

Bright and Medd.—LIBER PRECUM PUBLICARUM ECCLESIÆ ANGLICANÆ. A GULIELMO BRIGHT, S.T.P., et PETRO GOLDSMITH MEDD, A.M., Latine redditus. [In hac Editione continentur Versiones Latinæ—1. Libri Precum Publicarum Ecclesiæ Anglicanæ; 2. Liturgiæ Primæ Reformatæ; 3. Liturgiæ Scoticanæ; 4. Liturgiæ Americanæ.] *Small 8vo.* 7s. 6d.

Browne.—AN EXPOSITION OF THE THIRTY-NINE ARTICLES, Historical and Doctrinal. By E. H. BROWNE, D.D., formerly Bishop of Winchester. 8vo. 16s.

Campion and Beamont.—THE PRAYER BOOK INTERLEAVED. With Historical Illustrations and Explanatory Notes arranged parallel to the Text. By W. M. CAMPION, D.D., and W. J. BEAMONT, M.A. *Small 8vo.* 7s. 6d.

Carter.—Works edited by the Rev. T. T. CARTER, M.A., Hon. Canon of Christ Church, Oxford.
THE TREASURY OF DEVOTION: a Manual of Prayer for General and Daily Use. Compiled by a Priest. 18mo. 2s. 6d.; *cloth limp*, 2s.; *or bound with the Book of Common Prayer*, 3s. 6d. *Large-Type Edition. Crown 8vo.* 3s. 6d.
THE WAY OF LIFE: A Book of Prayers and Instruction for the Young at School, with a Preparation for Confirmation. Compiled by a Priest. 18mo. 1s. 6d.
THE PATH OF HOLINESS: a First Book of Prayers, with the Service of the Holy Communion, for the Young. Compiled by a Priest. With Illustrations. 16mo. 1s. 6d.; *cloth limp*, 1s.
THE GUIDE TO HEAVEN: a Book of Prayers for every Want. (For the Working Classes.) Compiled by a Priest. 18mo. 1s. 6d.; *cloth limp*, 1s. *Large-Type Edition. Crown 8vo.* 1s. 6d.; *cloth limp*, 1s.

[continued.

Carter.—Works edited by the Rev. T. T. CARTER, M.A., Hon. Canon of Christ Church, Oxford—*continued.*
SELF-RENUNCIATION. 16mo. 2s. 6d.
THE STAR OF CHILDHOOD: a First Book of Prayers and Instruction for Children. Compiled by a Priest. With Illustrations. 16mo. 2s. 6d.

Carter.—MAXIMS AND GLEANINGS FROM THE WRITINGS OF T. T. CARTER, M.A. Selected and arranged for Daily Use. *Crown 16mo.* 1s.

Chandler.—THE SPIRIT OF MAN: An Essay in Christian Philosophy. By the Rev. A. CHANDLER, M.A., Rector of Poplar, E., *Crown 8vo.* 5s.

Church's Seasons (The), and other Verses. BY YOLANDE. *Crown 8vo.* 4s. 6d.

Conybeare and Howson.—THE LIFE AND EPISTLES OF ST. PAUL. By the Rev. W. J. CONYBEARE, M.A., and the Very Rev. J. S. HOWSON, D.D. With numerous Maps and Illustrations.
LIBRARY EDITION. *Two Vols.* 8vo. 21s.
POPULAR EDITION. *One Vol. Crown 8vo.* 3s. 6d.

Copleston.—BUDDHISM—PRIMITIVE AND PRESENT IN MAGADHA AND IN CEYLON. By REGINALD STEPHEN COPLESTON, D.D., Bishop of Colombo. 8vo. 16s.

Devotional Series, 16mo, Red Borders. *Each* 2s. 6d.
BICKERSTETH'S YESTERDAY, TO-DAY, AND FOR EVER.
CHILCOT'S TREATISE ON EVIL THOUGHTS.
THE CHRISTIAN YEAR.
FRANCIS DE SALES' (ST.) THE DEVOUT LIFE.
HERBERT'S POEMS AND PROVERBS.
KEMPIS' (À) OF THE IMITATION OF CHRIST.
WILSON'S THE LORD'S SUPPER. *Large type.*
*TAYLOR'S (JEREMY) HOLY LIVING.
* —— —— HOLY DYING.
These two in one Volume. 5s.

Devotional Series, 18mo, without Red Borders. *Each* 1s.
BICKERSTETH'S YESTERDAY, TO-DAY, AND FOR EVER.
THE CHRISTIAN YEAR.
FRANCIS DE SALES' (ST.) THE DEVOUT LIFE.
HERBERT'S POEMS AND PROVERBS.
KEMPIS' (À) OF THE IMITATION OF CHRIST.
WILSON'S THE LORD'S SUPPER. *Large type.*
*TAYLOR'S (JEREMY) HOLY LIVING.
* —— —— HOLY DYING.
These two in one Volume. 2s. 6d.

Edersheim.—Works by ALFRED EDERSHEIM, M.A., D.D., Ph.D., sometime Grinfield Lecturer on the Septuagint Oxford.

THE LIFE AND TIMES OF JESUS THE MESSIAH. *Two Vols.* 8vo. 24s.

JESUS THE MESSIAH : being an Abridged Edition of 'The Life and Times of Jesus the Messiah.' *Crown* 8vo. 7s. 6d.

PROPHECY AND HISTORY IN RELATION TO THE MESSIAH : The Warburton Lectures, 1880-1884. 8vo. 12s.

TOHU-VA-VOHU ('Without Form and Void') : being a collection of Fragmentary Thoughts and Criticism. *Crown* 8vo. 6s.

Ellicott.—Works by C. J. ELLICOTT, D.D., Bishop of Gloucester and Bristol.

A CRITICAL AND GRAMMATICAL COMMENTARY ON ST. PAUL'S EPISTLES. Greek Text, with a Critical and Grammatical Commentary, and a Revised English Translation. 8vo.

I CORINTHIANS. 16s.	PHILIPPIANS, COLOSSIANS, AND
GALATIANS. 8s. 6d.	PHILEMON. 10s. 6d.
EPHESIANS. 8s. 6d.	THESSALONIANS. 7s. 6d.
PASTORAL EPISTLES. 10s. 6d.	

HISTORICAL LECTURES ON THE LIFE OF OUR LORD JESUS CHRIST. 8vo. 12s.

Epochs of Church History. Edited by MANDELL CREIGHTON, D.D., LL.D., Bishop of Peterborough. *Fcap.* 8vo. 2s. 6d. each.

THE ENGLISH CHURCH IN OTHER LANDS. By the Rev. H. W. TUCKER, M.A.

THE HISTORY OF THE RE-FORMATION IN ENGLAND. By the Rev. GEO. G. PERRY, M.A.

THE CHURCH OF THE EARLY FATHERS. By the Rev. ALFRED PLUMMER, D.D.

THE EVANGELICAL REVIVAL IN THE EIGHTEENTH CENTURY. By the Rev. J. H. OVERTON, M.A.

THE UNIVERSITY OF OXFORD. By the Hon. G. C. BRODRICK, D.C.L.

THE UNIVERSITY OF CAM-BRIDGE. By J. BASS MULLINGER, M.A.

THE ENGLISH CHURCH IN THE MIDDLE AGES. By the Rev. W. HUNT, M.A.

THE CHURCH AND THE EASTERN EMPIRE. By the Rev. H. F. TOZER, M.A.

THE CHURCH AND THE ROMAN EMPIRE. By the Rev. A. CARR.

THE CHURCH AND THE PURI-TANS, 1570-1660. By HENRY OFFLEY WAKEMAN, M.A.

HILDEBRAND AND HIS TIMES. By the Rev. W. R. W. STEPHENS, M.A.

THE POPES AND THE HOHEN-STAUFEN. By UGO BALZANI.

THE COUNTER-REFORMATION. By ADOLPHUS WILLIAM WARD, Litt.D.

WYCLIFFE AND MOVEMENTS FOR REFORM. By REGINALD L. POOLE, M.A.

THE ARIAN CONTROVERSY. By H. M. GWATKIN, M.A.

6 A CATALOGUE OF WORKS

Fosbery.—Works edited by the Rev. THOMAS VINCENT FOSBERY, M.A., sometime Vicar of St. Giles's, Reading.
VOICES OF COMFORT. *Cheap Edition. Small* 8vo. 3s. 6d.
The Larger Edition (7s. 6d.) *may still be had.*
HYMNS AND POEMS FOR THE SICK AND SUFFERING. In connection with the Service for the Visitation of the Sick. Selected from Various Authors. *Small* 8vo. 3s. 6d.

Garland.—THE PRACTICAL TEACHING OF THE APOCALYPSE. By the Rev. G. V. GARLAND, M.A. 8vo. 16s.

Gore.—Works by the Rev. CHARLES GORE, M.A., Principal of the Pusey House; Fellow of Trinity College, Oxford.
THE MINISTRY OF THE CHRISTIAN CHURCH. 8vo. 10s. 6d.
ROMAN CATHOLIC CLAIMS. *Crown* 8vo. 3s. 6d.

Goulburn.—Works by EDWARD MEYRICK GOULBURN, D.D., D.C.L., sometime Dean of Norwich.
THOUGHTS ON PERSONAL RELIGION. *Small* 8vo, 6s. 6d.; *Cheap Edition,* 3s. 6d.; *Presentation Edition,* 2 vols. small 8vo, 10s. 6d.
THE PURSUIT OF HOLINESS: a Sequel to 'Thoughts on Personal Religion.' *Small* 8vo. 5s. *Cheap Edition,* 3s. 6d.
THE CHILD SAMUEL: a Practical and Devotional Commentary on the Birth and Childhood of the Prophet Samuel, as recorded in 1 Sam. i., ii. 1-27, iii. *Small* 8vo. 2s. 6d.
THE GOSPEL OF THE CHILDHOOD: a Practical and Devotional Commentary on the Single Incident of our Blessed Lord's Childhood (St. Luke ii. 41 to the end.) *Crown* 8vo. 2s. 6d.
THE COLLECTS OF THE DAY: an Exposition, Critical and Devotional, of the Collects appointed at the Communion. With Preliminary Essays on their Structure, Sources, etc. 2 vols. *Crown* 8vo. 8s. *each.*
THOUGHTS UPON THE LITURGICAL GOSPELS for the Sundays, one for each day in the year. With an Introduction on their Origin, History, the Modifications made in them by the Reformers and by the Revisers of the Prayer Book. 2 vols. *Crown* 8vo. 16s.
MEDITATIONS UPON THE LITURGICAL GOSPELS for the Minor Festivals of Christ, the two first Week-days of the Easter and Whitsun Festivals, and the Red-letter Saints' Days. *Crown* 8vo. 8s. 6d.
FAMILY PRAYERS compiled from various sources (chiefly from Bishop Hamilton's Manual), and arranged on the Liturgical Principle. *Crown* 8vo. 3s. 6d. *Cheap Edition.* 16mo. 1s.

Harrison.—Works by the Rev. ALEXANDER J. HARRISON, B.D., Lecturer of the Christian Evidence Society.
PROBLEMS OF CHRISTIANITY AND SCEPTICISM; Lessons from Twenty Years' Experience in the Field of Christian Evidence. *Crown* 8vo. 7s. 6d.
THE CHURCH IN RELATION TO SCEPTICS: a Conversational Guide to Evidential Work. *Crown* 8vo. 7s. 6d.

IN THEOLOGICAL LITERATURE. 7

Holland.—Works by the Rev. HENRY SCOTT HOLLAND, M.A., Canon and Precentor of St. Paul's.
PLEAS AND CLAIMS FOR CHRIST. *Crown 8vo.*
CREED AND CHARACTER : Sermons. *Crown 8vo.* 3s. 6d.
ON BEHALF OF BELIEF. Sermons preached in St. Paul's Cathedral. *Crown 8vo.* 3s. 6d.
CHRIST OR ECCLESIASTES. Sermons preached in St. Paul's Cathedral. *Crown 8vo.* 3s. 6d.
LOGIC AND LIFE, with other Sermons. *Crown 8vo.* 3s. 6d.

Hopkins.—CHRIST THE CONSOLER. A Book of Comfort for the Sick. By ELLICE HOPKINS. *Small 8vo.* 2s. 6d.

Howard.—THE SCHISM BETWEEN THE ORIENTAL AND WESTERN CHURCHES. With special reference to the addition of the *Filioque* to the Creed. By the Rev. G. B. HOWARD, B.A., sometime Scholar of St. John's College, Cambridge. *Crown 8vo.* 3s. 6d.

Ingram.—HAPPINESS IN THE SPIRITUAL LIFE; or, 'The Secret of the Lord.' A Series of Practical Considerations. By the Rev. W. CLAVELL INGRAM, M.A., Vicar of St. Matthew's, Leicester. *Crown 8vo.* 7s. 6d.

INHERITANCE OF THE SAINTS, THE; Or, Thoughts on the Communion of Saints and the Life of the World to come. Collected chiefly from English Writers by L. P. With a Preface by the Rev. HENRY SCOTT HOLLAND, M.A. *Crown 8vo.* 7s. 6d.

Jameson.—Works by Mrs. JAMESON.
SACRED AND LEGENDARY ART, containing Legends of the Angels and Archangels, the Evangelists, the Apostles. With 19 etchings and 187 Woodcuts. *Two Vols. Cloth, gilt top,* 20s. net.
LEGENDS OF THE MONASTIC ORDERS, as represented in the Fine Arts. With 11 etchings and 88 Woodcuts. *One Vol. Cloth, gilt top,* 10s. net.
LEGENDS OF THE MADONNA, OR BLESSED VIRGIN MARY. With 27 Etchings and 165 Woodcuts. *One Vol. Cloth, gilt top,* 10s. net.
THE HISTORY OF OUR LORD, as exemplified in Works of Art, Commenced by the late Mrs. JAMESON; continued and completed by LADY EASTLAKE. With 31 Etchings and 281 Woodcuts. *Two Vols.* 8vo. 20s. net.

Jennings.—ECCLESIA ANGLICANA. A History of the Church of Christ in England from the Earliest to the Present Times. By the Rev. ARTHUR CHARLES JENNINGS, M.A. *Crown 8vo.* 7s. 6d.

Jukes.—Works by ANDREW JUKES.
    THE NEW MAN AND THE ETERNAL LIFE. Notes on the Reiterated Amens of the Son of God. *Crown 8vo.* 6s.
    THE NAMES OF GOD IN HOLY SCRIPTURE: a Revelation of His Nature and Relationships. *Crown 8vo.* 4s. 6d.
    THE TYPES OF GENESIS. *Crown 8vo.* 7s. 6d.
    THE SECOND DEATH AND THE RESTITUTION OF ALL THINGS. *Crown 8vo.* 3s. 6d.
    THE MYSTERY OF THE KINGDOM. *Crown 8vo.* 2s. 6d.

Keble.—MAXIMS AND GLEANINGS FROM THE WRITINGS OF JOHN KEBLE, M.A. Selected and Arranged for Daily Use. By C. M. S. *Crown 16mo.* 1s.
    SELECTIONS FROM THE WRITINGS OF JOHN KEBLE, M.A. *Crown 8vo.* 3s. 6d.

King.—DR. LIDDON'S TOUR IN EGYPT AND PALESTINE IN 1886. Being Letters descriptive of the Tour, written by his Sister, Mrs. KING. *Crown 8vo.* 5s.

Knowling.—THE WITNESS OF THE EPISTLES: a Study in Modern Criticism. By the Rev. R. J. KNOWLING, M.A., Vice-Principal of King's College, London. *8vo.* 15s.

Knox Little.—Works by W. J. KNOX LITTLE, M.A., Canon Residentiary of Worcester, and Vicar of Hoar Cross.
    SKETCHES IN SUNSHINE AND STORM: a Collection of Miscellaneous Essays and Notes of Travel. *Crown 8vo.* 7s. 6d.
    THE CHRISTIAN HOME. *Crown 8vo.* 6s. 6d.
    THE HOPES AND DECISIONS OF THE PASSION OF OUR MOST HOLY REDEEMER. *Crown 8vo.* 3s. 6d.
    CHARACTERISTICS AND MOTIVES OF THE CHRISTIAN LIFE. Ten Sermons preached in Manchester Cathedral, in Lent and Advent. *Crown 8vo.* 3s. 6d.
    SERMONS PREACHED FOR THE MOST PART IN MANCHESTER. *Crown 8vo.* 3s. 6d.
    THE MYSTERY OF THE PASSION OF OUR MOST HOLY REDEEMER. *Crown 8vo.* 3s. 6d.
    THE WITNESS OF THE PASSION OF OUR MOST HOLY REDEEMER. *Crown 8vo.* 3s. 6d.
    THE LIGHT OF LIFE. Sermons preached on Various Occasions. *Crown 8vo.* 3s. 6d.
    SUNLIGHT AND SHADOW IN THE CHRISTIAN LIFE. Sermons preached for the most part in America. *Crown 8vo.* 3s. 6d.

IN THEOLOGICAL LITERATURE. 9

Lear.—Works by, and Edited by, H. L. SIDNEY LEAR.

FOR DAYS AND YEARS. A Book containing a Text, Short Reading, and Hymn for Every Day in the Church's Year. 16mo. 2s. 6d. *Also a Cheap Edition*, 32mo. 1s.; *or cloth gilt*, 1s. 6d.

FIVE MINUTES. Daily Readings of Poetry. 16mo. 3s. 6d. *Also a Cheap Edition*. 32mo. 1s.; *or cloth gilt*, 1s. 6d.

WEARINESS. A Book for the Languid and Lonely. *Large Type*. Small 8vo. 5s.

THE LIGHT OF THE CONSCIENCE. 16mo. 2s. 6d. 32mo. 1s.; *cloth limp*, 6d.

CHRISTIAN BIOGRAPHIES. *Nine Vols. Crown 8vo. 3s. 6d. each.*

MADAME LOUISE DE FRANCE, Daughter of Louis XV., known also as the Mother Térèse de St. Augustin.	THE REVIVAL OF PRIESTLY LIFE IN THE SEVENTEENTH CENTURY IN FRANCE.
A DOMINICAN ARTIST: a Sketch of the Life of the Rev. Père Besson, of the Order of St. Dominic.	A CHRISTIAN PAINTER OF THE NINETEENTH CENTURY.
	BOSSUET AND HIS CONTEMPORARIES.
HENRI PERREYVE. By A. GRATRY.	FÉNELON, ARCHBISHOP OF CAMBRAI.
ST. FRANCIS DE SALES, Bishop and Prince of Geneva.	HENRI DOMINIQUE LACORDAIRE.

DEVOTIONAL WORKS. Edited by H. L. SIDNEY LEAR. *New and Uniform Editions. Nine Vols.* 16mo. 2s. 6d. each.

FÉNELON'S SPIRITUAL LETTERS TO MEN.	THE HIDDEN LIFE OF THE SOUL.
FÉNELON'S SPIRITUAL LETTERS TO WOMEN.	THE LIGHT OF THE CONSCIENCE.
	SELF-RENUNCIATION. From the French.
A SELECTION FROM THE SPIRITUAL LETTERS OF ST. FRANCIS DE SALES.	ST. FRANCES DE SALES' OF THE LOVE OF GOD.
THE SPIRIT OF ST. FRANCIS DE SALES.	SELECTIONS FROM PASCAL'S THOUGHTS.

Library of Spiritual Works for English Catholics. *Original Edition. With Red Borders. Small 8vo. 5s. each. New and Cheaper Editions.* 16mo. 2s. 6d. each.

OF THE IMITATION OF CHRIST.	OF THE LOVE OF GOD. By ST. FRANCIS DE SALES.
THE SPIRITUAL COMBAT. By LAURENCE SCUPOLI.	THE CONFESSIONS OF ST. AUGUSTINE. *In Ten Books.*
THE DEVOUT LIFE. By ST. FRANCIS DE SALES.	THE CHRISTIAN YEAR. 5s. *Edition only.*

A CATALOGUE OF WORKS

Liddon.—Works by HENRY PARRY LIDDON, D.D., D.C.L., LL.D., late Canon Residentiary and Chancellor of St. Paul's.

LECTURES AND ESSAYS. *Crown 8vo.*

THE EPISTLE TO THE ROMANS. 8vo.

SERMONS ON OLD TESTAMENT SUBJECTS. *Crown 8vo. 5s.*

SERMONS ON SOME WORDS OF CHRIST. *Crown 8vo. 5s.*

THE DIVINITY OF OUR LORD AND SAVIOUR JESUS CHRIST. Being the Bampton Lectures for 1866. *Crown 8vo. 5s.*

ADVENT IN ST. PAUL'S. Sermons bearing chiefly on the Two Comings of our Lord. *Two Vols. Crown 8vo. 3s. 6d. each. Cheap Edition in one Volume. Crown 8vo. 5s.*

CHRISTMASTIDE IN ST. PAUL'S. Sermons bearing chiefly on the Birth of our Lord and the End of the Year. *Crown 8vo. 5s.*

PASSIONTIDE SERMONS. *Crown 8vo. 5s.*

EASTER IN ST. PAUL'S. Sermons bearing chiefly on the Resurrection of our Lord. *Two Vols. Crown 8vo. 3s. 6d. each. Cheap Edition in one Volume. Crown 8vo. 5s.*

SERMONS PREACHED BEFORE THE UNIVERSITY OF OXFORD. *Two Vols. Crown 8vo. 3s. 6d. each. Cheap Edition in one Volume. Crown 8vo. 5s.*

THE MAGNIFICAT. Sermons in St. Paul's. *Crown 8vo. 2s. 6d.*

SOME ELEMENTS OF RELIGION. Lent Lectures. *Small 8vo. 2s. 6d. ; or in paper cover, 1s. 6d.*
  The Crown 8vo Edition (5s.) may still be had.

SELECTIONS FROM THE WRITINGS OF H. P. LIDDON, D.D. *Crown 8vo. 3s. 6d.*

MAXIMS AND GLEANINGS FROM THE WRITINGS OF H. P. LIDDON, D.D. Selected and arranged by C. M. S. *Crown 16mo. 1s.*

DR. LIDDON'S TOUR IN EGYPT AND PALESTINE IN 1886. Being Letters descriptive of the Tour, written by his Sister, Mrs. KING. *Crown 8vo. 5s.*

Luckock.—Works by HERBERT MORTIMER LUCKOCK, D.D., Canon of Ely.

AFTER DEATH. An Examination of the Testimony of Primitive Times respecting the State of the Faithful Dead, and their Relationship to the Living. *Crown 8vo. 6s.*

[continued.

IN THEOLOGICAL LITERATURE.

Luckock.—Works by HERBERT MORTIMER LUCKOCK, D.D. Canon of Ely—*continued.*

THE INTERMEDIATE STATE BETWEEN DEATH AND JUDGMENT. Being a Sequel to *After Death. Crown 8vo.* 6s.

FOOTPRINTS OF THE SON OF MAN, as traced by St. Mark. Being Eighty Portions for Private Study, Family Reading, and Instructions in Church. *Two Vols. Crown 8vo.* 12s. *Cheap Edition in one Vol. Crown 8vo.* 5s.

THE DIVINE LITURGY. Being the Order for Holy Communion, Historically, Doctrinally, and Devotionally set forth, in Fifty Portions. *Crown 8vo.* 6s.

STUDIES IN THE HISTORY OF THE BOOK OF COMMON PRAYER. The Anglican Reform—The Puritan Innovations—The Elizabethan Reaction—The Caroline Settlement. With Appendices. *Crown 8vo.* 6s.

THE BISHOPS IN THE TOWER. A Record of Stirring Events affecting the Church and Nonconformists from the Restoration to the Revolution. *Crown 8vo.* 6s.

LYRA GERMANICA. Hymns translated from the German by CATHERINE WINKWORTH. *Small 8vo.* 5s.

MacColl.—CHRISTIANITY IN RELATION TO SCIENCE AND MORALS. By the Rev. MALCOLM MACCOLL, M.A., Canon Residentiary of Ripon. *Crown 8vo.* 6s.

Mason.—Works by A. J. MASON, D.D., formerly Fellow of Trinity College, Cambridge.

THE FAITH OF THE GOSPEL. A Manual of Christian Doctrine. *Crown 8vo.* 3s. 6d. *Also a Large-Paper Edition for Marginal Notes.* 4to. 12s. 6d.

THE RELATION OF CONFIRMATION TO BAPTISM. As taught in Holy Scripture and the Fathers. *Crown 8vo.* 7s. 6d.

Mercier.—OUR MOTHER CHURCH: Being Simple Talk on High Topics. By Mrs. JEROME MERCIER. *Small 8vo.* 3s. 6d.

Molesworth.—STORIES OF THE SAINTS FOR CHILDREN: The Black Letter Saints. By Mrs. MOLESWORTH, Author of 'The Palace in the Garden,' etc. etc. With Illustrations. *Royal 16mo.* 5s.

A CATALOGUE OF WORKS

Mozley.—Works by J. B. MOZLEY, D.D., late Canon of Christ Church, and Regius Professor of Divinity at Oxford.

ESSAYS, HISTORICAL AND THEOLOGICAL. *Two Vols.* 8vo. 24s.

EIGHT LECTURES ON MIRACLES. Being the Bampton Lectures for 1865. *Crown* 8vo. 7s. 6d.

RULING IDEAS IN EARLY AGES AND THEIR RELATION TO OLD TESTAMENT FAITH. Lectures delivered to Graduates of the University of Oxford. 8vo. 10s. 6d.

SERMONS PREACHED BEFORE THE UNIVERSITY OF OXFORD, and on Various Occasions. *Crown* 8vo. 7s. 6d.

SERMONS, PAROCHIAL AND OCCASIONAL. *Crown* 8vo. 7s. 6d.

Mozley.—Works by the Rev. T. MOZLEY, M.A., Author of 'Reminiscences of Oriel College and the Oxford Movement.'

THE CREED OR A PHILOSOPHY. *Crown* 8vo.

THE WORD. *Crown* 8vo. 7s. 6d.

THE SON. *Crown* 8vo. 7s. 6d.

LETTERS FROM ROME ON THE OCCASION OF THE ŒCUMENICAL COUNCIL 1869-1870. *Two Vols. Cr.* 8vo. 18s.

Newbolt.—Works by the Rev. W. C. E. NEWBOLT, M.A., Canon and Chancellor of St. Paul's.

THE FRUIT OF THE SPIRIT. Being Ten Addresses bearing on the Spiritual Life. *Crown* 8vo. 2s. 6d.

THE MAN OF GOD. Being Six Addresses delivered during Lent at the Primary Ordination of the Right Rev. the Lord Alwyne Compton, D.D., Bishop of Ely. *Small* 8vo. 1s. 6d.

THE VOICE OF THE PRAYER BOOK. Being Spiritual Addresses bearing on the Book of Common Prayer. *Crown* 8vo. 2s. 6d.

Newnham.—THE ALL-FATHER: Sermons preached in a Village Church. By the Rev. H. P. NEWNHAM. With Preface by EDNA LYALL. *Crown* 8vo. 4s. 6d.

Newnham.—ALRESFORD ESSAYS FOR THE TIMES. By Rev. W. O. NEWNHAM, M.A., late Rector of Alresford. CONTENTS :— Bible Story of Creation—Bible Story of Eden—Bible Story of the Deluge—After Death—Miracles : A Conversation—Eternal Punishment —The Resurrection of the Body. *Crown* 8vo. 6s.

IN THEOLOGICAL LITERATURE. 13

Newman.—Works by JOHN HENRY NEWMAN, B.D., sometime Vicar of St. Mary's, Oxford.

PAROCHIAL AND PLAIN SERMONS. *Eight Vols. Cabinet Edition. Crown 8vo. 5s. each. Popular Edition. 3s. 6d. each.*

SELECTION, ADAPTED TO THE SEASONS OF THE ECCLESIASTICAL YEAR, from the 'Parochial and Plain Sermons.' *Cabinet Edition. Crown 8vo. 5s. Popular Edition. 3s. 6d.*

FIFTEEN SERMONS PREACHED BEFORE THE UNIVERSITY OF OXFORD. *Cabinet Edition. Crown 8vo. 5s. Popular Edition. 3s. 6d.*

SERMONS BEARING UPON SUBJECTS OF THE DAY. *Cabinet Edition. Crown 8vo. 5s. Popular Edition. Crown 8vo. 3s. 6d.*

LECTURES ON THE DOCTRINE OF JUSTIFICATION. *Cabinet Edition. Crown 8vo. 5s. Popular Edition. 3s. 6d.*

THE LETTERS AND CORRESPONDENCE OF JOHN HENRY NEWMAN DURING HIS LIFE IN THE ENGLISH CHURCH. With a Brief Autobiographical Memoir. Arranged and Edited by ANNE MOZLEY. *Two Vols. 8vo. 30s. net.*

*** *For other Works by Cardinal Newman, see Messrs. Longmans & Co.'s Catalogue of Works in General Literature.*

Osborne.—Works by EDWARD OSBORNE, Mission Priest of the Society of St. John the Evangelist, Cowley, Oxford.

THE CHILDREN'S SAVIOUR. Instructions to Children on the Life of our Lord and Saviour Jesus Christ. *Illustrated. 16mo. 2s. 6d.*

THE SAVIOUR-KING. Instructions to Children on Old Testament Types and Illustrations of the Life of Christ. *Illustrated. 16mo. 2s. 6d.*

THE CHILDREN'S FAITH. Instructions to Children on the Apostles' Creed. *Illustrated. 16mo. 2s. 6d.*

Oxenden.—Works by the Right Rev. ASHTON OXENDEN, formerly Bishop of Montreal.

PLAIN SERMONS. *Crown 8vo.*

THE HISTORY OF MY LIFE : An Autobiography. *Crown 8vo. 5s.*

PEACE AND ITS HINDRANCES. *Crown 8vo. 1s. ; sewed, 2s., cloth.*

THE PATHWAY OF SAFETY ; or, Counsel to the Awakened. *Fcap. 8vo, large type. 2s. 6d. Cheap Edition. Small type, limp. 1s.*

THE EARNEST COMMUNICANT. *New Red Rubric Edition. 32mo, cloth. 2s. Common Edition. 32mo, 1s.*

OUR CHURCH AND HER SERVICES. *Fcap. 8vo. 2s. 6d.*

[*continued.*

Oxenden.—Works by the Right Rev. ASHTON OXENDEN, formerly Bishop of Montreal—*continued.*
FAMILY PRAYERS FOR FOUR WEEKS. First Series. *Fcap.* 8*vo.* 2*s.* 6*d.* Second Series. *Fcap.* 8*vo.* 2*s.* 6*d.*
    LARGE TYPE EDITION. Two Series in one Volume. *Crown* 8*vo.* 6*s.*
COTTAGE SERMONS; or, Plain Words to the Poor. *Fcap.* 8*vo.* 2*s.* 6*d.*
THOUGHTS FOR HOLY WEEK. 16*mo, cloth.* 1*s.* 6*d.*
DECISION. 18*mo.* 1*s.* 6*d.*
THE HOME BEYOND; or, A Happy Old Age. *Fcap.* 8*vo.* 1*s.* 6*d.*
THE LABOURING MAN'S BOOK. 18*mo, large type, cloth.* 1*s.* 6*d.*

Paget.—Works by FRANCIS PAGET, D.D., Dean of Christ Church, Oxford.
THE SPIRIT OF DISCIPLINE: Sermons. *Crown* 8*vo.* 6*s.* 6*d.*
FACULTIES AND DIFFICULTIES FOR BELIEF AND DISBELIEF. *Crown* 8*vo.* 6*s.* 6*d.*
THE HALLOWING OF WORK. Addresses given at Eton, January 16-18, 1888. *Small* 8*vo.* 2*s.*

PRACTICAL REFLECTIONS. By a CLERGYMAN. With Prefaces by H. P. LIDDON, D.D., D.C.L., and the Bishop of Lincoln. *Crown* 8*vo.*
Vol. I.—THE HOLY GOSPELS. 4*s.* 6*d.* | THE PSALMS. 5*s.*
Vol. II.—ACTS TO REVELATION. 6*s.* | THE BOOK OF GENESIS. 4*s.* 6*d.*

PRIEST (THE) TO THE ALTAR; or, Aids to the Devout Celebration of Holy Communion, chiefly after the Ancient English Use of Sarum. *Royal* 8*vo.* 12*s.*

Pusey.—Works by the Rev. E. B. PUSEY, D.D.
PRIVATE PRAYERS. With Preface by H. P. LIDDON, D.D. 32*mo.* 1*s.*
PRAYERS FOR A YOUNG SCHOOLBOY. With a Preface by H. P. LIDDON, D.D. 24*mo.* 1*s.*
SELECTIONS FROM THE WRITINGS OF EDWARD BOUVERIE PUSEY, D.D. *Crown* 8*vo.* 3*s.* 6*d.*
MAXIMS AND GLEANINGS FROM THE WRITINGS OF EDWARD BOUVERIE PUSEY, D.D. Selected and Arranged for Daily Use. By C. M. S. *Crown* 16*mo.* 1*s.*

Reynolds.—THE NATURAL HISTORY OF IMMORTALITY. By the Rev. J. W. REYNOLDS, M.A., Prebendary of St. Paul's. *Crown* 8*vo.* 7*s.* 6*d.*

IN THEOLOGICAL LITERATURE. 15

Sanday.—THE ORACLES OF GOD: Nine Lectures on the Nature and Extent of Biblical Inspiration and the Special Significance of the Old Testament Scriptures at the Present Time. By W. SANDAY, M.A., D.D., LL.D., Dean Ireland's Professor of Exegesis and Fellow of Exeter College. *Crown 8vo.* 4*s.*

Seebohm.—THE OXFORD REFORMERS—JOHN COLET, ERASMUS, AND THOMAS MORE: A History of their Fellow-Work. By FREDERIC SEEBOHM. *8vo.* 14*s.*

Stanton.—THE PLACE OF AUTHORITY IN MATTERS OF RELIGIOUS BELIEF. By VINCENT HENRY STANTON, D.D., Fellow of Trinity Coll., Ely Prof. of Divinity, Cambridge. *Cr. 8vo.* 6*s.*

Stephen.—ESSAYS IN ECCLESIASTICAL BIOGRAPHY. By the Right Hon. Sir J. STEPHEN. *Crown 8vo.* 7*s. 6d.*

Swayne.—THE BLESSED DEAD IN PARADISE. Four All Saints' Day Sermons, preached in Salisbury Cathedral. By R. G. SWAYNE, M.A. *Crown 8vo.* 3*s. 6d.*

Tweddell.—THE SOUL IN CONFLICT. A Practical Examination of some Difficulties and Duties of the Spiritual Life. By MARSHALL TWEDDELL, M.A., Vicar of St. Saviour, Paddington. *Crown 8vo.* 6*s.*

Twells.—COLLOQUIES ON PREACHING. By HENRY TWELLS, M.A., Honorary Canon of Peterborough. *Crown 8vo.* 2*s. 6d.*

Welldon. — THE FUTURE AND THE PAST. Sermons preached to Harrow Boys. By the Rev. J. E. C. WELLDON, M.A., Head Master of Harrow School. *Crown 8vo.* 7*s. 6d.*

Williams.—Works by the Rev. ISAAC WILLIAMS, B.D.
A DEVOTIONAL COMMENTARY ON THE GOSPEL NARRATIVE. *Eight Vols. Crown 8vo.* 5*s. each. Sold separately.*

THOUGHTS ON THE STUDY OF THE HOLY GOSPELS.
A HARMONY OF THE FOUR GOSPELS.
OUR LORD'S NATIVITY.
OUR LORD'S MINISTRY (Second Year).
OUR LORD'S MINISTRY (Third Year).
THE HOLY WEEK.
OUR LORD'S PASSION.
OUR LORD'S RESURRECTION.

FEMALE CHARACTERS OF HOLY SCRIPTURE. A Series of Sermons. *Crown 8vo.* 5*s.*
THE CHARACTERS OF THE OLD TESTAMENT. *Crown 8vo.* 5*s.*
THE APOCALYPSE. With Notes and Reflections. *Crown 8vo.* 5*s.*
SERMONS ON THE EPISTLES AND GOSPELS FOR THE SUNDAYS AND HOLY DAYS. *Two Vols. Crown 8vo.* 5*s. each.*

[continued.

Williams.—Works by the Rev. ISAAC WILLIAMS, B.D.—*continu*
PLAIN SERMONS ON CATECHISM. *Two Vols. Cr.* 8*vo.* 5*s.* ea
SELECTIONS FROM ISAAC WILLIAMS' WRITINGS. *Cr.* 8
3*s.* 6*d.*
THE AUTOBIOGRAPHY OF ISAAC WILLIAMS, B.D., Author several of the 'Tracts for the Times.' Edited by the Venerable GEORGE PREVOST, as throwing further light on the history of Oxford Movement. *Crown* 8*vo.* 5*s.*

Woodford.—Works by J. R. WOODFORD, D.D., Bishop of Ely.
THE GREAT COMMISSION. Addresses on the Ordinal. Edit with an Introduction, by H. M. LUCKOCK, D.D. *Crown* 8*vo.* 5*s.*
SERMONS ON OLD AND NEW TESTAMENT SUBJECT Edited by H. M. LUCKOCK, D.D. *Crown* 8*vo.* 5*s.*

Woodruff.—THE CHILDREN'S YEAR. Verses for t Sundays and Holy Days throughout the Year. By C. H. WOODRU B.C.L. With an Introduction by the Lord Bishop of SOUTHWE *Fcap.* 8*vo.* 3*s.* 6*d.*

Wordsworth.
For List of Works by the late Christopher Wordsworth, D.D., Bishop Lincoln, see Messrs. Longmans & Co.'s Catalogue of Theological Wor 32 pp. Sent post free on application.

Wordsworth.—Works by ELIZABETH WORDSWORTH, Princip of Lady Margaret Hall, Oxford.
ILLUSTRATIONS OF THE CREED. *Crown* 8*vo.* 5*s.*
ST. CHRISTOPHER AND OTHER POEMS. *Crown* 8*vo.* 6*s.*

Wordsworth.—Works by CHARLES WORDSWORTH, D.D., D.C.1 Lord Bishop of St. Andrews, and Fellow of Winchest College.
ANNALS OF MY EARLY LIFE, 1806-1846. 8*vo.* 15*s.*
PRIMARY WITNESS TO THE TRUTH OF THE GOSPEL, which is added a Charge on Modern Teaching on the Canon of t Old Testament. *Crown* 8*vo.* 7*s.* 6*d.*

Younghusband.—Works by FRANCES YOUNGHUSBAND.
THE STORY OF OUR LORD, told in Simple Language for Childre With 25 Illustrations from Pictures by the Old Masters, *Crown* 8: 2*s.* 6*d.*
THE STORY OF GENESIS, told in Simple Language for Childre *Crown* 8*vo.* 2*s.* 6*d.*
THE STORY OF THE EXODUS, told in Simple Language Children. With Map and 29 Illustrations. *Crown* 8*vo.* 2*s.* 6*d.*

Printed by T. and A. CONSTABLE, Printers to Her Majesty,
at the Edinburgh University Press.

www.ingramcontent.com/pod-product-compliance
Lightning Source LLC
Chambersburg PA
CBHW032354230426
43672CB00007B/692